A LIFETIME WITH MARK TWAIN

To Miss Mary Lawton

with the best wishes of her friend

Mark Twain

A LIFETIME WITH MARK TWAIN

The memories of Katy Leary, for thirty years his faithful and devoted servant

Written by
MARY LAWTON

With Many Illustrations

APPLEWOOD BOOKS
CARLISLE, MASSACHUSETTS

. . . and the elements
So mixed in him, that Nature might stand up
And say to all the world,
This was a Man!

JULIUS CAESAR.

Originally published in 1925

978-1-4290-9366-8

Cover photo of Katy Leary courtesy of
The Mark Twain House & Museum, Hartford, CT

Thank you for purchasing an Applewood book. Applewood reprints America's lively classics—books from the past that are still of interest to modern readers. Our mission is to build a picture of America's past through its primary sources.

To inquire about this edition or to request a free copy of our current catalog featuring our best-selling books, write to:

Applewood Books
P.O. Box 27
Carlisle, MA 01741

For more complete listings, visit us on the web at:
www.awb.com

MANUFACTURED IN THE UNITED STATES OF AMERICA

TO

CLARA CLEMENS GABRILOWITSCH
AND TO THE IMPERISHABLE YEARS
OF OUR FRIENDSHIP

THIS book would not be complete without my grateful acknowledgment to Arthur T. Vance, Editor of *Pictorial Review*, whose rare vision and understanding brought about the first publication of these articles in his magazine.

MARY LAWTON.

An Introduction to the New Edition of Mary Lawton's

A Lifetime with Mark Twain:

The Memories of Katy Leary, for Thirty Years His Faithful and Devoted Servant

by Steve Courtney

SOMETIME around 1903 or 1904, Samuel L. Clemens— Mark Twain—and his wife, Olivia, living in New York, made the acquaintance of a young actress named Mary Lawton. In her early thirties, she was training for a career on the stage. She was later to spend a decade on Broadway, meet the playwright George Bernard Shaw, and act in several of his plays, along with one silent movie. She was also an artist's model: Her bold, attractive visage stares from the seated statue of Athena by Daniel Chester French on the steps of Columbia University's Low Library.

She quickly became the fast friend of the Clemenses' daughter, Clara, and describes in *A Lifetime with Mark Twain* how she encountered the family's Irish-American maid, "a handsome, smiling, stalwart, unique, and very kindly figure on that gracious threshold."

Catherine Leary was by then about fifty and had served

the family for more than two decades. Lawton noted her "funny stories and quaint sayings, her searching observations of life, her lightninglike perceptions of people." Clemens himself, she says, regretted that "Katy" did not have the literary skill to "put down the doings of this family." Two decades later, Lawton decided to remedy this, seeking out Lawton and transcribing her vivid speech. The result is this extraordinary book, first published in 1925.

In 1880, the Clemens family lived in the great house they had built in Hartford, Connecticut, and summered routinely in Olivia Clemens's hometown of Elmira, New York. That year they hired Leary, a twenty-four-year-old from Elmira. For thirty years she worked as their seamstress, nursemaid, nanny, and lady's maid.

"Katy was a potent influence, all over the premises," Samuel Clemens wrote of her. "Fidelity, truthfulness, courage, magnanimity, personal dignity, a pole-star for steadiness—these were her equipment, along with a heart of Irish warmth, quick Irish wit, and a large good store of the veiled & shimmering & half surreptitious humor which is the best feature of the 'American' brand—or of any brand, for that matter."

As she describes in *A Lifetime with Mark Twain*, Leary also provided important personal support for the family, being present and attentive at the deaths of daughter Susy in 1896, Olivia Clemens in 1904, daughter Jean in 1909, and finally Samuel Clemens himself in 1910. "I didn't think of the money I was earning," she writes, "and I never interfered in any way with them. I wouldn't ever do it—they came first—and I did it because I loved them and they was so good to me—just like I was one of their own."

A Lifetime with Mark Twain sheds important light on the details of the life of the author who was both Mark Twain the funnyman and Samuel Clemens the devoted father, husband, and employer. Its reappearance now is a major event in broadening our knowledge of his eventful and sometimes tragic life. But it also brings back to life the "searching observations" and "lightninglike perceptions" of a rare woman.

Steve Courtney is the author of *Joseph Hopkins Twichell: The Life and Times of Mark Twain's Closest Friend* (Georgia) and *"The Loveliest Home That Ever Was": The Story of the Mark Twain House in Hartford* (Dover).

Foreword

From the very beginning of my intimacy in the Clemens household, the doings of that delightful family were an everlasting joy to me.

In that House of Enchantment—for so it always seemed—besides the magic figure of Mark Twain, the gentle presence of Mrs. Clemens, and those three diverting children, Susy, Clara, and Jean, was another figure: the unique figure of Katy Leary, for more than thirty years their faithful and devoted servant.

Katy Leary, whose quaint sayings and philosophies and funny stories of the family happenings bubbled up like the Fountain of Life, and were an unfailing source of delight to all who heard them. Long before it actually grew into a resolve, the idea was often vividly in my mind that Katy's inimitable story of Mark Twain and his daily thrilling adventures was something to reckon with—something to treasure.

What a romance it was! How unlike anything else! One glimpsed another world—one breathed a better air. It was something too precious to be lost. Something must be done about it. I felt sure, even then, that that eager, devoted public of Mark Twain's would love it as much as I did. Some day, somehow, it must be written. And then—then my youthful imagination soared gayly at the thought, that some day I would write it! That some day I would gather up those golden sheaves, and write the stories as Katy used to tell them, in all their cozy, funny, homely, tragic, and tender intimacy.

My mind went back to my first and unforgettable visit to the Clemens household where afterwards I spent so many joyous days, and I remember that it was Katy Leary herself that opened the door. I can see her now as vividly as she stood then—a handsome, smiling, stalwart, unique, and very kindly figure on that gracious threshold. Her flashing black eyes still flashed, although behind large spectacles. Her thick wavy hair, that must have been in the early days as black as the proverbial "raven's wing," was iron-gray. A fine ruddy color burned in her welcoming face—a face that was firm and round and happy as a girl's. In fact the first impression that Katy Leary gave was one of happiness, bubbling happiness, and after that the flash of her humor was the thing that struck one most, and made one feel that it would be an amusing and enlightening experience to talk with Katy Leary.

She seemed so a part of the household—so vital and yet so unobtrusively a factor in the life of the family, that as Mark Twain once said of her, "Why, Katy is like the very paper on the walls—she's always there!" Indeed, one could not picture the house without her. Even in that first glimpse I could not imagine the door being opened by any one else. And that is Katy Leary as she looked; but when she spoke—ah, then it was that you began to laugh with and love Katy Leary. The things she said in her soft, deep, and rather quiet voice were inimitable! The Irish wit of her—the Irish quickness of her—the Irish deftness of her—and sometimes, when necessary, the Irish blarney of her—was something to think over, something to laugh over, and something sometimes, alas, to weep over!

And how it all came tumbling out—her funny stories and quaint sayings, her searching observations of life, her lightninglike perceptions of people! What a riot of words! And words unforgettably her own: funny, humble, gay, illiterate—as she herself says—eloquent and searching and so magnificent when occasion warranted. What a mixture it all was—and what a language!

How often in our talks together Clara Clemens (the best beloved of all my friends) has said to me, "Oh, Mary, if only Katy's story of my father's life could be written just as she tells it!" And how often I have answered back, "Oh, Clara, if only I could write it in her own words!" And then the day when Mark Twain himself said to me, "Now, if Katy only knew how to write, and could put down the doings of this family, we should indeed have a document worth having!"

Perhaps it was that—those fateful words of his (I like to think so) that swept my early flickering hope into a full-grown resolve, that some day I'd find a way and write the great story. Well, the "some day" came—the psychological "some day." It came, and Katy with it—Katy ready to tell it to me and I ready to write it. And what a wonder story it is—her life in the Clemens household! From youth to old age she stood at her post—in storm and in stress, in laughter and in tears. How vital her sharing of their joys and triumphs—their sufferings and losses, as they came! How stanchly she weathered the years! How devotedly she served, how tenderly she cared, their servant and their friend. For thirty years, until that last great break of all, when Mark Twain himself, adored and laughed with throughout the world, laid his hand forever on our hearts—and left us.

Here is the story as Katy and I lived it again together not long since in her little house in Elmira, where she was born nearly seventy years ago. There I found her—older, sadder, I must admit, but still one glimpsed the Katy Leary of old. The quaint sayings and funny stories that used to come all tumbling out, now hung haltingly—the unforgettable riot of gay words seemed hushed forever—the precious memories lay scattered through the twilight of the years, and only the thin flame of the past glowed in that quiet room.

For anxious days that flame burned low and fitfully and then—out of the smoldering embers, the fires leaped up once more; the years were swept away, and the magic of those happy, laughing days came back again—and Katy with them! She bloomed under it all like a sturdy rosebush in a deserted garden. She flowered and flamed into life once more—the life of those incomparable days in that lovely Clemens household, so charming and so vanished in this time of stress and loss.

In that little quiet room they lived again, her beloved "family": Mr. Clemens and his laughter—Mrs. Clemens in her gentleness and beauty—and Susy and Clara and Jean, little children again, children in Katy's arms.

It is all here—the dear funny story; and here at last it lives and speaks again. I lay it now before you all—on the Altar of Affection—in cherished memory and grateful tribute to these peerless friends.

MARY LAWTON.

List of Illustrations

List of Illustrations

A LIFETIME WITH MARK TWAIN

A LIFETIME WITH MARK TWAIN

First Part

I WILL begin when I first got my position. Well, at this period—I was born in Elmira, and went out sewing by the day—I was seventeen years old, and was earning fifty cents a day then. I could sew very good, you know (I learned my trade as dressmaker) and I went out sewing, mostly making baby clothes. I was copying some of Mrs. J. Sloat Fassett's baby's clothes when Mrs. Stanchfield come in. Mrs. Stanchfield was a great friend of Mrs. Clemens. She visited there. She was there half a year as a rule. She was the wife of John B. Stanchfield—who got to be a very smart lawyer afterwards. Well, she come in and looked at my sewing and admired it very much and says, "Why, Katy, wouldn't you like to leave Elmira?" And I said, "Yes, I would; I've nothing chaining me here!" So she says, "I know somebody would love to have you. She lives in Hartford, and Hartford is a beautiful place; she has three children and her name is Mrs. Clemens. She is a perfectly wonderful, lovely woman, and you would like her—and I think she'd like you." She said she would see Mrs. Clemens and tell her about me and I would hear from her later.

Well, I didn't think it would come to nothing—but it did. In a couple of weeks I had a letter from Mrs. Clemens asking me to come and see her (she was at Quarry Farm then); and she would go to her mother's, Mrs. Langdon's, and see me there on a Sunday evening.

So I went over to see her (Mrs. Clemens), I did. I was settin' in the library waiting, and this wonderful, wonderful woman appeared, and she startled me with all her beauty—she was like an angel, almost. She wore a white silk dress and her hair was perfectly plain, you know, combed down plain and done in a coil; but her face and her manner was wonderful, and I felt like she was something from another world.

"Why, is this Katy Leary!" she says. I told her "Yes." Then she says to me, "Would you like to come and live with me?" "Oh, yes!" I says. "Yes, I would."

"Well, when could you come?" and I says, "Well, I need about a week or ten days to get ready." "Why, you could come about . . ." (I don't know what the month was, but she made it the 19th.) And I said, "Yes, I'll be ready; I'll come to Hartford then." So she said, "Mr. Langdon will give you all the details of the traveling." (Mr. Langdon was her father.)

Of course, I'd never traveled anywheres then. I was green as a monkey. Well, she said Mr. Langdon would give me the details, and then she called somebody in the hall:

"Youth, Youth, dear, will you come in here?"

And he came in, and I looked at Mr. Clemens for the first time. But I didn't know who Mr. Clemens was, never knew that he wrote a book nor didn't know anything about him; then Mrs. Clemens said:

"Now this is Katy Leary that is coming to live with us in Hartford."

Well, then he gave me the once-over pretty quick, looked at me pretty sharp, I can tell you.

"Have you got any money?" he said. "How much will you need?" Of course, I didn't know how much I needed, so he pulled out five dollars. "If that isn't enough," he said, "you can charge it to us when you come to Hartford; but," he says, "I think maybe that will buy your ticket anyway." So that was the end of that.

Well, then I went to Hartford. I left Elmira Sunday and I arrived Monday morning; and when I got to the house, you know, I kind of thought I would have a brass band to meet me (I was so set up and excited with my new job—I was in a dream almost), but I didn't! I got a carriage to take me to the house and my trunk too, and I went to the front door and the butler opened it (he was a colored boy)—George, his name was, colored George.

"My name is Katy Leary," I says. "I'm expected here. Didn't you know it?"

"No," he said, "I didn't know nothing about it."

"Is Mrs. Clemens in?"

"No," says George, "she ain't!"

"Well," I says, "I've got my trunk out here on this cab, and I want it brought in, and I don't know how I'm to get it in."

"Well," he said, "I don't know neither."

But he called somebody—I don't know who it was, and they said: "Why, yes! It's Katy Leary! She's coming to live with us. Take her trunk right into the kitchen." (You see, the front of the house was the kitchen part.) Then we told the cabman to take it in there and I set down for a while to rest myself—and this colored boy stood looking at me and staring and wondering, "Well, what sort of a thing is she, anyway?"

Pretty soon Mrs. Clemens come in, and of course made me feel right at home and happy. First thing she did was to take me upstairs to the nursery to show me the children, and the three of them was there, huddling in a group—Susy, Clara, and Jean was a baby in the nurse's arms. So I saw the children, got acquainted with them, and then Mrs. Clemens took me to my own room, and left me there, to rest myself and have my supper.

Well, after I had been there a while (I think I will put this in now because it was the first time that Mr. Clemens said what I looked like), he said to Mrs. Clemens:

"So you hired that girl after me giving you the money?" "Yes," she says.

"Well, did you notice them wide, thick, black eyebrows of hers?" "No," Mrs. Clemens said. "No, I didn't."

"Well, you know," he said, "she's got a terrible fierce temper, I believe; nothing halfway about her. Yes, I think you'll find she *has* a temper. She's Irish!"

But Mrs. Clemens only laughed and said, "Yes, maybe—we'll see."

Well, after that first day I began my regular work. I was Mrs. Clemens' maid. I used to comb her hair every morning. Such beautiful hair! Beautiful long hair—dark brown, it was—and she combed it perfectly plain, as you see in her picture. I liked to comb and brush it for her. Oh, I loved to do that! I used to comb and braid it every night, too, when she went to bed; and then I used to sew the rest of the time.

Well, the day would begin like this: We had breakfast about half-past seven, and at that time the family—meaning Mr. and Mrs. Clemens—never came down for their breakfast till about eleven o'clock. They didn't get up so early, but I used to go in when Mrs. Clemens would ring for me and brushed her hair and helped her dress and then they would come down to breakfast say about eleven o'clock, and then Mr. Clemens (he never eat any lunch, you know), he'd go to his billiard room to write. He left strict orders not to have anybody disturb him—oh, for nothing! Some days he worked harder than others; but every day not to disturb him as he was a very busy writer. Well, he would appear again about half-past five (they had dinner at six o'clock in those days). He'd come down and get ready for dinner and Mrs. Clemens would get ready too. Mrs. Clemens always put on a lovely dress for dinner, even when we was alone, and they always had music during dinner. They had a music box in the hall, and George would set that going at dinner every day. Played nine pieces, that music box did; and he always set it going every night. They brought it from Geneva, and it was wonderful. It was foreign. It used to play all by itself—it wasn't like a Victrola, you know. It just went with a crank. George would wind it up and they'd have pretty music all during the dinner. Oh, it was lovely! And the children was just delighted with it.

Afterwards they all gathered together in the library and set around the great open fireplace, if it was in the winter time. Mr. Clemens and they all set down on big chairs or even set on the floors sometimes (that is, Susy and Clara did), and Mr. Clemens would have Browning or Dickens and would read aloud to them. Well, Clara, she wanted to read like her father too—she was so ambitious, you know. So she'd get a big book (though she couldn't read at all), but she guessed what was in the book. She'd get this book in front of her—she was so little you couldn't even see her on that big chair; and she'd set way back with her feet all curled up, and read away in her broken English, pronouncing all them big words wrong. When her father had stood it about as long as he could, I guess, he'd tell her to lay down the book and listen to *him* read. He used to read until nine o'clock every evening.

The children was always very nice about going to bed—didn't make any fuss. And after that, Mr. Clemens, he'd have his hot—(I think I'll tell this)—he used to have a hot Scotch every night at nine o'clock. George, the butler, would bring in a pitcher of hot water and a bottle of the best Scotch whisky, and Mrs. Clemens would have her tea at the same time. That was English then—that was foreign, too. They had just come from the other side at that time. After they'd had the tea and the toddy, they would set and talk and laugh—happy and contented; and then they'd go to bed about ten o'clock, and that would finish the day.

After the children were a little older, Mrs. Clemens taught them herself. She began to get up a little earlier when she started giving them their lessons, and she'd have breakfast about half-past eight, and teach them all the morning, you know—every morning from nine until twelve in the schoolroom. The schoolroom was right off the nursery, and Mrs. Clemens taught them there herself. She taught them for a couple of winters like this and then got a governess—a teacher called F—. She was a nice girl then—she wasn't a Christian Scientist in those days nor a Spiritualist, either. She got that later. That spoiled her!

Yes, Mrs. Clemens taught them for several winters before the governess come. They never were home in the summer time, you know—they always left Hartford in June and went to Quarry Farm in Elmira, where her father lived. Mr. Clemens went right up there and Mrs. Clemens would look after the children a little more there than she did at home. She was a very busy woman, a wonderful housekeeper, and wonderful with the children. If ever they were sick she would get them out of the nursery and bring them right in to her own bed, and Mr. Clemens—well, he'd have to go into another room. I'd go and set up with her and keep the fire (they always kept the fire all night in her room) and help her take care of the sick baby. Oh, the children! They used to *love* to be sick, because they loved to be taken into their mother's room. She had a great large bed (I think Clara has that now). It was an old Dutch bed, four-poster, and there was four little smiling, fat cherubs, one on each post; and the children would play with them cherubs. They used to have them taken down and put on the bed with them. (They'd come off the posts—unscrew, you know.) They was delighted with that, and delighted to be sick, too, just to be in their mother's room—that is, if they wasn't too sick.

Clara had croup a good deal and had to be kept covered up. Of course, then she couldn't play with the little fat cherubs, and her disappointment was something awful; she'd holler bloody murder!

Now, first I must tell you a little about the Hartford house. It was really wonderful. I'd never been in anything like it before. I guess I told you when I first come there I noticed the kitchen was in the front of the house, which hit me as kind of funny. But Mr. Clemens used to say the reason they had the kitchen in the front, was so's the servants could watch the parades and circuses go by without having to run into the front yard!

Well, the Library was a beautiful room and all the furniture was very elegant all through the house, and so was the pictures and hangings and curtains and things. There was a carved wooden mantelpiece in the library that Mrs. Clemens had brought from some place in Europe—from some old castle, I suppose—and there was a brass plate on it that had a motto, and the motto said that the best thing in a house was the friends that come into it—or something like that—I don't remember the exact words, but anyhow, that was the meaning to the thing. And oh! There was another beautiful room downstairs, called the Mahogany Room; and then at the top of the house was the famous Billiard Room where Mr. Clemens used to do all his writing (and I did the dusting!), and where we used to fight over them precious manuscripts of his. Yes! and there was pretty little balconies opening out of the Billiard Room where you could set if you wanted to. Almost everybody—all Mr. Clemens' friends that come there—admired the house very much. They all thought 'twas wonderful, and Mr. Howells used to say that there warn't never another house in the whole world like that one, and I guess what they all meant was, the great reason it was so wonderful was 'cause Mr. Clemens himself was in it. It was beautifully managed, too, because Mrs. Clemens always attended to everything herself.

Now, I must tell you all about them precious manuscripts. Mr. Clemens always did all his writing up in the Billiard Room. He had a table there, you know, and Mrs. Clemens used to go up and dust that table every morning and arrange his manuscript and writing, if he didn't arrange it himself, which he sometimes used to do. He took good care of it—he thought he did, anyway! Oh, he was very particular! Nobody was allowed to touch them manuscripts besides Mrs. Clemens. But one day I was up there and I says:

"Oh, Mrs. Clemens! I don't see why you have to come way up these stairs every morning just to dust that table. I could do that, I think, and save you the trouble."

"Yes," she said, "I know you could, Katy, but Mr. Clemens is so fussy about his manuscripts—"

"Well," I says, "you just tell him I didn't *actually* dust them—I just dust *around* them." And so Mrs. Clemens said I might try. Well, I had been doing the dusting for a year almost, when he caught me one morning! He come up quite sudden and said, very fierce:

"Katy, what are *you* doing up here?"

I was so startled I could hardly speak at first, because I never wanted him to catch me around that precious table. But I finally says:

"I am dusting this table."

"*You* don't dust that table," he says. "I have for about a year," says I.

"Oh, no!" says Mr. Clemens. "Mrs. Clemens takes care of that. *She* is the only one that can come up here!"

"But I thought it was kind of hard for her," I says. "I could help her that much anyway, then she wouldn't have to climb up them three flights of stairs every morning."

Well, that was enough for him, as he never wanted any trouble put on her, because anything he thought would tire Mrs. Clemens or bother her, he didn't want. But of course he didn't think of that at the time, while she was doing it, you know, till I brought it to his mind—which is the way with men—even the best of them, I've found out.

Well, after that, of course, if there was anything missing, I was called and he'd say, very fierce and excited, "Katy, what did you do with all that manuscript I left on the table last night?"

"I didn't do anything with it; I didn't touch it. Isn't it where you left it?"

"No," he'd answer. "No, I suppose it's burned! *You* burned it this morning! That's what you've done—burned it!"

"Well," I said, "I'll look on the table. It wasn't there this morning when I come up. There was no manuscript on that table—only them few letters."

"Well, it was on that table when I left last night, Katy!"

"It wasn't there this morning, anyway," I said; and after that I'd get so worried over us contradicting each other, I'd kind of start to go away and he'd call out, in a terrible voice:

"Well, you burned it—I know you did! It's gone, anyway. It's lost—burned!! That's the end of it!"

Well, he'd come around perhaps at dinner time, he'd go downstairs to the bathroom and wash his hands for dinner (he always washed his hands for dinner). I used to be combing Mrs. Clemens' hair. She set in front of the mirror, where she could see him as he'd come out of the bathroom (he'd have a towel wiping his hands, maybe); and he'd look at me in the glass over her head (I was standing behind her, fixing her hair) and I'd look at him, and I used to know by his wink that he *found* the manuscript himself. Then he'd say, kind of sheepish:

"I found it, Katy." And I'd say, "Well, I knew you would," and Mrs. Clemens would start up and say, "What's that? What is it?"

"Oh, nothing!" he says, careless like, "I was just telling Katy something."

"Oh, this is nothing new to me, Mrs. Clemens, but it *was* something—it was a great deal," I says.

WHERE MARK TWAIN WAS BORN, NOVEMBER 30, 1835, FLORIDA, MISSOURI
(Courtesy A. B. Paine and Harper & Brothers)

Gunney

MARK TWAIN, ABOUT 1869
(Courtesy Harper & Brothers)

W. Knowlton's, Elmira

MRS. CLEMENS AS A YOUNG GIRL

"No, no," said Mr. Clemens, "it's nothing! Don't make such a fuss about it, Katy. I just kind of thought you destroyed some of my manuscript, that's all."

"Oh, Mrs. Clemens!" I said, "if it wasn't for *you*, I'd be on my way back to Elmira to-night, because he accused me of taking his manuscript, burning his manuscript and destroying it! I told him I knew he'd find it—and he has. He's all the time scolding me for burning his manuscript."

"Oh, Youth dear," Mrs. Clemens said, "you mustn't scold Katy. Why do you scold her like that when she wouldn't destroy any of your manuscript for anything in this world? She knows what it is—and she's very careful about it."

"Well," he said, "I couldn't find it anyway. I never can find it after *she's* been dusting my table!"

"But you did find it," I said.

"Well, yes," says he, kind of sheepish again. "I found it in a pigeonhole just now."

And then he'd turn and go away pretty quick before anything else could be said to him. By and by he'd come back all smoothed down and then Mrs. Clemens said:

"I suppose I'll have to go up there again and dust that table myself."

"No, Livy darling, no, no," he said. "That's all right. Katy's all right as long as she doesn't *touch* anything!"

So he used to mark with his foot how near I could go

to that precious table, and he'd put a mark about a foot away from it.

"Now," he'd say, "do you see that? Don't you dare go inside that mark, Katy, never!"

"All right, Mr. Clemens, all right," I says—but I'd go there just the same! But that precious manuscript was always a trouble between us and sometimes he used swear words when he thought anything was lost—but I don't want to say the words he used. Oh, he'd say anything! Sometimes he'd say, "I know that's a damn lie," when I told him I hadn't touched any of his writing; then I'd say:

"Oh, Mr. Clemens, you told me I was a liar!" But I didn't say what *kind* of a liar he called me. You couldn't say it before Mrs. Clemens, oh, no! You couldn't make a swear word before her (though he did sometimes, if he thought she didn't hear him!). But he always found the manuscript in the end, after all the swearing and fighting. Finally I says to him one morning:

"Now, Mr. Clemens, I want to say to you that I never destroyed one item of paper that you ever have a sign of writing on. I never destroy it—never—I put it away," I says. "When I first began to dust your table, I made a great big bag and it's in there—in the closet; and I put every little scrap in it—every scrap you ever wrote anything on, from the first time I began to dust your table. I know how valuable it is and how disturbed you get for fear your manuscript might be lost or destroyed. I am very particular about it," I says, "very particular."

Well, of course we had a good many tough fights, but after a while he didn't say anything more to me. He had to trust me and I can prove it, too, because when he wrote *Tom Sawyer* (he wrote part of it up at Quarry Farm)— Yes, it was the manuscript of *Tom Sawyer*, I think, if I remember right—but whatever it was, it was one of his most valuable manuscripts and he sent it home in a trunk—back to Hartford—sent it to *me*, and wrote that he was sending his precious trunk in my name and I didn't need to open it because there was manuscript in it. Well, by that time manuscripts was something wonderful to me! Oh! I think I had six or seven letters he wrote me about that trunk with the manuscripts in. Well, you know, it came safe and sound and of course nobody opened it until he arrived. I opened it the day he came —had it up in the Billiard Room all ready for him.

"Now, Mr. Clemens," I says, "your manuscript is all right, and safe here—it's up in the Billiard Room; I opened the trunk a little while ago, as you can see it when you go up."

"Oh," he said, very polite, "thank you—thank you very much, Katy. I knew if I sent it to *you*, it would be all right!"

Just think of that! After all the scoldings he give me about them manuscripts, he did depend on me a little bit (he had to) finally. If he thought of anything in the middle of the night, you know, he would jump up out of bed and go right upstairs and write it—write sometimes two and three hours up there. He always gave Mrs. Clemens the manuscript to read first. She always had a pile of manuscript right by her bed. Every night he laid them there. I think she read everything as fast as he wrote it—and when he was writing he had plenty for her, I can tell you. She looked it all over and scratched some out, and gave it back to him to fix up again, because what she scratched out would sometimes spoil as much as two or three pages. Mr. Clemens always listened to everything Mrs. Clemens said. She always made every plan and did everything, you know. He would often say to her, "Well, I think it would be nice maybe if we give a dinner party" (there were so many wonderful gentlemen he liked to invite, and their wives, too); and so she planned it and fixed it all up, and made it a very elegant dinner for him. Oh, she was a wonderful, wonderful woman to get up anything like that, you know! They used to have the most beautiful dinners that I ever heard of before or since; and she had the colored butler, George, to top it all off. And I used to help the butler some in those days, that is, take the extra dishes off—that first winter I was there. To them dinners we always had a fillet of beef and ducks as a rule, canvasback, they called them. Oh, and this is one thing that I must tell you!

It was when we was having that silly old "chestnut"

joke. Well, I used to pass the vegetables, and one night we had mashed chestnuts; and when I passed the dish to Mr. Clemens he looked in it and whispered, "What is that, Katy?"

"Chestnuts," says I, "chestnuts."

But he looked at me and said, "Katy, I asked you *what* was in that dish"; and I said "Chestnuts" again, and told him to take some because they was *good* chestnuts. But he didn't—he thought I was just playing a joke on him—and he wouldn't touch them. Well, at those dinners, as I was telling you, we had soup first, of course, and then the beef or ducks, you know, and then we'd have wine with our cigars, and we'd have sherry, claret, and champagne, maybe— Now what else? Oh, yes! We'd always have crême de menthe and most always charlotte russe, too. Then we'd sometimes have Nesselrode pudding and very often ice cream for the most elegant dinners. No, never plain ordinary ice cream—we always had our ice cream put up in some wonderful shapes—like flowers or cherubs, little angels—all different kinds and different shapes and flavors, and colors—oh! everything lovely! And then after the company had eat up all the little ice-cream angels, the ladies would all depart into the living-room and the gentlemen would sit (*lounge,* I think they called it) around the table and have a little more champagne (maybe) while we passed the coffee to the ladies in the drawing-room, where they'd drink it and then set down and gossip awhile.

Wonderful people come, like Mr. and Mrs. Charles Dudley Warner, also there was W. D. Howells—he was a writer, too—and his wife, come up from Boston, and Mr. and Mrs. Cheney, from West Hartford, and Dr. and Mrs. Twitchell—he was the minister—the children called him Uncle Joe. And T. B. Aldrich—he was an editor—and Bret Harte—and Mr. Cable—and— Oh, it's so hard for me to remember all the names—there's no end to them.

Well, speaking of famous people, I must tell you about Lawrence Barrett. He was an actor, Irish—a gallant Irishman—which interested me—being Irish myself! He come to call one day and they didn't ask him (I don't know why—they didn't think of it, I suppose)—they didn't ask him to dinner; so he just had to call and go away, and was very disappointed. When Mr. Clemens heard how bad he felt, he went and asked him if he would be in town the next day, and Barrett said he didn't know; maybe—he'd see. So then Mr. Clemens said:

"Now, we'd like to have you stay over tomorrow night and perhaps you could meet some of our friends at a nice dinner party."

"Oh, I'd love to," he says, very pleased. So he stayed and they gave a lovely dinner for him to make up for his disappointment.

Lawrence Barrett was a very fine actor—he used to act with Booth, I believe, who was very famous then. He was a very nice gentleman, Barrett was, Irish—though he sounded quite English when he talked. I suppose that's because he was on the stage and used elegant language. I don't think anybody very extra come to this dinner they gave him,—just the family and a few friends, but they told lots of funny stories and had a grand time, and he was well satisfied after that.

You know, Mr. Clemens used to tell a story called "My Golden Arm." Well, it seems that when he was a little boy that they had two slaves in the family,—two old colored servants, and this old colored Mammy used to tell Mr. Clemens (little "Sam" as she called him) and his little brothers and sisters lots of blood-curdling, hair-raising stories, that would frighten the children almost to death! Mr. Clemens says they used to set around the fireplace, his father and his mother and all the children, and then when it got kind of dark that colored Mammy'd begin and tell the children them stories—and that's where he got the Golden Arm story from. She used to tell it to him. I suppose, of course, Mr. Clemens kind of fixed it up and made more of it—made it more dramatic—but anyway, it was one of his most famous stories, and he used to tell that almost every dinner, and at his lectures, too. I can't tell it very good—not the way he did. I only remember it was a story about a man whose wife had her arm cut off, and they gave her a nice gold one in its place. When she died her husband couldn't stand the idea, I guess, of that gold arm being buried along with her and wasted. So he sneaked off in the night and dug her up—took away the golden arm and put it under his coat and rode off quick with it. It was an awful stormy, windy night, and as he was rushing along, he kept hearing a voice—like a ghost or something—his conscience, I guess 'twas,—whispering and wailing right in his ear through the wind:

"Who's got my golden arm? Who's got my golden arm?"

The faster he went, the louder the voice whispered:

"Who's got my golden arm? Who's got my golden arm?"

Oh, it's a terrible story! It's in Mr. Clemens' biography. Well, when Mr. Clemens come to that part where the voice kept whispering, *"Who's got my golden arm? Who's got my golden arm?"* he began very soft and then come out louder and louder, then very loud and hard toward the end—when he used to rise right up out of his chair, and lean way forward over the table very sudden, and point with his finger straight at somebody, and cry *"YOU'VE got my golden arm!"*—in the most blood-curdling tones,—the kind he always used for that story. Oh, my! It would frighten any one almost to death, the way he said it. When Mr. Clemens told that story (he was always telling it at dinner parties) he would frighten everybody stiff. The company always said the shivers went straight down their spines—they felt like they was freezing to death! It made what you call a sensation!

There was another story he used to tell about a little baby that was born in England. He was invited there to the christening, and the minister, he came to the pulpit and said (the baby laid in the minister's arms—it was so little he could almost blow it from one hand to the other), "Well," the minister says, "it's a little mite of a thing, but it *may* be wonderful, it may grow up to be a great member of Parliament, it may be a great President, it may be . . ." Oh, well, he told all the great things it might be! Then he turned to the mother and he said, very polite, "And what is his name?"—and she said "Mary Ann!" My goodness! That just took the wind out of his sails! He didn't say anything about its growing up to be a wonderful *woman!* Oh, no! He didn't make any more remarks after that splurge! He quieted right down. That's a pretty good story, I think, when you really take it in.

Then we had Henry Irving there in Hartford when he was playing at the theater. We had lots of famous people in them days. Irving—why he was just plain Henry; he wasn't a Sir then, he got his title afterwards—well, he was playing in Hartford and stayed with us three nights, but Ellen Terry didn't come to us—she used to stay at the hotel. And then we had Elsie Leslie, too. She was a child actress, you know. She stayed with us all the time she acted in Mr. Clemens' play, *The Prince and the Pauper*, when it played in Hartford. You know, Elsie Leslie played the two parts, the Prince and Tom Canty. It was a terrible exciting time when the rehearsing was going on, because the Clemens children was just crazy about it—the theater—and Susy wrote a little play of her own at that time and they put it on one Thanksgiving night and Clara and Jean and Margaret Warner was in it, too. Oh, it was lovely! And Mr. Clemens was just wild over it and he had them do that play two or three times, he liked it so much. He was telling everybody how proud he was of Susy—for writing that play—and how talented she was.

Elsie Leslie was a little mite of a thing when she acted in Hartford that time, why, she used to play with Clara and Susy up in the hay loft and sometimes she didn't want to go to the theater at all to do her part—she just wanted to stay and play with the children, and then Mr. Clemens, he'd have to coax her and tell her stories and take her there himself sometimes, because she was an awful stubborn little rat—but then, you couldn't blame her none because she was nothing but a child. William Gillette, the actor, he was awful fond of Elsie Leslie, and he was always over to the Clemens house, you know. He thought she was very talented, and she was an awful cunnin' little thing. Mr. Clemens just loved her.

Well, there was an awful funny thing happened about her one time. Mr. Clemens and Mr. Gillette thought they'd give her a present—something they made themselves (as a joke, I guess). So they embroidered her a pair of slippers. Each one had a slipper to embroider all himself. Oh, my! You should have seen the awful mess they made of it! Mr. Clemens was always carrying his around with him and had a great big needle and embroidery silk, working on that slipper, and my land! them slippers was big enough for a giant and the funniest-looking things you ever saw! But then, of course it was all done as a joke, as I said before.

Now, I have spoken about William Gillette quite a number of times, because he was there an awful lot and I was just crazy about him. I thought he was the handsomest man I ever had looked at. The first time I seen him, I didn't know who it was and I couldn't hardly take my eyes off him, and I says to Mrs. Clemens when I went upstairs after he'd gone, I says, "Why, who is that man—that handsome man—the best-looking man I ever laid an eye on?" And she laughed and said: "Why, Katy, don't you know? That's William Gillette, the actor. He is handsome," she says—and he was! He became very famous afterwards. And Joseph Jefferson, too—he was another one. He was a great actor—one of the very best, and he used to come and stay at the house a lot—sometimes stay three and four days. He used to come at the same time William Gillette did, and they used to play billiards together.

Joe Jefferson was a little mite of a man, and I remember once it was awful cold when he come there, and Mr. Clemens made him put on his big fur coat. Everybody that come to Hartford had to put on that fur coat of Mr. Clemens if they was cold. Joe Jefferson was kind of lost in it—it was so big for him. But he could talk, I tell you, and crack jokes, too—and he used to tell awful funny stories at dinner. He was a very good actor, they said, about one of the greatest that America ever produced—although I never seen him myself. He did one play all the time—*Rip Van Winkle*, that was.

As I told you before, the Clemens children was just crazy about the theater. They was always having charades in the early Hartford days. They loved that and they always had nice costumes to rig themselves up in. Their father used to play with them and he was a grand actor, and the children used to have wonderful times with him. The Warners and the Twitchell children used to come over, too. Yes, Mr. Clemens was certainly very dramatic and would have made a great actor if he'd gone on the stage. He always loved the theater right up to the day of his death, and we always had lots of famous actors at our house, and Henry Irving, as I said before, was among the best of the lot.

Henry Irving, he used to tell wonderful stories, too,

you know, at our dinners. He was very entertaining—good company to be with, though he was very quiet.

Well, Mrs. Clemens always had a new dress for every dinner. She wore brown a good deal, silks and velvets. She had one dinner dress that was a wonderful dress. Madame Fogarty (she was a great dressmaker in New York) made all her dresses, made her wedding dress and made her dresses right up to the time she died. She made the dress she was buried in—but, oh! I can't speak of that now! . . . Well, she had this beautiful brown dress of satin and velvet, and the satin was all puffed out and made fringy, you know; and the skirt had panels to it. Oh, beautiful they was—they trailed on the ground. She always used to wear high collars too—never wore low neck.

Mr. Clemens never appeared in his famous white suit in those days. That come afterwards. His hair never was red in my time, either. No, he always had gray hair. He was married ten years when I went there and he had gray hair then. He used to have a feeling that if his hair was massaged every day it would stay in—that he wouldn't ever get bald. He had a horror of being bald-headed. I went to Boston with Miss Clara once and I studied massaging the head there, because she said, "Father'll like this, Katy, when we get home, because then you can massage his head and he'll never get bald."

So I used to massage his head every morning. He'd

ring for me at a certain time to massage his head—even up to the time he died. He used to think it helped his hair to stay in—and it did! And nobody had more beautiful hair than he had.

Mr. Clemens was a very good-looking man—oh, very good-looking, indeed. He had nice eyes and he was lovely and kind and very much—well, he looked like a person very much devoted to his wife—which I found out afterward he was. It struck me that way the first time I saw him. You can always tell. He had such nice manners, too, and was so interested in everything. He looked just like all his pictures, too; and he had such deep, interesting eyes. Somebody asked me one time what *kind* of eyes Mr. Clemens had. Well, I thought for a moment and then I said, "Now, really, I can't tell." So I was talking with Mrs. Clemens one morning, and I asked:

"What *kind* of eyes has Mr. Clemens?"

And she says, "Why, Katy, don't you know?"

"No, I don't," I says, "because sometimes when Mr. Clemens is very jolly and happy his eyes are *blue* to me; but when he gets angry or upset at anything, like losing his wonderful manuscript, his eyes are very fierce and *black*."

And Mrs. Clemens laughed and laughed, and said: "Yes, I guess that's true, Katy; but his eyes are really blue."

But I couldn't tell actually, because he had two kinds of eyes, to me. He always dressed very nice. He used to wear a Prince Albert when he was dressed up good, and had gray striped trousers, but I don't know what kind of a waistcoat he wore—I guess it was black like his coat. And he wore nice little low collars with a pretty little black tie—a bow, like in one of his pictures—and oh! he didn't wear shirts buttoned in front like they used to wear in them days. He didn't like those shirts, so he had a man in Hartford make his shirts special for him, with the buttons on the back, but he wanted the collar on the shirt, sewed on half way, one of those little collars, turned over, so that it was easy for him to get into (without swearing), I guess!

It was while they was living in Hartford they put *The Prince and the Pauper* on the stage (that was Mr. Clemens' play from his book). Mrs. Clemens did it herself, got it up all herself for the children.

Well, as I told you, we had a wonderful house in Hartford in them days, with a conservatory, too. In the back end was a living-room, and Mrs. Clemens thought it would be nice to have the play there. Mr. Clemens was away and she thought it would be nice to surprise him with this play when he come home, so she got everything ready. She got the actresses and actors together and Susy was the Prince and Daisy Warner (she was Charles D. Warner's niece—William Gillette's niece, too), she was in it, too. He was a great friend—came over every day when he was in Hartford—as I told you before.

Well, Daisy Warner was the Pauper, and Clara was Lady Jane Grey—and she was wonderful! Jean was one of Lady Jane's maids, and they had beautiful costumes, made exactly to picture the thing. I was in it, too. And the scenery was wonderful, real painted scenery that Carl Gerhardt did. I guess I'd better tell you now about Carl Gerhardt.

Well, Carl Gerhardt was a young fellow that worked in Pratt & Whitney's Machine Shop. Mr. Clemens got interested in him and sent him to Europe to learn to be a sculptor, because he was really a natural-borned artist, and he sent him over there and paid all his expenses. So Carl, he went over there and began to study. He made a bust of somebody for his lessons (they had to see how long it took the pupils to make a bust)—they had samples, I suppose, to work from—and Carl, he got the first prize from his sample; and he sent it on to Mr. Clemens, and Mr. Clemens was pleased because he had helped him. Then Carl came back to America and he also got to be quite a painter, too. So he painted all this scenery for the *Prince and the Pauper* play; that's why I'm telling about him now.

Well, the play was done in the drawing-room and the conservatory was the Palace garden, and it looked just like a real palace. Oh, it looked brilliant and lovely!

Bundy, Hartford

KATY LEARY AS A YOUNG WOMAN WHEN SHE WORKED FOR MARK TWAIN IN HARTFORD

MRS. CLEMENS WITH CLARA AND SUSY
(Courtesy of Mrs. Ossip Gabrilowitsch)

All the audience set in the living-room and dining-room. Mr. Clemens was in it, too, and he was so funny, just his walk was funny—the *way* he walked! He made out he was quite lame when he was walking out in the play. (He was Miles Hendon.) Then he rang the bell for me to bring the pitcher of water in, and he poured it out the wrong way—by the handle and not by the nose—and of course that took down the house! They roared at him when it was over. Then he made a few remarks, telling how his wife got up this thing to surprise him, and it did surprise him, because it was the most wonderfully got up thing he'd ever seen. It couldn't have been got up better by a regular artist in the theater, he said—and that was so; and Mrs. Clemens was so happy, after all her hard work, just 'cause he was pleased.

There was always funny things happening in that household and one of the funniest was about the picture agent. That's an old story—it was kind of a stand-by in the family—it's been told pretty often and I guess there's been some "embroidery" added to it from time to time, as Mr. Clemens would say; but anyway, this is the way I remember it: Well, it seems one day some of the pictures (the wires got loose and rusty) was falling down off the wall. So Mrs. Clemens thought she'd have George put new wires on. So they took a lot of them pictures down and laid them around on the floor and up against the wall, and had the room full of them pictures, when a gentleman come to call on Mr. Clemens.

Well, that morning, it seems, Mr. Clemens said to George not to disturb him under any circumstances, "Not if the Holy Ghost comes" he says—not to call him down! So when this man came and gave his card to George, poor George, he didn't know what to do. So he took the card to Mrs. Clemens. She looked at it and says: "Oh, yes! Take it up to Mr. Clemens, and he'll come right down."

"He said not to disturb him," George says, "not even if the Holy Ghost comes—not to disturb him."

"But," she said, "you tell him these are my wishes." So George went up and told Mr. Clemens there was a nice gentleman down in the parlor and would he come down and see him. I don't think Mr. Clemens even looked at the card at all, he was so mad and upset.

"No, no," he says to George, "no, I don't want to see anybody—it's some book agent, I suppose! I won't see him."

Well, it seems this gentleman was wonderful to them when they was up in Onteora one summer, and did everything for them to make them comfortable. That's why Mrs. Clemens wanted Mr. Clemens to see him. But, of course, Mr. Clemens didn't know anything about that—that this was the same man. But when George told him that Mrs. Clemens wanted him to come down, he said, "Oh, well, he'd go—but he'd be damned if he'd buy anything!"

So he hurried down. He didn't even look at the man

when he come into the room, because the first thing his eye lit on was them pictures lying on the floor, and he says right out, before the man could speak a single word:

"No, no, no! We don't want any of your damned old truck!" he said. "We've got all and more than we can take care of now. Take it away! Take it away!"

Well, this gentleman, of course, didn't know what on earth to make of it, so he tried to be very polite and he says he did hope Mrs. Clemens was well. Mr. Clemens thought that was pretty fresh and funny, and so he says, very cross:

"Oh, yes, she's well enough!"

So the poor gentleman didn't know what to make of that, either—not knowing Mr. Clemens thought he was a picture agent! So he sort of set down for a minute on the edge of the chair and picked up one of them pictures—to hide his embarrassment, I guess. And—my goodness! When Mr. Clemens seen that, he just went on a regular rampage, he got terrible mad. He says: "No, I tell you, no! We don't want that! We've got that one! We don't want any of them pictures of yours. I told you to take all that truck away with you, and clear out! We don't want any of the damned old stuff. Take it away! Don't bother me with it!"

Well, by this time the poor man (his name was Martin) didn't know where to look nor what on earth to make of it; so he jumped up and rushed right out of the room without another word. When Mrs. Clemens came in a few minutes afterward and seen he wasn't around, she called George.

"Did Mr. Clemens see that gentleman, George?"

"Yes," George said, "he see him, but he insulted him something terrible; told him to take those pictures in the living-room and get out! He thought they were *his!* He thought he was a picture agent." So she sent for Mr. Clemens right away and says, "Oh, Youth dear, did you know *who* that was?"

"Why, no!" he said. "Who was it?" Then she told him who it was and he felt terrible! He said: "George, I heard him ask you for some house—Charles Dudley Warner's. Has he gone over there?"

"Yes," George said, "he's gone over there."

Well, Mr. Clemens just had on his old slippers and no hat, but he ran over to the Warners' house as fast as he could and he brought the gentleman right home and they gave him a wonderful dinner that night, to make up for sending him off that way.

And another afternoon Mr. Dickens—old Dickens' son—and his wife appeared there. Well, they gave another wonderful dinner for them. They got it up right that night, so it was a hurried dinner; but there was a Mrs. Perkins, lived in Hartford (she was a Beecher, sister of the lady that wrote *Uncle Tom's Cabin*), who came that night. It was Harriet Beecher Stowe, you know, that wrote that book, *Uncle Tom's Cabin*, and it was a wonderful book, that was. 'Twas all about slavery, and it created a great impression all over the world, they said. She used to come to the Clemens a great deal in the old Hartford days. She kind of lost her mind a little bit when she got older, but she was very nice. She used to go out every day for a walk and every one she'd meet, she'd stop and talk with them very pleasant and ask them if they'd read her book *Uncle Tom's Cabin*, and some of them would have a blank face on, and didn't know what she was talking about. "Really," she'd say, "you should read it. What's your name and address? I'll write to my publishers and have them send you a copy right away." Then, of course, everybody would say they hadn't read it, because they all wanted one of them books free! She used to write her autograph in all her books, and her autograph was: "Love the Lord and do good." That's pretty, ain't it? "Love the Lord and do good."

She loved flowers, and she loved roses the best of all; and she used to come over to our conservatory and help herself, pick the flowers herself—snap them right off, the roses, but Mrs. Clemens always said to let her do as she liked—let her pick all the roses she wanted herself, and so she would always go away with a big bunch of them. She just loved flowers and couldn't see one without wanting to pick it. That was her way of doing things. She always wanted to help herself—never wanted anybody to give her anything. I was always very much interested in her and I read her book, too, but in those early days, authors didn't hit me so much as they do now, because I didn't know enough to appreciate them. Now I can understand them, and know that they are different and have to be treated different, but then—why, of course, I thought they was just like anybody else.

Anyway, to go back to the dinner party, this lady was at that dinner for Dickens, and she told some wonderful stories and so did Mr. Dickens. I remember about it, for I helped wait on the table. I always helped George wait on table if there was over twelve at the dinner. Mr. Clemens wouldn't be expected, at a regular dinner party, in them days, to get up and walk around and talk—the way he used to later on; but he did walk about sometimes at dinner when the family was all alone—walked and talked. He loved that. When Mr. Clemens used to get up and walk and talk at the dinner table, he used to always be waving his napkin to kind of illustrate what he was saying, I guess. He seemed to be able to talk better when he was walking than when he was settin' down. He always asked the guests to tell stories, too, at these grand dinner parties, you know, he would ask everybody, but his stories was the best of all, of course, and all the guests wanted him to tell them—and he just loved that, too, and always had a fresh supply on hand.

His story-telling always seemed just like acting to me. I think myself he would have made a great actor—'cause he was always so very dramatic—about everything. Henry Irving it was, I think, that said so too—that Mr. Clemens had the makings of a very great actor in him.

George and I always used to listen to them stories—listen through the crack of the door at all the grand dinner parties. Oh! we just loved them—and George used to laugh very loud at all the jokes. Sometimes George would laugh right out in front of the company while he was waiting on the table. I'll tell you about that later on, 'cause 'twas awful funny, though it used to make Mrs. Clemens feel terrible; but there was no stopping George when he started to laugh!

Mrs. Warner was a great story-teller and so were lots of others. John McCullough, too. He was a famous actor that used to come to our house very often in them days. He come one night and he acted kind of sad and queer, and Mr. Clemens asked him what it was that made him feel so bad—thought there must be something troubling him, you know. He had a wife and he'd got rid of her, and maybe that was what was troubling him. He was losing his mind, that was the amount of it—which he did shortly after he left. He wasn't himself at all at that time, and didn't have anything to say hardly, and before that he was always very jolly, told stories and made everybody laugh and laughed loud himself, too; but this time he didn't. He felt very bad. It was a sad affair, for he was a very good actor. It was in New Haven, I think, the last time he acted, that he came right out on the stage and he began sneezing on the stage (instead of acting), and that was the first the audience thought there must be something wrong, you know, because he wouldn't come out on the stage just to sneeze at them. Well, he couldn't finish his act—he went right back behind the curtain and never come out again, not any more. It sounds funny, the sneezing part, but it was really very sad, for he was a great actor in the old days, and everybody admired him very much, including Mr. Clemens.

Henry Irving, as I told you, used to come to the house a lot. He always seemed like one of those old Quakers to me, with his long hair and long face. He was—well, Quaker-like, don't you know—very quiet. But he seemed very nice and pleasant always. He played billiards a good deal, and Mr. Clemens would keep him all the day playing billiards, and he never said a word when he was playing—quite different from Mr. Howells, who used to laugh all the time.

There was another famous character and writer—he wrote stories—used to come there, too. Everybody knows him—Bret Harte, his name was. And he come and made quite a long visit there once, and he and Mr. Clemens wrote a play together. It didn't last very long, but they said it was good while it did last, and of course Mr. Clemens was crazy about it. Then afterwards I heard it was put on in New York, but it really didn't go. It was kind of a fizzle. Mr. Clemens wrote quite a number of plays, but none of them amounted to much except *Pudd'nhead Wilson.* That was a great success.

Yes, we used to have all kinds of famous people in

Hartford in the old days, and dinner parties all the time. Mr. Howells used to come very often to visit, and they would all laugh from the time he come in till he went out. He used to come up from Boston in them days. He was a writer himself, and very famous. Well, you couldn't hear a thing from the Billiard Room but peals of laughter from them two men when he was visiting there. Oh, how they'd laugh! Mr. Clemens and Mr. Howells. They'd tell jokes all day long. He used always to be joking Mr. Clemens and everybody, and so did Mr. Clemens. Mr. Howells was a very nice man, a nice fatherly kind of a man, and he had a wonderful smart daughter—"Pilla," they called her, but her name was really Mildred; and then he had a son, too, a nice boy named John. I'll tell you about him later. But Mr. Howells was such a nice fatherly man. He was just kind of ordinary, don't you know, to look at him, but you liked him just to see him. They loved each other very dearly and Mrs. Clemens was a great friend of Mrs. Howells, too.

Charles Dudley Warner, he was there all the time. He was a neighbor, too. He was quite a famous writer—though not as famous as Mr. Clemens. He was a fine man and he was asked to every dinner party and Mrs. Warner was a great friend of Mrs. Clemens, and they were always together. All those wonderful people were at everything that happened in Hartford.

One winter they had a reading class of Dickens. Mr.

Clemens used to read every Wednesday morning to a lot of ladies that come there. The ladies was Mrs. Trumble (Ann Trumble), and Mrs. Warner (both the Warners), and—oh, yes, Mrs. Twitchell. She was there a great deal and was always a great help to Mrs. Clemens entertaining the people. Mrs. Robinson too, and she was kind of sensible—and Mrs. Whitmore was another one. Oh, lots of ladies in Hartford come. They'd all come—all that was invited. They'd go up to the Billiard Room and sit there while Mr. Clemens read to them—read aloud from Dickens. He read about an hour or so every Wednesday morning, and they all was so delighted—they'd go away laughing and telling what a lovely time they'd had. Then they used to have what they called a Saturday Morning Club, too, when they'd go to different people's houses. They had a big party once, a lot of women in Hartford, and one Saturday morning they had their lunch at our house. We served it out in the arbor—a great big place on the lawn, and Mrs. Clemens gave the luncheon out there. It was a very nice luncheon—a very pretty affair, and Mr. Clemens, he come along while they was eating and stopped at every table and made a few remarks and they was delighted. I remember one table he stopped at he said: "Now, ladies, ladies, look here! This won't do! I don't believe you're eating all these nice expensive things we're giving you—you're leaving too many good things on your plates. I want you to eat up *everything*—because, if you don't, why, I'll have to eat all the stuff myself after you've gone! I'll have to eat cold food for the rest of the week—so I want you to eat up every scrap yourselves—to save me from that terrible fate!" Of course they all roared at it, then eat up every single thing to please him!

Oh, those was happy, happy times! It seemed so wonderful to me the things they did. It was a wonderful life they led, Mr. and Mrs. Clemens. Yes, they had a wonderful life. I realized it then—even if I hadn't had any life before that, you know. I always thought it was wonderful from the beginning—to live with such people. Why, just to hear them talking was happiness to me.

Now I must tell you about Friday night and the billiard playing. Mr. Clemens always reserved Friday nights for his billiards. He had company every Friday night—he invited this company himself. Mr. Whitmore and Mr. George W. Robinson (he was Governor then) and Edward Bunce (he was quite prominent, too) and lots of others I can't remember. Well, they used to play billiards every Friday night and sometimes there'd be a few ladies. Mr. Clemens always invited the wives to come and keep Mrs. Clemens company down in the Library, and Mrs. Clemens would have tea there, and Mr. Clemens would have beer and hardtack in the Billiard Room—that's what he treated his friends to—and played billiards till about ten o'clock, and laughed and told stories and you could hear them all over the house laughing, you know, and having such a good old time coming downstairs. Little Jean used to hear them coming down—her room was right on the landing—it always used to wake her up.

I think I'll tell the story now about Jean and her praying. She was about six years old, I should say, and everything she wanted she would pray to God for nights, for she had a way of praying for everything she wanted (never got anything, though!). This is the prayer she began with. I listened to her for, oh, a month almost, then I thought it was too good to listen to alone any longer, so I called the family in. She used to sleep in the nursery. Her bed was right near the fireplace and I think she used to talk up the fireplace—it sounded like it anyway. She'd begin: "Dear Jesus and dear God! I wish you'd bring me a pair of ponies and nice cart and a harness and everything that goes with it, and get it here—oh, well, you needn't get it here so very early in the morning, but if you get it here say about nine o'clock that would do, and I could help my mother a great deal. She could get the rugs from the rug man's and if they didn't fit I could take them back in my little cart—so, dear Jesus and dear God, I hope you won't forget it." Then she'd say: "I know you're far away, but mamma says you can hear everything I say; so if you'd just bring the ponies and the cart around in the morning, why, of course, that'd be all right and make me happy. Don't forget, please, please! Good night, dear Jesus and dear God."

There was a lady there the night that I called Mr. Clemens up to listen to that prayer. He listened for a long time and was very much—well, you know, depressed, and affected by it. I don't know what you'd call it—he was crying and the tears was running down his face. "Oh, the little darling," he says. "The little darling!"—the faith she had so touched him. This lady that was visiting there said when she went back downstairs, she says, "Why, if I had to hunt all over Hartford, all over New York, I would get those ponies and that cart and have them here some morning."

Mr. Clemens says, "Yes, and I'll go and get them in the morning." But Mrs. Clemens said:

"No, Youth dear. Don't do that," she said. "I would be so glad if she could have them, but I don't want to give them to her just because we could afford to get the ponies and the cart, for," she says, "if they were downstairs in the morning and then Jean would ask for something else that we *couldn't* get, maybe—then she'd lose the faith she has; that if God could give her one thing he ought to give her *everything*, no matter what she asks for."

Wasn't that sensible? Whoever 'twas there visiting I don't remember, but she didn't have such good sense as Mrs. Clemens. Jean never got the ponies then, but she kept right on praying. She'd pray for everything and anything. Why, I heard her say once, "Dear Jesus and dear God: Couldn't you please make it so's I could eat corn-beef hash with potatoes in it?"

She kept it up, her praying, all the winter. I always used to listen when I'd be passing by and she would have something new every night to pray for, but the ponies were the greatest thing.

The children were always up to something, especially Clara. We had a coachman, Patrick. He was a funny man and Irish. He had a cow that had a calf, and the calf Clara named Jumbo. Now, Clara wanted a pony at that time. She wasn't more than seven or eight years old, but she wanted a pony terrible bad; but her mother wouldn't get her one—she was afraid she'd get killed on it, so Patrick said: "Now, Miss Clara, I'll tell you what we'll do. If you do just as I tell you we'll make this little calf turn straight into a pony! It will grow right into a pony, and then you will have a nice little one all your own." "Oh! what must we do, Patrick?" said Clara, terrible excited. "Well, in the first place," says Patrick, "you must curry it every day yourself—like I do the horse. You must also be very careful about his feet to wash them thorough every day, and keep him very nice and clean, just like I do the horse." "Oh, all right!" said Clara, delighted. So she began to work on Jumbo and cleaned him up good every morning. Then Patrick said to her—"Now, you will have to have a suit made to work in." "What kind of a suit?" says Clara. "Well," says he, "perhaps your mother could buy you a hat and a pair of trousers so you can come out every morning and clean the stable, too, when you clean Jumbo." Well, she got the suit somehow or other, and every morning she took off her clothes on the porch under the little laundry, and put on that suit and stole out to the stable and curried off Jumbo. She'd wash his feet good and thorough (washed her own at the same time, too!) and then,—well, there was always something new that Patrick was putting her up to. The next thing Patrick said—she must have a blanket for the calf to keep him warm. Of course she couldn't buy these things—couldn't ask for anything because she was keeping it a secret—that the calf was going to turn into a pony! She wanted to be perfectly independent—and to have this horse for her own, and didn't want the family to know anything about it. So she came to me and said, "Katy, have you got anything that I could make a blanket for my calf?" I thought for a minute, then I says: "Well, I'll tell you. There's a cover in the storehouse, an old cover to a billiard table, green cloth, that's all torn and dirty. You can have that, I guess."

So she went and looked at it and said: "Oh, Katy! That will be just the thing! Will you help me make it?" So I began to take the measures. We went and got the measure around Jumbo's neck and back, down to his tail, so it would cover him all up good. We got the blanket fixed—and then Patrick got her a halter to lead him, and oh! it made him look funny, for Jumbo was a red calf and she put a green blanket on him! Every day she took him out for a run in the lane and her father and mother used to watch her from the house. They used to think that calf would go so fast that she'd bound right over the rocks and kill herself. There was a hill and the brook below it, and Mrs. Clemens used to say:

"Oh! That calf will certainly throw Clara into the river."

"Oh, no," said Mr. Clemens, laughing. "No, he won't. I'll trust her with Jumbo. Jumbo's all right!"

She kept doing that to get Jumbo used to running with the halter. Well, the days went on and she got pretty anxious to know *when* he was going to turn into a pony.

"Patrick," she says, "we ought to get him a saddle now, don't you think, just to try him? It will frighten him if he gets much older and don't know how a saddle feels on his back."

So Patrick kept up the joke. He had an old saddle that belonged to somebody in the army, an old thing all in tatters, but Patrick fixed it up and made a saddle small enough to fit that calf's back—half fit, anyway. Well, he had the saddle fixed and one morning she started to take a ride. She got the calf up to the front door of the stable, and Patrick helped her on his back. There was a road near the stable and a row of evergreens growing there, and suddenly, without any warning, Jumbo kicked up his hind feet and he throwed her right into that bunch

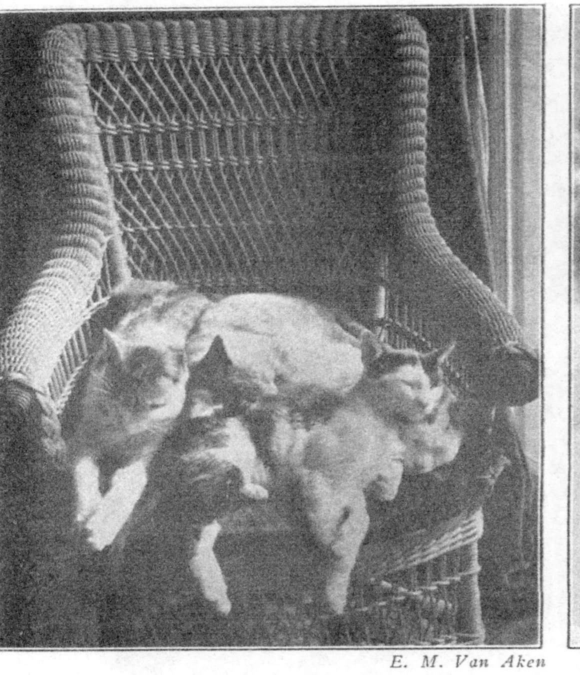

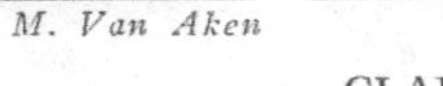

E. M. Van Aken

MARK TWAIN'S CATS

Gessford, N. Y.

CLARA AND THE CALF JUMBO, WHO WAS GOING TO TURN INTO A PONY

Alfred Ellis

MARK TWAIN, OF HARTFORD DAYS

of evergreens, and there she sprawled, all over them there evergreens! She hurt her hand, and scratched her arms and legs; but she never said a word nor cried nor anything. She didn't lose faith even then in him turning into a pony. Then she tried it again and got on his back, and we had a great big jardinière setting in front of the driveway, and Jumbo, when he seen that, he went right up to it and dumped her down in that thing, and almost smashed her head this time! After that mess she didn't get on his back any more. And then—oh, my! Suddenly he began to show signs of having horns! Patrick came in one morning when she was currying and washing him and she said: "Oh, Patrick! Jumbo, my horse, is going to have horns! What does that mean, Patrick?" "Oh, no," he says. "Why, no! That don't amount to nothin'. After they get a little mite longer, I'll just cut 'em off." Everything he told her was just to keep on deceiving her—to keep on currying and washing that calf, to make him turn into a horse!

Finally her mother said one morning when she come in to breakfast: "Oh, Clara! I can't stand this awful smell of the stable when you come into the room." "Why," says Clara, "what do you mean, mamma? Do I smell of the stable? Oh, mamma, I think it is delicious!" She'd stand anything if she'd get that calf to turn into a pony! Well, this went on for some time; then Patrick lost interest in the joke, and one day a man come along that wanted a nice little calf and Patrick just up and sold little Jumbo and the man took it away to his house. He took Jumbo away without anybody noticing it. Clara used to go over every night the last thing to say good night to Jumbo, and that evening she went out and didn't find him. She called Patrick. "Oh, Patrick, where's my Jumbo?" "Well, Miss Clara," says Patrick kind of cross and sick of the joke, "I sold him! I had so many cows I couldn't take care of him, so I sold him." "You sold my Jumbo!" says she. "Sold Jumbo!" And she screamed and screamed, cried so loud (the Billiard-Room windows were open and her father heard her, she made such a noise) and Mr. Clemens came running down and says, "What's the matter?" Clara says: "Oh, oh! What do you think, papa? Patrick has sold my Jumbo—sold my Jumbo, before he turned into a pony!" And she screamed as though her little heart was broken. Her father was very angry, and asked Patrick why he sold Jumbo without saying anything to him. "Why did you sell it, Patrick?" Then he said: "Now you must go right out and bring that calf back." So Patrick had to go buy Jumbo right back! By that time I guess Clara knew Jumbo would never turn into a pony, never turn into anything but a cow!

Well, Jumbo did turn into a cow, but a wonderful cow; and she kept it until they left Hartford. Patrick had deceived her all that time for nothin'—just for a joke! When it was all over, she says to Patrick: "I don't think you ever told me the truth about that calf in the beginning. You knew that Jumbo could never turn into a horse, though you said he would if I kept on working on him."

So she lost all faith in that anyway—and I think it was real mean of Patrick to deceive her. I've got a little picture of her and the calf. I'll give it to you. Anyway, she got her faith back, some of it, for when she got a little older, her father got her a real pony all her own; but I guess she never thought as much of it as she did of Jumbo—the calf that wouldn't turn into a horse! I thought that was terrible of Patrick to deceive Clara. I wouldn't deceive one of the children—oh, for nothing! They always seemed just like my own to me. In fact, the whole family seemed just as if they belonged to me, my own people. It was always so from the beginning, from the first day I went there. I never felt like their servant—they never made me feel like that.

I always loved them just like my own, more than my own, because my life, my whole life, as it turned out, was spent with them.

When I first left home to work for Mrs. Clemens and I told my mother I was going to Hartford, she didn't want me to go—didn't want me to leave home.

"Oh! I have to!" I said. "This woman is perfectly wonderful! She's so lovely," I said. "I know I'll be happy there. I want to go. I *want* to live with her."

Well, my mother said, "I'd like to see her first," so I think I must have sent word some way to Mrs. Clemens that my mother wanted to see her, and instead of her asking my mother to come and see her as most people would, she came to see my mother herself.

My mother told her that she didn't like me to leave home because I was too young and never was away before.

"Oh!" Mrs. Clemens said. "Now, Mrs. Leary, don't worry about Katy. I'll take good care of her—I'll take just as good care of her as I would of my own children. I'll always look after her," she said. "Nothing will happen to her; and if she's sick, I'll take care of her, and when she's well, I'll take care of her just the same"—which was a bad thing for me in one way when I wanted to "gad" around, for of course I had to ask her every time I went out and tell her who I was going with. I always said I was going with the cook! I didn't have anybody else really and she was a good girl, and Mrs. Clemens liked her very much. She thought I was all right when I went with Delia. But she didn't know one thing that Delia did to me once.

One night Delia and her beau asked me out with them. We passed by Heiblind's hotel where they used to keep a saloon in the back. Heiblind's is a famous hotel in Hartford. It's still there. Well, there was a big porter (he used to have a big fat stomach) standing in the door that opened right back into the saloon. You could go inside the saloon through that door. Then Delia's beau said:

"Let's go in here and have a glass of lemonade."

So we went in (that was the ladies' entrance), and this big fat porter-man appeared, and when I seen him I says: "Why," I says, "why, this is no place for lemonade! This is a saloon! Heiblind's saloon!"

"Oh, no, no!" said Delia and her beau, laughing. "This ain't a saloon; this is a place for ladies to come to. Don't you see the Ladies' Entrance?"

"But," I says, "there's the big porter-man that always stands out at the front door. He's the sign for every one to come in to Heiblind's Saloon."

Oh, my! They laughed at that very hearty—thought it was a great joke that I was so green and so proper that I thought it was terrible to even go into a saloon. So we went in and they just ordered a glass of lemonade for me (out of respect for my innocence, I guess); but they had beer for themselves—good and plenty.

I had never tasted beer in my life then, never. It wasn't till after I went to Europe, I learned to drink beer. We used to have to have beer in all them foreign gardens. Why, you couldn't get a chair to set in unless you took a glass of beer; but I didn't like it very much, and used to throw it under the table when the waiters weren't looking. And Jean used to get so mad when I did that. No, I never drank much beer; but I drank wine, of course, later on.

I was going over on a French steamer once and we had a bottle of wine, and at first I put a little bit of wine in a glass and filled it up with water, but after I was over there for a while—well! I put a little bit of water in the glass and filled it up with wine!

So, you see, I learned to drink wine very quick after all. I took to it natural, I guess.

Of course I loved Mrs. Clemens so much that I always wanted to do just what she thought best. Once I was invited to a ball by a man quite a bit older than myself. He wasn't a regular beau, he just used to hang round a little. Well, one night he asked me if I would go to a ball. It was a Hibernian Ball, and you know what Hibernian means—high Irish society! Well, he wanted to know if I wouldn't go with him and meet some of the gallant Irishmen. I said, "Why, yes, I'd go," that is, of course I'd love to go, but I'd have to ask Mrs. Clemens first.

"Why," he says, "can't you tell now whether you can go or not?"

"No, I must ask her first." Then he says: "Well, I never! Who's your boss?" I said, "Well, I've got one, and I must ask her anyway."

So I told Mrs. Clemens about it—that I was invited to a ball—and, "Can I go?" says I. And she says, "Who's going, Katy?" And I told her Delia and her beau, and this young man that was going to take me.

Then Mrs. Clemens says, "Is it a nice ball, Katy?"

"Why," I says, "it's a Hibernian Ball. The Hibernians are all right; they're high Irish, you know."

Well, Mrs. Clemens laughed and says, "Yes, if Delia is going, of course you can go with her." So I went to the ball and had a grand time, but I don't think I went to another very soon, because I don't think any one asked me.

You see, I never got very much chance to see people or to go out, in the early days. I was very much set up for this first ball, I can tell you, and I dressed myself up fine for the occasion. I had a red silk dress covered with black lace, and I took the red out from under the lace sleeves because my arms was red enough to make it look like a piece of the dress anyway. I thought it looked very nice and was very much pleased with myself.

We danced all them old square dances. I never danced round dances, you know, because the Catholic Church didn't approve of round dancing in them days. Jazz hadn't struck the world then! So we did, well, just money musk, lanciers, and quadrilles—we danced lots of them dances and we had a grand old time—at least it seemed so to me then, before I had many good times and seen so much of Europe and Royalty—which is no joke! The Royalty kind of spoils you—makes a place like Elmira and the people there seem pretty tame, and I guess that's what my foreign travel done for me—as I found out afterwards. I told Mrs. Clemens all about it—how I had met some very nice men, all gallant Irish, and she laughed and said that was nice, but she didn't know whether I'd better go again, very soon, because she thought I might be even *asking* some one to take me—I was so crazy for dancing.

I didn't get another chance that winter, as I told you, but I went to the theater a good deal. She liked me to go to the theater. That was all right. She thought I learned something there.

Yes, Mrs. Clemens, she was wonderful and kind—but I could have had a great deal better time going out, if she didn't take *quite* such good care of me!

But I loved her and wouldn't do anything she didn't want me to—because she was always so good to me. I wouldn't do anything that I thought would displease her, no matter how much I wanted to myself. I told her everything—all my secrets, though I didn't have many to tell then.

Oh, yes, we used to have lovely talks every night after she got in bed. She used to get in bed right after I combed her hair and then she'd say, "Now, tell me, Katy, what kind of books are you reading?" And then she'd begin and we'd have nice little talks—about everything; about books and about my life and she'd ask so many questions, you know, and of course, she'd select my books for me. She wouldn't let me read anything she didn't know about, or didn't give me herself; and she would give me the books that she thought I ought to read and would like and understand.

And then the next night, after she had given me something, I'd tell her how far I was in that book and what

I thought of it; how it struck me. Of course, I was very ignorant! She never said so, but she must have thought I had quite a narrow life. I didn't read anything as a rule that she didn't give me; but one time I found a book up in the Billiard Room, that was a fast book—a bad book. I can't remember the man's name that wrote it, but it was quite a gay book. Yes, a French book, and of course, right away I picked it up and brought it down into my room and began reading it. I read it very quick, too—because it was kind of gay and I guess I liked it. Yes, I took in every word, and it explained everything very plain. I could understand it, I tell you. It was in English and I could understand it—the bad part, and I enjoyed it, too. Well, one night she took me unawares and said:

"Katy, what are you reading?"

Now, when she asked that I felt so guilty I just went and told her the name of the book straight off!

"What?" she says. "Why, Katy, where did you get that?" And I told her I found it in a package of old books in the Billiard Room. She said, "Bring that book to me at once," and I did, but with a heavy heart. She knew what it was, but I hated to give it up before I'd read the whole story. But I never finished it—I couldn't, when she exclaimed so. She made me feel as though I had committed a murder to begin it at all! So I didn't dare to finish it. She took it and I never saw it again. Wasn't that too bad now? It was by a Frenchman, but I can't remember the name—maybe it was Balzac. He was a famous writer, too. I used to hear Mr. Clemens talk about his books. He thought they was wonderful. When I told her I was reading it, oh! I felt bad! It just seemed to pop out, because I was reading it on the sly, when she thought I was reading something she had given me—Dickens or *John Halifax*, or something dull and good like that. I had a guilty conscience, I guess. She tried to make me read the *Tale of Two Cities* (that was by Dickens) and I tried my darndest to read that book, but I couldn't get interested in it at all. I used to say to her:

"Why, I can't remember even what I read last night! I don't understand it at all." And she'd say: "Oh, Katy, what is it? What's the trouble?" "No trouble," I says, "but I can't understand it. I'm sorry but I'll try again."

And then I'd try and try, but 'twasn't no use! I knew the characters—at least some of them—but I really couldn't worry through the book. It wasn't until we went to France and seen the Tuillieries and the Bastile and the things that was in that book that I wished I could have read it. Then I said: "Oh, wouldn't I like to have the *Tale of Two Cities* now! *Now* I could understand it." So we got it again. Mrs. Clemens' sister, Mrs. Crane, got it. She wanted to read it, too. She wasn't any better than I was, because she never could read it in America, either; but she read it there, and I read it as soon as she was through with it. Why, I was just crazy about it then. Yes, it makes quite a difference after you have seen the places and know about the people. That's what foreign travel does for you. You find out the world is a pretty big place.

Yes, the family kept a pretty strict watch over me—which was probably a good thing. I didn't have no real beaux in them days that I cared anything about, but there was one young fellow that came pretty regular every evening, only he had to go home always at ten o'clock sharp. You see, Mr. Clemens always used to lock up the house in the old days at ten o'clock. There was an alarm clock in the house and he used to turn it on every night for ten o'clock, and if the doors weren't fastened then, he used to call down, "Ten o'clock, ten o'clock!" And one night I knew that old alarm was going off and I had a beau setting there. "Well," I says, "you'd better get your hat quick and get ready to go; that alarm clock is going off in a minute."

There was a little porch that opened right out of the kitchen, so I shoved him right outside the door and says good night to him in a hurry, for Mr. Clemens was calling: "Katy, Katy, the alarm is ringing. It's ten o'clock!" Then when I come upstairs, Mr. Clemens says, "Well," he says, "did you send that young man away?" I says, "Why, yes, Mr. Clemens, I had to, because you said the alarm was going off!"

"Well," he said, "Katy, that was kind of hard on the

young man! If I'd known that," he said, laughing, "I might have given you another ten minutes!" And I guess he would have, too. You see, I lived a very regular kind of a life in a way—just like I was in a convent.

No, I didn't have any real beaux them days, so Mrs. Clemens never talked to me about getting married, because I didn't show any signs of it then. She used to tell me to be good and kind and truthful and talked just like the priest when you went to confession. It had a great influence on my life—she was so gentle, you know. She would go right into your heart, right into the depths of your heart, and advise you and sympathize with you and tell you what to do. If you were in any trouble you could always tell her. You could tell her anything; she was always ready to receive anything and to help everybody, even people that wasn't living with her she would help; and I think it used to worry her, too, sometimes,—all the people that would come to her. You know, some people you can't tell them anything; then there's other people you can tell everything, because they sympathize with you and know just what to do for you; and she was one of those that understood. Oh, she was wonderful—wonderful! All her friends admired her and used to come for miles (I was going to say) just to talk to her and get her views. She was so conscientious—and always saw the right thing to do. Oh! She was a lovely woman and there never was a happier couple lived in this world than they was. They never had a cross word—I don't think they ever spoke a cross word to each other, and she was so kind, and so sweet and true. She would teach you a lot, just from being herself, you know. As I said before, she used to talk to me every night, little talks before I went to bed. I never had any education, and she told me so many things that I ought to know; she used to give me what she felt would be an "inspiration" (as she called it)—that is, teach me something. Once she gave me a book called *Jane Eyre.* I liked that book and read it—and then I used to tell her what I thought of it. It was written by a woman called Charlotte Brontë. Well, she seemed a wonderful writer to me, and when Mrs. Clemens explained that she was just a poor minister's daughter, that had never heard anything or been anywheres, and then to be able to use the words she used—wonderful words—hard words, too, to make it stronger (I can't imagine how she ever heard them in a minister's house!)—well, it seemed remarkable to me that a poor, ignorant girl like that could write such a grand book as *Jane Eyre.*

In all the years I was with her, Mrs. Clemens never lost her patience with me once, and was always kind and thoughtful about everything. I was so ignorant then, as I look back upon it, and so blunt with everything—that it made it more remarkable how she could like me and put up with me at all. I didn't do much thinking them days. No, I didn't reason things out very much—I kind of just acted on my impulse, because I never was nice—

never could be—to people I didn't like. I always had a reason, of course. 'Twas something *I felt*, I guess, but I couldn't be nice to people I didn't like, and I always knew I didn't like them by what you call "intuition"—that's the way Mrs. Clemens explained it to me.

I've told you so many things now about Mr. and Mrs. Clemens, but I haven't told you yet their pretty little wedding story and how Mr. Clemens first fell in love with his wife.

Mr. Charles Langdon and Mr. Clemens, before he was married, was both avoyage on the *Quaker City*. That was a wonderful steamer and full of wonderful people. It was on its first voyage around the different ports of the world, and they stopped at all them foreign places. Mr. Clemens was just a young writer then, and 'twas from this trip that he made up his first and most famous book, *Innocents Abroad*.

Well, Charles Langdon went on that voyage, too. He was quite a young man and Mrs. Clemens' brother. She was Olivia Langdon, you know, before she married Mr. Clemens. Young Langdon, it seems, had his sister's picture in his pocket and he showed it, one day, to Mr. Clemens, and Mr. Clemens was so impressed, he asked to see it again. And the second time he seen it, he said, right out loud, "Well, that young lady is going to be my wife!"

Of course Mr. Langdon laughed at him for thinking of such a thing so sudden, but Mr. Clemens kept on being good friends with him all the way back—on purpose, I guess—because when they was landing he said to Mr. Langdon, "Would'nt you please invite me up to your house so I could meet your sister?"

"Well, I don't know," Mr. Langdon said. "Maybe. You can give me your address, anyway."

You see, he really didn't know anything about Mr. Clemens then—who he was nor nothing. He had no name, no money—nothing. As I told you, he was just getting the material for that book, *Innocents Abroad*. So Mr. Langdon said, "Well, when I get home, I'll tell them all about you, anyway." Of course, I don't know what he told his family. There wasn't much to tell about him, because he wasn't known then. But I guess he told them about how this young man had fell in love with the picture of his sister at sight. So Charles Langdon wrote to Mr. Clemens and asked him to come to Elmira—that his people would be glad to meet him. But that wasn't until some time later. It seems Mr. Clemens first really met Olivia Langdon at a party at some house in New York, and fell in love with her right on the spot—just as he'd done with her picture before. So when he got that invitation to go to Elmira, he was delighted and started right off. Mr. Charles Langdon, the brother, met him just a little ways out of Elmira and brought him safely to the house. And Mrs. Clemens said she liked him as soon as she seen him—the very first minute. That was, of course, the first time he'd ever seen her in her father's house, and he stayed for a week, and they begun courting each other right away, I suppose. When she first met him it was on New Year's Day in New York (they was having a reception, you know) and Mr. Clemens was so different from all the rest of the men that night. She really liked him just for that. He didn't talk about the weather when he came in, like all the rest of the people, or something stupid like that, and she thought he was different from all the men she had ever seen—so brilliant and fascinating. She liked his being unusual and bright. She told me that one day when she was talking about him years afterwards.

Well, as soon as he got there he went right to her father (on that first visit) to fix up everything then, and asked for the hand of his daughter. "But I don't know anything about you," Mr. Langdon says, "I don't want you to be engaged to my daughter yet, because I don't really know much about you nor your prospects."

Then Mr. Clemens, he says: "Well, you can find out all about me and I'll tell you how. I used to be a newspaper writer to a man in Kansas City. He'll tell you all about me. If you'll write to that man, he'll lie for me, good and plenty, because I've often lied for him!"

Well, Mr. Langdon thought that was pretty clever, I guess. He laughed and said: "Well, now, I'll tell you what I'll do: I'll put you both on probation for a while (but you can't write nor see each other during that time) and if my daughter feels the same way later on that she does now, well," he says, "you can have the engagement. Yes," says Mr. Langdon, "that's what I'll do."

Of course Mr. Clemens had to agree to that, but in the meantime he'd written something that was giving him quite a little notoriety. Mr. Langdon, of course, never wrote to that man in Kansas City; he just took that as a good joke, but he had heard something of Mr. Clemens from a little pamphlet that told what a great writer Mr. Clemens was going to be. So they became engaged, but there was no time set then for the wedding.

It was while he was there on his second visit that they became engaged, and when the time came for him to go, he felt terrible about leaving, so he fixed up a scheme with the coachman so that he would be tipped out of the carriage when he started to go to the station. He says to the coachman: "Now, when we start from the house, you take the trap and fix the back seat so it'll tip right over the minute anybody sits in it! I used to be able to do that," Mr. Clemens says, "when I was a boy. We had a trap at my father's house, and I'll show you how, if you don't know." So the coachman, he caught on to the joke and fixed the seat so that when they started up the carriage, the seat would tip right over backwards and spill the person who was sitting in it, out on the ground.

Well, the carriage drove up and Mr. Clemens jumped in and set on the back seat. He set there all alone, where he could look at Miss Langdon with all his eyes. The family was all standing on the porch and waving their hands, and then Doyle started up the horses very sudden. "Get up," says he, and the seat tipped right over back and out went Mr. Clemens on the ground! My, they were scared! They all ran out and picked him up and made a terrible fuss; they thought his neck was broken and made a great to-do. But he never was hurt a mite—he just made believe he was. They got a doctor and put him to bed and Mrs. Clemens (Miss Langdon, she was then) nursed and cared for him and he stayed two weeks longer—right there in bed—just on purpose! Think of that! He did that just to stay a little mite longer, because he hadn't seen enough of her on that visit—which was very sweet, I think.

Why, they used to write each other letters every day, even when they was in the same house. Years afterwards, when I went to live with them in Hartford, there was a green box that used to go to the bank every year with the silver and other valuables. And one day I says to Mrs. Clemens:

"Mrs. Clemens," I says, "there isn't a thing in this house I don't know what's in it and that I haven't seen the inside of, except that green box, and I certainly am wondering what can be in that." Well, Mrs. Clemens, she laughed and kind of blushed, and then she says, very soft, "Well, Katy, that's one thing I'm sure you never will see the inside of, because that box holds all my love letters."

"Oh!" says I. "Well, of course I know I can't see them." And you can see from this that they was treasured very much, them letters, because they went to the bank for safe keeping every year.

Once when somebody was there writing an article about Mr. Clemens, that was to have access to all his papers (that was years afterward, of course, after Mrs. Clemens was dead) this person got hold of that box. Mr. Clemens didn't know what was in it either, and so he said not to bother if they didn't have the key, to just break it open. When I heard that, I ran as fast as I could to Miss Clara and told her, and I says, "Are you going to let them love letters of your mother's be seen?" I says. "'Cause they're going to break that box open now and see what's in it." And Clara says, "No, Katy, no, of course not. Can you carry it?"

"You bet I can," I says.

"Well," says Clara, "bring it right in here to me, then, quick." So I brought the green box to Miss Clara, and I never seen it since. I guess she's treasuring it just like her mother did.

Well, to get on with the wedding: They was married the second day of February and they was going to live in Buffalo to be near Mr. Clemens' publishing house. He was having his first book published then. Mrs. Clemens' father bought a house as a surprise for him, for a wedding present. They got it all furnished that winter before the wedding. She and her mother went to

New York and picked out the furniture and everything lovely. And they sent a man up from New York to do the decorating, and it was beautiful. The furniture was all satin-covered—light blue satin, most of it. She had a bedroom with a blue satin canopy over the bed and blue satin curtains hanging down, and all the chairs of blue satin, and she brought that bed to Hartford with her when they moved. It was a low bed, all upholstered in that beautiful blue satin. I used to admire it very much. Well, the house was furnished, every detail of it, by Mr. Langdon, and everything was all ready, in perfect order, before the wedding. Why, they even had the coachman that she used to have at home—that was Patrick—I told you about him; and then they took the cook up, too. Even the coal was in the cellar and everything all ready to the bacon and eggs, so's they could sit right down and have breakfast in their own house the next morning.

They didn't have a very big wedding, and they was married very quiet in Elmira by Thomas L. Beecher, the brother of Henry Ward Beecher. They was married at the Langdon residence and they didn't go on the honeymoon then, but they went the next day in a private car right up to Buffalo. Mrs. Clemens' father had a private car hitched on the same engine and invited up a lot of friends of Mrs. Clemens to go to Buffalo that same day with him, to surprise her. Mr. Clemens and his bride got there first, and was met by a gentleman who knew about the surprise party. He met them with a carriage and told the driver where to go. Of course he didn't want to get Mr. Clemens to the house before the rest of the party. He wanted Mr. Langdon and the friends to get there first and secreted and hidden in their places behind the curtains before Mr. Clemens got there. So they kept on riding and riding till Mr. Clemens finally said, well, he didn't know what on earth they was doing—driving all over Buffalo like that, unless they was trying to find some house down in the slums to take him to! But finally they arrived at this very fine house and the coachman pulled up at the door and a very nice woman appeared. She was got there for the occasion on purpose. She ushered Mr. and Mrs. Clemens right in and when Mr. Clemens seen that beautiful house and all that beautiful furniture and everything, he was perfectly amazed. He said to this woman, "Well, madam, this is no ordinary boarding-house, and I'm afraid I'm not able to pay the bill here," he said, "but if I'm not able to by the time I'm leaving, well, you can hold our trunks!"

"Oh, no," says she, "no, that'll be all right, Mr. Clemens." So they went into the parlor, Mrs. Clemens first and Mr. Clemens right after her, and then all that party that was hid behind the curtains just burst out laughing and talking, and kissing the bride and shaking hands with Mr. Clemens. There was a terrible to-do. It was really a great surprise, and everybody was delighted and Mr.

Clemens was just struck dumb, they said, for once! I guess that's one time he didn't have anything to say—that is, for a minute.

Well, Mr. Langdon (Mrs. Clemens' father) was there and all the Langdon family, and lots of friends, and they had supper and the jolliest time you could think of. And when they told Mr. Clemens that this wonderful house and all the things in it was a present from Mr. Langdon, his father-in-law, well! they said he was just overcome and couldn't speak for a minute and that he went up to Mr. Langdon and says, shaking hands, "Well, Father Langdon, I certainly don't know how to thank you, I never shall be able to thank you, but I want to say this: that whenever you're passing through Buffalo—don't matter how often or at what time—you can come right here and stay with us as long as you like—and it won't cost you a cent!" Well, of course, I suppose they all just roared over that, 'cause 'twould make anybody laugh.

So that was the end of the wedding and the beginning of their new life and the wonderful happiness that was waitin' for them—which lasted to the very end of their days—beautiful from beginning to end, as I've been telling you.

From the first minute I went to live with them at Hartford when I was as green as grass, it struck me that way, and nobody could know better than I could, 'cause I was living right in the midst of it. There was only one sad thing that happened then—those first years in Buffalo—and that was when the first little baby (a boy too)—died.

He only lived a few months—he had diphtheria—and oh! it nearly killed Mr. and Mrs. Clemens—'cause it was their first-born—you know.

And so after that they moved away from Buffalo—and left that house. Then they went to Hartford—decided to take a house and live there—and that's where I went to them later on, after the girls was born.

Of course I was with Mrs. Clemens a great deal in the early days and she had a great influence on my life, as I told you before. But I guess in the long run it wasn't any greater than his—Mr. Clemens'. He was always lovely to me, always nice except, of course, when he fought with me about that precious old manuscript; but that wasn't always, and didn't last long, as I told you. Yes, he was awful nice to me, nice and funny, too, and he used to argue with me about everything under the sun—and a good deal about my religion. Why, he told me one time he was very sorry for me—that I was brought up wrong from the beginning; of course I appeared all right on the surface, he said, but inside I was all wrong; and he would try and change me, change my opinion on religion—'cause I was a Catholic.

After one of our great arguments I come to him and I says: "Well, Mr. Clemens, you know I think we understand each other at last. I think you believe the way I do."

"Oh," he says, "have I got you at last, Katy?"

"Well," I says, "I don't know whether you got me or I got you, but I know you do believe the way I do: you believe there *is* a God, no matter what you say! I know it."

"Here, here, Katy, none of that kind of talk, none of that," he says.

But although he was always arguing and joking about religion and they all said he was an unbeliever, I don't think he was. I know he wasn't. I know he wasn't, because when Jean died, years afterwards, and we stood looking at her, he says to me:

"Oh, Katy! She's in heaven with her mother."

Now, if he hadn't believed in heaven or a hereafter, he wouldn't say that, would he? Oh, I think—I am *sure* he believed in the hereafter. But he was pretty serious in arguing about religion. It interested him very much to argue, and one day he said:

"Well, Katy, what will Father Hardy (he was the priest) say to me if he knows that I'm talking to you the way I am?" I says, "Well, Mr. Clemens, he would say something you wouldn't want to hear." And then, of course, he laughed hearty and said, "Well, I wouldn't like *that*—because I like *him!*" And that ended the argument—for that day, anyway.

He was very charitable, too, you know. He gave away everything and the Christmases they used to have was something wonderful. The way they used to make everybody happy! Baskets and packages all over the place. Mrs. Clemens would be fixing baskets in the Billiard Room off the Library (they always used to do the Christmas things there) and she used to do up about fifty baskets herself. She always had a crowd of people, children and old people and grown-up people, too, depending on her and she fixed them up wonderful baskets with a big turkey and cans of peas and tomatoes and vegetables and then, oh, a bottle of wine and a great big box of candy, and nuts and raisins, and then there was always some stockings and underwear and a few pretty things, too. She used to give every one of them a present, individual-like, extra. She knew, it seems to me, just what each person wanted most and she shopped for weeks before Christmas, doing up all those things and having all those baskets ready, and then when Christmas morning come, if it was cold and snow on the ground, Mr. Clemens would start out to distribute the things. He'd put on his big fur overcoat, take the sleigh and the two children with him, Susy and Clara, and they'd start early in the morning with them great baskets. The children would read the names and then Mr. Clemens would lift out the baskets and Patrick would take them into the house.

Mr. Clemens looked just like Santa Claus, you know, with that great big fur coat with a white fur collar on it, and he and the children had such fun over it. Then Mrs. Clemens, she'd have presents besides for every one in the house, and a great big tree for the children and their stockings hung up the night before, and really a wonderful Christmas for them all. Oh, what Christmases and Thanksgivings we had! Thanksgiving was most as wonderful as Christmas. Mrs. Clemens always had all the people to a great dinner that day—people that wasn't very well off, poor people—not her own friends specially. Then in the evening the Warners would have a great dinner (and the Twitchells used to go over to the Warners for that). Then on their way back Mr. Twitchell and his wife and the nine little Twitchells used to stop at our house and then we used to play charades. The dining table was always loaded with all the candy that there was —about ten dishes of candy—set all around the table near the edge, just where the little Twitchells could reach up their hands to get it and there was the little Twitchells' hands going around that table as fast as they could go until all the candy was gone. They'd empty all them dishes in no time! There was nine in the family, and no wonder!

Mr. Clemens always took part in everything and he helped everybody and he was just so good to the children. He was charming with them. He loved all children and they loved him and used to abuse him, too (that is, Susy and Clara did). They used to sit on his lap and pull his hair and pull him all over the house, you know, and he was always ready to crawl on his hands and knees or lie on his back or do anything to make them laugh. Clara always called him "Grenouille"—which means "frog" in French.

"Now, papa, you've got to do so-and-so this evening."

"All right," he'd say, "we'll play horse or anything you like." So he'd get down on his knees and she'd get up on his back and pull his hair for the lines—and pull it good and hard, too, I can tell you. Then he used to sing to them, and oh! it was beautiful to hear him. He'd sing after dinner (he had a nice voice) and he'd sing nigger Spirituals and act them out, too, for the grown folks as well as the children. And then, sometimes, he'd play on the piano—try to anyway.

He used to sing one song that was so lovely that I always used to sneak in and listen to it: "In the Days of Old When Knights was Bold." That was the song he used to sing and play on the piano himself. Oh, the children would stand round just adoring him when they heard that! They had a lovely, happy time. It used to strike me as heavenly. 'Twas a home just like you'd make for yourself—like a dream house, don't you know, that you would like more than anything else in the world. A happy, happy home—happiness budding all over—everybody always happy. Our life—it just rolled on like a smooth sea—wasn't a thing for eleven years—not a bit of sadness of any kind. There was always fun and excitement, especially when Mr. Clemens was around. He used to go on a rampage about his shirts, though. If he found a shirt in his drawer without a button on, he'd take every single shirt out of that drawer and throw them right out of the window, rain or shine—out the bathroom window they'd go. I used to look out every morning to see the snowflakes—anything white. Out they'd fly! It was my duty to keep buttons on his shirts, and he'd swear something terrible if I didn't. Oh! He'd swear at anything when he was on a rampage. He'd swear at his razor if it didn't cut right, and Mrs. Clemens used to send me around to the bathroom door sometimes to knock and ask him what was the matter. Well, I'd go and knock; I'd say, "Mrs. Clemens wants to know what's the matter." And then he'd say to me (kind of low) in a whisper like, "Did she hear me, Katy?" "Yes," I'd say, "every word!" Oh, well, he was ashamed then, he was afraid of getting scolded for swearing like that, because Mrs. Clemens hated swearing. There was two doors into Mrs. Clemens' room, one opened at the head of her bed and one opened so you could go in without seeing the head of the bed. Well, the morning that he swore like that (if she heard him) he would always come in by the door where she couldn't see him—kind of sneak in—and say "Good morning," careless-like, as if he was in a terrible hurry, and then he'd go right out. Oh, he didn't want to see them cold blue eyes she turned on him. That would be all she'd have to do, was to look at him once. He said she had a blue eye like steel, you know, that would go right through him.

Well, he'd always try to steal out this back door, after he'd been swearing, and one morning she called him back and said,

"Aren't you going to say good morning, Youth dear?"

"Oh, I forgot," he says, "I forgot, Livy."

"Oh," she said, "you know better than that; you didn't forget." Well, he couldn't say anything, couldn't deny it, of course. He kind of laughed it off in his way. But you couldn't get mad at Mr. Clemens about anything, even when his shirts would be all outdoors and I'd have to go and bring them back in—I wasn't mad at him; though he never wanted one of those shirts put back. He used to say to me: "I see my shirts are getting kind of bad. There was no buttons in the shirt I wanted to put on this morning." That was why he'd throw them out the window, to remind me, I suppose.

He always had three sets of cuff buttons and shirt buttons fixed, so there'd be always a shirt ready for him. My goodness! I used to have to fix three shirts at the same time, because if he found one shirt that didn't have the proper cuff buttons in, he'd tear it up.

"Now, don't put those shirts back in my drawer, Katy," he'd say. "They're getting old. I'll have to go and get some new ones." But of course I didn't pay any attention to him. I brought 'em all in and put the buttons back and mended them up, and of course he never knew—he wore them!

Mr. Clemens wore nightshirts, too. He never would

put on pajamas—they wasn't fashionable in them days—short nightshirts was what he wore. Well, when I first went there to work, he used to have short nightshirts—just boughten ones, and he would jump out of bed often and go up in the Billiard Room without putting on his double gown; and I used to think he'd catch cold that way—his legs would be all bare—he very seldom stopped to put on his slippers even. So I said to Mrs. Clemens that I should think if Mr. Clemens would have some nice, *long* nightshirts it would be very nice, and she said:

"I've often thought that too, Katy, but I don't know whether he'd wear them or not."

I said, "Well, I'll make some anyway, and we'll see—we'll try it."

So I made a long nightshirt for the experiment, and I put trimming on it, rickrack, red—brought it all down the fold in front. I put the nightshirt on his bed the night it was finished and when he seen it he said:

"Livy, I think Katy made a mistake. She's put *your* nightdress over here instead of mine!"

But Mrs. Clemens laughed. "No, Katy made that for you, Youth dear."

"What!" he says. "What! with all that red trimming on?"

"Yes," says Mrs. Clemens, "she thought a nice, *long* nightshirt would keep you warm when you jump up to write in the night."

Well, of course he made a terrible fuss at first, but

he finally put it on and he liked it very much, Mrs. Clemens said, and walked around in it. He walked around the room in it, very gay, and he liked it and the next morning he said it was really the most comfortable nightshirt he ever had because it covered his feet good in the night, you know, and he never wanted to wear anything else. But after a few years he got kind of cold one time, and then he thought he'd like a *flannel* nightshirt, so Mrs. Clemens got the loveliest flannel she could find and I made him one of those nightshirts out of that. Then he used to wear the flannel nightshirts. He wouldn't give up the nightshirts with the trimming on, though. He had got used to it and liked it. I trimmed them all with different colors. I had pink and red and blue. The white ones was a great success, but the flannel ones was the greatest success of all. You see, he was comfortable all the rest of his life with those nightshirts, so I don't think I have lived in vain. I've made *one* man comfortable, anyway!

I think now I'll tell you about Mr. Clemens and the clocks—putting all them clocks out of the house in his nightshirt. You know, he was on a lecture tour, and he got little Mr. Cable (George W. Cable) to go with him on this tour (and he was lecturing, too)—reading from their books.

Major Pond—he run a famous Lecture Agency—managed Mr. Clemens and Mr. Cable on that tour, and they had a great time of it. Mr. Clemens, he owned the show, of course, and they say he paid Mr. Cable as high as $500 a week sometimes for his part in it.

Mr. Clemens and Cable was great friends, although they was very different and never could agree about anything. Mr. Cable was very prim and conventional. He hated to travel on Sundays, too, and of course that would make Mr. Clemens mad. Sometimes, they said, Cable used to take more than his share of the time telling his stories, and I suppose there was a good deal of argufying; but in spite of that, it didn't amount to nothin' and they had a great success and made lots of money, although, of course, Mr. Clemens was the mainstay in the lecture and the one that people came to hear.

Well, when they got all through with their lecture tour, the last place they went was in New Jersey and they stayed overnight with a friend of Mr. Clemens', by the name of Nast—Thomas Nast was his name. He was a famous artist; made pictures—cartoons, they call them—in the newspapers. He was very well known and a great friend of Mr. Clemens. Well, they stayed there overnight at his house. There was lots of clocks in that house, it seems, and several alarm clocks too. They set them alarm clocks, because Mr. Clemens was going to get up to take an early train in the morning. After Mr. Clemens had gone to bed, he got tired of the ticking of them damned clocks—he said he couldn't stand the ticking of 'em—it made him nervous—set him crazy. Mr. Cable didn't mind the ticking, I guess—he could sleep

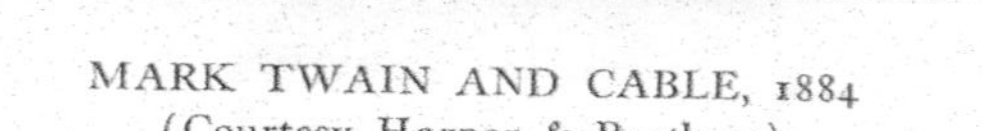

MARK TWAIN AND CABLE, 1884
(Courtesy Harper & Brothers)

H. G. Smith, Boston

THE AMERICAN HUMORISTS
JOSH BILLINGS MARK TWAIN PETROLEUM V. NASBY

THE HARTFORD HOUSE
(Courtesy Harper & Brothers)

THE BUFFALO HOUSE, PRESENTED BY MR. LANGDON
(Courtesy Harper & Brothers)

through anything—but Mr. Clemens made up his mind that he'd put those old clocks right out of the house, then, that night; so he moved them right out and even put some of them into the front yard, I heard! There was one or two long clocks—tall ones—in the house. That was the kind they used in them days. Grandfathers' clocks, they called them.

Well, Mr. Clemens he began to move those clocks too, moving them right out himself. Then he made Cable get up and help him (they was so heavy he couldn't move them alone), and they put four or five clocks out on the front lawn of the house together. Well! Mr. Nast seen 'em pulling them out, he and Mr. Cable, in the night, but he just didn't say anything then—let them do it (because he was famous, I guess), though they'd stop anybody else but Mr. Clemens.

Well, Mr. Nast told Mr. Clemens the next morning that if he'd told him how he felt, he'd gladly put them out himself for him, but he says, "I'd advise you, Mark, the next place you visit, if you don't like the sound of the clocks ticking, you'd better say something about it to the *family* first, because it spoils clocks to yank them about the way you've been doing!"

Of course Mr. Clemens didn't care. He didn't care a damn! He didn't want them in his room or anywheres he could hear them tick. He never could stand the ticking of a clock and, of course, when Mr. Clemens couldn't stand anything—he just didn't have it, that's all. Some of the clocks was very heavy—that's why he had to haul little Mr. Cable out of bed, to help him lug them out. And it was one of my nightshirts with the trimming on he was wearing when he was pulling out them clocks! It was long and must have trained on the ground, and he must have looked awful funny going round the house and down the stairs, lugging a great clock in that trailing nightshirt. Wasn't that a funny thing to do? It was awful—really—but that was one of the things he did, that nobody else would dare do, would they? Of course Mr. Cable and Mr. Clemens missed their train next morning because I guess the alarm clocks they set for it went off on the lawn! It was a great joke in the Nast family and he and Mr. Clemens roared over it. Nast drew a funny picture about Mr. Clemens in his nightshirt, putting out them clocks. Everybody seen that picture because it was published in the newspapers once. It was very funny and you could see that one of my nightshirts was drawn in that picture.

Well, after that episode they got back to Hartford. They arrived on Saturday night and Sunday morning Mr. Cable waked up very sick with a sore throat. Mr. Clemens said it must be "Lecture" Sore Throat. Mr. Cable was suffering terrible. He said if we could make bags of hot salt to put on him he'd be better, so I was his nurse for the day and I made bags of hot salt to put on him. He put 'em up to his jaw—it was all swelled right through—and he says to me,

"We better tie 'em on, Katy." As I was tying 'em on him he'd say, "A little tighter—just a little tighter, Katy." And then I give it a good hard pull to shut his wind off, so he couldn't keep saying, "A little tighter, Katy." I thought I'd tie it tight enough to stop him talking—for once! Mr. and Mrs. Clemens stayed up all night with him, fussing about him, and putting on hot cloths, and doing everything they could for him; and then Mr. Clemens sent for a doctor, he wanted to send for a nurse—for two nurses or three nurses—anything to get him well! So they got a nurse from the hospital, and she began to minister to him and the doctor come, but he couldn't find out what did ail him. They doctored him for a week for a sore throat, and Mr. Clemens worried so at one time he was going to send for Cable's wife (you know they lived way down South), and he thought he'd feel better if they sent for her. But he finally got better anyway and sat round the house and began telling stories again for a few days to Jean and Clara. They sat on a chair near him—close to him (he was such a little man, you know, that they could get very close to him!). He stayed there a few days after he got better, and then went home. But after he left Clara came down with the mumps, for that's what he had—the mumps! Then Jean got them, then the nurse that was taking care of him and she had 'em too. That old blooming doctor never knew what was the matter with Mr. Cable. He was doctoring him all the time for a sore throat, but what he had was the mumps! And little Mr. Cable did a good job, too. He did it up brown. He give everybody in the house the mumps, and the children was really very sick. Clara was very sick and so was Jean. They was just as sick as they could be with Cable's mumps. I guess Mr. Clemens blessed him then good and hard, but, poor man, he couldn't help it. I didn't have the mumps myself, because I never went near enough to him. I used to stand way back of him when I tied up his head. He was a nice man, though, and a great friend of Mr. Clemens. He came here for Mr. Clemens' Anniversary, after his death, and he preached a nice sermon in Carnegie Hall. They was always great friends as long as Mr. Clemens lived.

It was about this time that Clara began studying the piano. She was very ambitious and wanted to become a teacher, so she started out by giving us piano lessons—George, the colored butler, and me. She was only a little thing then, but that didn't make any difference. She started with George first—he was her first pupil. She had him in the schoolroom and made him begin with the finger exercises; then she taught me for a while. George used to have to leave sometimes before the lessons was up, because he'd have the table to set and his work to do, and her mother used to think that she was really taking too much of his time—time that he ought to be doing his work. But that didn't make no difference to Clara—she wanted to give him lessons anyway. She thought an hour would be about the shortest lesson she ought to give. Then she started in to teach me, because I had a little more time. I was delighted and I went to her as a pupil. I could give her half an hour quite a number of times, so she decided we'd begin at once. Oh, my! What a teacher she was—a borned teacher, you know. Why, she'd make you do everything just as she said; make you see your mistakes and make you do them right over again. She'd get very cross sometimes, and hit the piano hard with her little pencil on the keys. She was such a mite of a thing, it was really funny to hear her scold, and her little hand wasn't near long enough to play good. Her fingers wasn't long enough to reach an octave. She had to use her other hand to help herself out, and then she said to me, "Oh, Katy, wouldn't I just love to have the great big stretch you have got in your hand!" But she never could manage that—though my big hands didn't make a piano player of me!

The first lessons I did was nothing but learn the scales —she never really got beyond that with me nor with George either, because when we only started, then she was leaving home for the summer. But she talked to us very serious and told us we must practice every day— practice half an hour a day regular. Of course we said we would, but we didn't do it. But George really liked it. He took great interest in it—more than I did, I guess. I kind of did it to humor her. You know the colored people are musical and George liked it very much, them lessons. He thought he could be a musician if she could only stay home to teach him; maybe he'd go on the stage. Then after she came home the next time she was a little older herself and had to practice harder herself, too. So she didn't say any more about our lessons. It kind of faded away.

George was really very nice for a colored boy, but he was very conceited in those days. Yes, George used to say he was the best-shaped man in Hartford, the very best-shaped. He said Ryan, the tailor, always sent for him when he wanted to try on clothes for a model. He was a nice-looking nigger, but he was a nigger just the same. We used to have great arguments about the niggers. We was always arguing—just like Mr. Clemens. He used to say:

"Well, Katy, they never could have plays or anything else that was funny, if it wasn't for the Niggers and the Irish." And I'd say to him:

"Uh! Don't talk to me that way about the niggers and the Irish. Don't you *dare* put the nigger *ahead* of the Irishman!" I says.

That used to make me mad when he did that. George was always very grand and he just adored Mrs. Clemens. He thought there wasn't anybody in this world like Mrs. Clemens; but even so, she couldn't stop him from laughing out loud at the dinner parties when they was telling stories and having them good jokes. Mrs. Clemens used to take George to task very often about this. If Mr.

Clemens or any gentleman was there at dinner and they was telling jokes, if there was anything very funny to laugh at, George would be the first one to laugh! He'd laugh right out loud, before Mrs. Clemens or anybody. He'd laugh right out before anybody could stop him—that colored laugh that was kind of loud. He'd laugh before he could even get his handkerchief out and put it up to his mouth to stop the laugh. He couldn't wait until he got to the pantry to roar. Mrs. Clemens would take him to task the very next morning and he'd promise to do better. But the next time it happened just the same. It always struck him so funny, them stories, that he couldn't help it and then, before anybody else, he would laugh. If he'd only waited until the company had laughed first, he wouldn't be heard quite so plain, but he always laughed *first*—he'd open the laugh, you might say, and it always made Mrs. Clemens feel terrible.

George and I was always great friends, even if he was black and I was white. He liked me, you see. In fact, everybody that I lived with always liked me. George had a very good opinion of himself and always used to brag about the girls he had—and how they used to bother him with their attentions.

"Why, they bother the very life out of me," he said. "Just let me step out (and I can't help myself)—they begin making advances to me—very bold!" Of course he pretended he didn't like it, but I guess it flattered him as much as it would any man. Anyway, George was always a loving, faithful servant to the Clemens family. He just adored them both to the end of his life. He was a terrible liar sometimes, though—not bad lies, just necessary lies. Most Niggers—in fact, most people—are like that. I think I'll tell you about the time when Mrs. Clemens took George to task and gave him a terrible dressing down for not telling the truth.

"George," she says, "you tell me so many lies that you give me an entirely different account of things that happen every day."

"Well, Mrs. Clemens," he says, "in a house like this, there's one person that's *got* to lie! If I was not the liar I am, there's not a person for miles around that would be speaking to anybody else." So that ended that argument!

Mr. Clemens used to say that George came there first to wash the windows, but he stayed over eighteen years! He was just the kind of a character that Mr. Clemens loved, and the children was crazy about him, too. Of course, Mrs. Clemens was fond of George, but she didn't approve of his lying. She was always taking him to task, as I told you, for the things he did. He was always betting and gambling, trying to make money, and he was pretty smart at it, too.

Once when Mrs. Clemens had given George a terrible dressing down, she was so upset that she said he really couldn't go on working there, so she discharged him right away. Well, the next morning—there George was, right there at the breakfast table, the same as usual—he didn't pay no attention to being discharged, you see. And when she saw him, Mrs. Clemens says, "Why, George, I discharged you yesterday, didn't I?"

"Well, yes, Mrs. Clemens," says George, "you did, but I know you really couldn't get along without me, so I thought I'd just stay right on anyway." So of course, after that there wasn't nothing more she could do about it.

George loved Mr. Clemens and he wouldn't have left him for anything—couldn't have driven him away.

Now, I must tell you something about the children going to school. Of course they had governesses to give them lessons and everything that any children could possibly have, but Mrs. Clemens thought it was the proper thing to send them to the public school. I was surprised at that, because I thought them children would never go to anything like a public school, but Mrs. Clemens used to say: "Oh, no! I must not deprive my children of anything like that. It will be a great experience for them to go to the public school." She never went to a public school herself, nor any of her people, but she believed the best thing that could happen to them little darlings of hers, was to send them right out to public school to mingle with the world so they could play with other children, not just their own kind. But she never carried out her plan, though, because they went off to Europe right after that and the children was educated abroad. That was her idea, though. She thought it was the best thing for them to do—to go out and mingle with the world when they was little. Mrs. Clemens was brought up very conventional, but she was always thinking ahead. She took an interest in things that was ahead of the time. She had a great deal of common sense and she always saw everything very clear. Oh, she was a lovely creature! She was clear herself and made everything clear about her. She was like a light—a little light that burned all the time—day and night.

Mr. Clemens had the most wonderful hospitality I think I ever seen any one have, before or since. Why, when any one come inside his house he was right there to entertain them, no matter who they was, no matter how busy he was, whether he liked them or not; he just devoted himself, you might say, to making them happy. And he did it, not because they was nice or interesting or anything like that, but just because they was his guests.

I remember one nice thing he did once to help a poor man—young Carl Gerhardt that I was telling you about. It seems the Warners was all settin' in their library one night at Mr. Charles Dudley Warner's house, when the doorbell rang and a very pretty young woman come in and she asked to see Mr. Warner. She was a nice blonde, a Swede. She says:

"Mr. Warner, I've got to see you about my husband that is working down in Pratt & Whitney's Machine Shop. He's an artist to his finger tips," she says, "and he wants to be a sculptor. He can't get no opportunity to get an education now, but he could be a wonderful sculptor, if he had the chance."

Then she took out a little image that he had done, to show Mr. Warner. "I've come to ask you what I can do," she says, "because I believe if he doesn't get help now, his whole life will be ruined; but I have two children and he's just a workman in the factory, and a foreigner."

Mr. Warner was greatly interested, so he says:

"Why, this is worth thinking about. We will see what can be done. I will see certain people I know, and talk it over."

Then she says, "Doesn't Mr. Clemens live next door?" And Mr. Warner says, "Yes, he does."

So the very next morning Mr. Clemens he went over to see Mr. Warner and he said:

"Charley, did a pretty Swedish girl come over here last night to see you about her husband?"

"Yes," said Mr. Warner, "she did."

"Well," Mr. Clemens said, "that young woman interested me very much and I'm going to find out about the thing." So Mr. Warner said, "Yes, Mark, find out all about it, and let me know."

So Mr. Clemens went to Pratt & Whitney's shop to see this young man, and when he got back he says to Mr. Warner:

"Well, Charley, I have fixed up everything for them good. They're going abroad—his wife and the children, too—and I am going to help him for four years. I will give him the money to study with in Europe."

Then Mr. Warner says, "But, Mark, don't you think you ought to let some of the rest of us chip in with you, too?"

"Oh, no! Nobody need chip in," says Mr. Clemens. "That man and his family are going to Paris and I am going to lend him the money."

Well, they went off to Europe and Carl he studied there, and one of the very first things he done was a picture of Mr. Clemens and Mr. Warner. He did it in what you call terra cotta. Then he sent over a splendid bust of Mr. Clemens. I think it was the best bust he ever had. It was a bronze bust. Then after that they come home, and Mr. Clemens says to him:

"Now, as soon as you can get on your feet, you can give that money back to me if you want to, but I don't want you to be worrying about it all the rest of your life unless it's easy for you to give it back."

And he did return the money to Mr. Clemens because he was a great success. And later on, he made a bust of General Grant when Mr. Clemens was publishing Grant's book. Mr. Clemens fixed that up. It was a very fine bust and most people thought it was the best likeness ever made of General Grant. Carl Gerhardt started that bust from a little picture of Grant, and then it was so good that Mr. Clemens he took him to Grant himself, when Grant was sick and lying in bed, and Carl began to work right then and there on it—right from General Grant himself. That's why it was so good. Everybody liked it and so did General Grant. Carl gave it, the first original bust, to the Grant family and they got it now, I guess. Yes, he got lots of jobs and when they was going to decorate the capitol in Hartford (Mr. Clemens and Mr. Warner was helping about it) they got him to do that job, too, and he done a lovely statue of Nathan Hale that they put up there. This was the same man, Carl Gerhardt, that I was telling you about—that painted the scenery for our *Prince and the Pauper* show.

You know, Mr. Warner lived right next door to the Clemenses in Hartford and, of course, they was the greatest friends. He'd come to every dinner that the Clemenses gave, almost. Why, it wouldn't be a real dinner excepting Mr. and Mrs. Warner was there. The children called them Cousin Susie and Cousin Charley. Mr. Warner, was a writer too, but he was a terrible letter writer—terrible handwriting. Sometimes when he'd send a note to Mr. Clemens he'd write it so poor Mr. Clemens used to call John (John was Mr. Warner's man who brought it over). "John," he'd say, "you go right back and tell Warner how in hell he thinks I am going to *read* that note! Tell him to read it to *you*, John, and then you can learn it and come back and tell me what it says, because nobody on earth could read it, and how he expects me to read it is more than I know!"

So John would take it back again to Mr. Warner very

solemn, and then come back and tell Mr. Clemens what was in the note. When John did that, then Mr. Clemens wouldn't fuss any more. He'd say: "Well, that's all I want."

I used to often hear Mr. Clemens ask Mr. Warner, "Where in hell did you learn to write, Charley?"

Well, Mr. Warner'd say, he didn't have any trouble with anybody else reading his handwriting. "Nobody ever complains but you, Mark," he says. "I never have any trouble with anybody but you, reading my handwriting." Then Mr. Clemens, he says, "Of *course* they have trouble reading it, but they don't know you well enough to tell you so, Charley, that's what it is! They're afraid to tell you the truth!"

Mr. Warner was a very fine-looking man in early days. Tall, with a gray mustache and gray hair. He was very pleasant-looking and nice. He was a great story-teller too. They was always happy when they was together. Of course, Mr. Howells was there about as much as anybody, though he lived in Boston. He had charge of some little magazine there—I think it was called the *Atlantic Monthly*—and it's still going. He was a nice-looking man, too, as I told you, and one of the very pleasantest men that ever lived. You could hear them for miles around, they talked and laughed so much when they was together. Mr. Howells was short and stout and jolly. One of those real jolly men, smiling all the time, no matter what happened. Mr. Clemens said to him one time, when he was going to take a kodak picture of him, he says to him very loud,

"Now look pleasant, damn you, look pleasant," he says, "if you can!!" Of course he was only joking, for Mr. Howells never looked any other way but pleasant; and when Mr. Clemens seen the picture and how smiling it was he says:

"Why, Howells, that's the best picture you ever had, because it's so unusual—so smiling." Of course that was one of Mr. Clemens' jokes, because Mr. Howells never looked any other way—even when he felt bad.

Mildred Howells, his daughter (Pilla, I told you they called her) was a very nice, bright girl. She traveled in Europe a good deal, she wrote poetry and drew pictures, too. She was very smart. She had a book of pictures that she drew, pictures of all the cathedrals in Rome. She kind of sketched them off in a book as she was traveling. People said they was very good when she showed them (they had to, I suppose), and very likely they were, 'cause she was really a very clever girl.

John Howells, he was her brother, and he got to be an architect. He was a very fine one, too, and made the plans for our Redding house years afterwards. He was a great friend of Miss Clara's, and all the family, and he was always at the house for all the jollifications. Everybody liked him—I did myself. He was a very nice young man. He and his sister was always great friends of the girls. Of course, the Clemens children (and by that I mean Clara and Susy) certainly had the most wonderful time that any children ever had in this world and everything to interest them and to make them happy.

When they was quite little, they had an awful cunnin' little playhouse up at Quarry Farm. 'Twas right up in a kind of a little bower—all vines and bushes and stuff, and so Mrs. Clemens said they'd build a little house for them there. It was a regular little cottage when it was finished—with little windows, a porch and a door and everything like a regular house. There was dishes and chairs and little curtains to the windows. It was an awful cunnin' little place. And they called it "Ellerslie"—out of some book I guess, but I don't remember what one. And they called that little tangle of bushes back of it "Helen's Bower." They was just crazy about it and played there all the time when they was at Quarry Farm. They loved them summers there. They lived out of doors all the time, and they used to have a little donkey to ride on, too, and they used to read with their mother sometimes. They was reading English history, I remember, one summer when they was getting ready to go to Europe; and then almost every day Clara and Susy used to sew a little mite, too. That is, they tried to, but it didn't amount to much. Jean was so little then, she was just kind of runnin' around, playing with the cats mostly, and she was always hungry—she was always asking her mother what she could have to eat! There was one summer that they had eleven cats up there at the farm. Mr. Clemens, you

LITTLE HOUSE WHERE MARK TWAIN WROTE "HUCKLEBERRY FINN" AND "TOM SAWYER," AT QUARRY FARM, ELMIRA, N. Y.

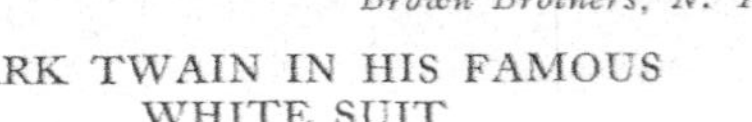

Brown Brothers, N. Y.

MARK TWAIN IN HIS FAMOUS
WHITE SUIT

MARK TWAIN ABOUT 1880
(Courtesy Harper & Brothers)

know, was so crazy about cats that he'd stop anything—even his writing, to speak to a cat! They used to have what he called a regular "cat procession" up at Quarry Farm, when he and Mrs. Clemens and all the children and the donkey, too, and all the cats bringing up the rear, would walk around the grounds. All the cats Mr. Clemens had seemed to understand everything he said to them—just like humans, they'd listen to him.

There was one particular summer at Quarry Farms that Susy and Clara used to have a good many quarrels, like children always do (especially sisters), and they used to get awful mad at each other and then they'd feel very bad and tell their mother about it, and wonder if there was any remedy for their quarreling, so's they could get over it. They didn't really want to fight each other, Susy said, but they couldn't help themselves; and one day their mother said that perhaps if they would just stop a minute and *pray* when they started to fight, God would help them.

So one day Mrs. Clemens said she was setting in her bedroom and she heard them come rushing upstairs and that they throwed themselves right down on their knees in front of her door and begun calling out, and praying, "Oh! please, dear God, stop me from fighting with Susy," said Clara; and then her mother looked out and seen Susy on her knees with her hands clasped, saying, "Please, dear God, just stop me from fighting with Clara."

It seems they was up in the hayfield when they got to quarreling, and then they remembered what their mother said and they ran right down to the house without stopping and begun to pray. They thought that would break up the fight maybe—that the prayer would finish the job; and I guess it did, for that time, anyway.

Both the girls was talented, and Susy, she could write very good, even when she was a little girl. She was what you might call a natural writer. I think if she'd lived she'd probably been a very famous author—like her father, maybe. Mr. Clemens thought she was very talented, too. She used to keep a diary and he was very proud of that. I used to hear a good deal about it in those days. It was what you might call a biography of her father—there was a great deal about him and the family and all their doings. She said in one part of her diary that her father was a very attractive man and was a very striking, strong character, and that he had a beautiful-shaped head and lovely manners and a very good figure, too; and that he was a very fine-looking man, indeed—even if he was her father, she'd have to say so.

Of course, Mr. Clemens and the children just adored each other, and he was just lovely about everything in the house—that is, except when he'd *lose* anything—just like his manuscript. He'd get terrible upset if he'd lose any of his things, and I remember once he got terrible mad at me and called me "a regular damned fool" for throwing away a long spike he had to clean his pipe with! It seems he couldn't find it and I'd throwed it away, and when he asked me where it was, I said, "Why," I said, "I threw it away; 'twas a dirty old spike, and I threw it away. I didn't know you wanted it."

"What!" he says. "Was you really fool enough to throw my beautiful spike away? Why," he says, "I wouldn't have lost that—I wouldn't sell it, or give it up," he says, "for fifty dollars—no, not for a thousand dollars, I wouldn't have lost that spike! It's the only thing I ever had to clean my pipe good. Where did you throw it?"

"Well," I says, "I threw it right down into the brook from the porch where I was standin'."

Well, when he heard that, he went on a terrible rampage; he felt terrible and so did I. I didn't know it was anything he cared about, of course; it looked like a little dirty old file on the mantelpiece and I says to myself: "Well, that's a dirty old thing. He'll never see that again, I'll throw it away." But when I found out how precious it was to him, and he got so mad and gave me "down the banks" for it, I went right out and got a little skewer from the butcher boy and I had him file it down fine like a knitting needle, you know, and then I went and gave that to Mr. Clemens.

"Well," he says, very gloomy, "I suppose you think

that's going to take the place of that nice one you threw away! It don't," he says; "it never will, either. But I'll use it, anyway. I'll have to."

But it took him a long while to get over the loss of that dirty old spike. He was always like that about any of his things.

It was shortly after the telephone invention that I went to Hartford. They just put it in about that time and it made Mr. Clemens so mad—"just to hear the damned thing ring," he said. Yes, that telephone used to make Mr. Clemens wild, because he would hear all right, but he couldn't give his message out good. It wasn't very good service them days, and he used to fight the telephone girls all the time. He'd say:

"Why, damn it, are you all asleep down there? If you don't give me better service you can send somebody right up here now and pull this thing out. I won't have this damned thing in the house—it's a nuisance!"

One night Mrs. Taft, the wife of Dr. Taft (lovely people that lived in Hartford), she called him up and George answered the telephone first and then he went and called Mr. Clemens. So Mr. Clemens went out to speak to her but he didn't know who was at the telephone, so he said "Hello! Hello!!" He thought it was one of them hello girls. Mrs. Taft didn't answer him quick enough, so he says, very loud, "What in —— the matter with you down there? Are you all asleep?" And then she said "Hello" and then he said "Hello," and then she says "Hello"—and finally he says, "Dammit, how many times more have I got to say 'Hello'?" Why, he was so mad by then, he didn't even hear Mrs. Taft, and he kept shouting, "If I don't get better service than this I am going to have this pulled right out of my house, if I don't get any better service from you hello girls down there!"

He was swearing and carrying on something awful, so Mrs. Clemens heard him and opened the dining-room door and put her finger up to her lips. Then, of course, he quieted down and poor Mrs. Taft had a chance to be heard at last! So she says very polite:

"Good evening, Mr. Clemens."

"Oh," he says, "is this you, Mrs. Taft? Well," he says, "well, well! I just this minute come to the telephone! *George* has been here trying to talk, and he's been having such a bad time with this old telephone, I had to come and help him and see what I could do!" Think of that! Of course she never let on—but pretended that she believed it.

"Oh, that's too bad, Mr. Clemens," she says. Then she went on with her talk, but she knew all the time it was Mr. Clemens carrying on like that and swearing to "beat the band." Of course he had to get out of it somehow and blamed it on George! But he was always ashamed after talking like that and felt terrible bad. He didn't swear any more after Mrs. Clemens opened the dining-room door and looked at him. He quieted down then, but of course his swearing never seemed really bad to me. It was sort of funny, and a part of him, somehow. Sort of amusing it was—and gay—not like real swearing, 'cause he swore like an angel!

But it took him a long while to get used to the telephone. He was always mad at it and always thought it was a nuisance. One time, just before New Year's, it was, he was wishing everybody in the whole world a Happy New Year—everybody—whether he knew them or not—rich and poor, white and black—everybody everywhere, the whole world (except Mr. Bell, the inventor of the telephone). "Because," he says, "the telephone's a damned nuisance and so I won't wish him a Happy New Year's!"

Mr. Bell wrote to him to have him take it back, but Mr. Clemens didn't want to. He still maintained that old instrument was a "damned nuisance"—that telephone invention of Mr. Bell's. He wrote a letter that was published in all the newspapers, and of course Mr. Bell saw it; so he asked him if he wouldn't take it all back and please to wish him a Happy New Year's too? It made him feel terrible bad to have everybody in the whole world wished a Happy New Year but him! Well, Mr. Clemens was very stubborn and wouldn't take it back then. He wrote to Mr. Bell and said he'd think it over, but he wouldn't take it back just then, anyway. He might in another hundred years—he'd see! But he did take it back later, though, when Mrs. Clemens' mother,

Mrs. Langdon, died in Elmira and Mr. Beecher was going to preach a wonderful sermon about her (he wasn't going to preach it at the funeral but he was going to preach it several months later); then Mr. Bell wrote Mr. Clemens and asked him if he couldn't do something for him about listening to that sermon without having to leave his house. Mrs. Clemens was sick and couldn't go up to Elmira, and Mr. Bell said he would put wires in at the Park Church right under Mr. Beecher's pulpit, and he would connect them up in the library in Hartford, so's Mr. Clemens could sit in the library with his family and be comfortable and hear the sermon without budging. Mr. Bell said he would put in seven or eight receivers and they could all set right there and listen to the sermon. Then Mr. Clemens wrote him and thanked him, and asked him what his charges would be, and Mr. Bell wrote right back, "Nothing—nothing at all! but just please to wish me a Happy New Year." So Mr. Clemens said, "Well, *now* you can have all the Happy New Years you want—Happy New Years for the rest of your life!" So you see, he did wish him a Happy New Year's after all! But that was Mr. Clemens' way—his bark was always worse than his bite—which was really no bite at all.

And then we went to Europe and I'll tell you why. It was then the trouble began, when the typesetting machine (that Mr. Clemens thought was going to make such a fortune) failed. The publishing house that he was connected with busted, too—that went first, on account of the typesetting machine, I guess. Mr. Clemens was kind of tired of writing, I think, so he wanted to be a publisher himself—try it, anyway. He got his niece's husband, Webster, and made him manager of that publishing company that he was interested in—I forget the name of it. They published some of Mr. Clemens' things and then by and by Mr. Clemens, he got General Grant to let him have his Life that he was writing, to publish. I can't tell very much about that—I only heard a little about it; but I knew it was very important and I think they did very well with that Grant book. They sold lots of copies. Mr. Clemens paid an awful big price for the Grant book in the beginning—a good deal bigger price than anybody else would pay, because he admired Grant so much and loved him so. He felt that he wanted to pay General Grant a lot of money for that book—he thought it would be a wonderful book and everybody would want to read it. He was always too generous about anything he believed in. I heard that General Grant was going to give it to some other publishing house, but when Mr. Clemens talked with him he said, "Why, General, that company isn't going to pay you *half* enough! That offer they make you isn't near enough for your book."

It seems that General Grant said he thought that the person that *first* give him the idea of writing his book was the one he ought to let publish it. Well, it seems

Mr. Clemens had given him that idea years ago. He suggested it to him—told him he ought to do it—and then when General Grant remembered that, why he just up and let Mr. Clemens have it for his publishing house. Of course Grant said Mr. Clemens was too generous—was paying too much for it; but Mr. Clemens wouldn't listen to him at all, and just drawed a great big check right then on the spot—twenty-five thousand dollars, I heard it was—to clinch the bargain. It was this firm, the Webster Company, that published Mr. Clemens' *Huckleberry Finn*, too.

Huckleberry Finn was drawn from life. One of the little boys he used to play with—I can't remember his name—was Huckleberry Finn; so all the doings in that story was true happenings. Everybody knows what a wonderful book that was. He made lots of money out of that, I guess, because everybody read it, and are still reading it.

It seems Mr. Clemens was right after all, for Grant's Life did make lots of money—more than any other book had ever made, they said. Business was flourishing, I can tell you, and then they set out to publish the life of the Pope, too. Mr. Clemens was terrible excited about that, and Mr. Webster went right over to Rome to see the Pope. It seems he had a grand audience with his Holiness and was awful set up by it because everybody was talking about it—it was so unusual at that time. Webster rode in a grand carriage in Rome, and fixed himself all up for his call on the Pope. They had a real good talk together and everything was settled satisfactory. The book was going to be written by somebody else and the Pope was going to approve of it. Of course they thought it would sell like hot cakes, just as much as General Grant's did, but it didn't! 'Twas kind of a fizzle. All the Catholics, they was counting on to buy it and read it—just didn't buy it, I guess. It wasn't such a great thing after all. It was a great splurge but didn't amount to much in the end.

Then things got kind of bad in the publishing house and Mr. Webster, he was taken sick and had to give up, and then a young fellow that was in the firm, he took charge of things and I guess he didn't run it very good, and that was the beginning of awful troubles, and of course, by that time Mr. Clemens was all deep in the typesetting machine, and he was putting all his money in that so he didn't have much left to help out the publishing company. That was the beginning of the end of that venture—that's all I can tell you about it, anyway.

Well, now I'll tell you about the typesetting machine. That's a long story. Mr. Clemens' heart was just set on that, he believed in it so. He was expecting such wonderful things from it. Why, he thought he could buy all New York. He was asking how much it would take to buy all the railroads in New York, and all the newspapers, too—buy everything in New York on account of that typesetting machine. He thought he'd make millions and own the world, because he had such faith in it. That was Mr. Clemens' way.

Well, that Paige machine, it swamped more money in Hartford than I can tell you. It was invented by a man named Paige. It was a machine for typesetting—could set the type and distribute it both. It would do the work of six or seven men, Mr. Clemens said—"do it better than six men ever could do it." It worked by itself, automatic, as they called it, and Mr. Clemens said it was the greatest invention ever contrived by man. That's what he thought of it, so no wonder he put all his money into it. Of course they was trying to bring it to perfection and it needed a lot of money for that, so they were trying to get rich men to go in it and invest like Mr. Clemens did.

The first typesetting machine was built somewhere else—but that didn't last very long. It wasn't any good, they said, so they threw the old machine away and built a new one in Pratt & Whitney's shop in Hartford,—built it from the ground up. It was a terrible undertaking. Mr. Clemens had such wonderful grand ideas about it and people wrote him from all over the world. He was always calculating all the millions that typesetting machine was going to bring in. All the newspapers all over the world was going to have one of them machines, and quite a good many bought stock and Mr. Clemens, he owned a lot of stock too; but still there was never enough money to feed that old machine. Paige was all the time thinking up something new that he would invent before it would be perfect, and Mr. Clemens had to give him money all the time. Oh, my! He sent him thousands of dollars. Used to send him each month a great big check to keep it going. They was just waiting for it to be perfect—to astonish the world. Of course Paige was always promising and expecting it would be all ready next month, and then poor Mr. Clemens, he'd send more money, and the next month it wasn't ready and that's the way it went. For years it went like that, and the family had to economize very much. It was about this time we went to Europe because we could live cheaper over there and help save for the typesetting machine; but Mr. Clemens never lost faith in it, no matter how much money it took and how many times it broke down—and it was always breaking down and having something the matter with it. Finally he got Senator Jones interested—Senator Jones from Nevada (they called him the "Silver King"). I remember him. He was very rich, had millions and millions and owned a silver mine. He was a Senator down in Washington then and quite a character, and was very famous, too. He come up to Hartford several times from Washington where he was Senator and one time he told Mr. Clemens that a couple of men he knew would spend a couple millions easy—"ready to put up a million," Senator Jones says, "if the thing was really good."

A lot of celebrated men was interested in that machine. Mr. Clemens, you know, was always trying to get people interested to put in money, just as he did, and among them was Carnegie. That is, Mr. Clemens kind of suggested to him that he ought to be interested in it. I really don't know whether he ever was or not, but I heard one time Mr. Carnegie said one awful smart thing about it, when Mr. Clemens said he'd better not put all his eggs into one basket, but kind of branch out into something else, and Carnegie told him:

"Oh, that's all right. It's a good thing," he says, "to put all your eggs in to one basket, only you must just sit down and watch your basket!"

I guess it was that kind of sense (and watching) he had, that made Carnegie the rich man he was! Of course that story is an old one and has been told by everybody—everywhere.

Then one time I heard it was arranged for some of them men to come up to Hartford on a certain day and look over the machine. Paige had got it all fixed up good. 'Twas in beautiful running order just for that morning. So all them big men come up and took lunch with Mr. Clemens. He was alone that time—the family was in Europe. He telephoned he was bringing them men to lunch and told the cook to get a very nice dinner ready and oh, my! she did cook an elaborate lunch for them all! and George did his best to make everything homelike and cozy. Well, they eat their lunch and had the jolliest time you ever heard of. They laughed and talked and eat hearty and drank (they had Roman punch for an appetizer, I believe). And they had champagne, too, and after they eat up everything, they went to Pratt & Whitney's factory to see the machine. And what do you think? If that darned old thing didn't break down right when those men was just looking at it! It broke right in front of their faces! The old thing busted itself and went to pieces! The machine was so fine it couldn't stand the pressure, I guess. Anyway, they all said it wasn't any good that time. They was terribly disappointed—and all got mad and said they wouldn't put twenty-five cents in it—which was quite a comedown from a million!

It almost killed Mr. Clemens. It was a hard blow on him, you know, to have it behave so right in front of Senator Jones and all them big men. But anyway, he still had faith in it. Nothing could make him lose faith in that old typesetting machine, so he went on with it alone. Senator Jones, he got out. He never said nothing more about it. He seen then, I guess, it wasn't any good. 'Twas a pity Mr. Clemens didn't see it at the same time.

Well, it went on for I don't know how long—about ten years, I guess. Always sort of coming up again, and he'd be full of hope and excited, grabbing at straws about it, but finally he had to give it up. He didn't give it any more money. He just had to let it go; and so everything kind of went to pieces at once,—the publishing business and that, too, and it was really a bad time with the family; so, as I said before, they stayed in Europe several years. They thought they could live cheaper there. Mr. Clemens spent nearly two hundred thousand dollars on that machine they said. My, that's an awful lot of money to throw away, but of course he didn't know he was throwing it away then. People never know, until it's too late. It's like everything else in the world, I guess—you got to take a chance.

Mrs. Clemens felt terrible, too, for she had put some of her money in it; said she was afraid they'd lost so much money they would have to cut down all their expenses. One day she was talking to me and said:

"Oh, dear! I am afraid I'll have to lose my help. I'll have to send them all away."

I said, "Oh, Mrs. Clemens, you won't have to send *me* off, for I won't go! If you just give me something to eat, never mind my pay—I'll stay."

Then big tears come to her eyes and she said: "Oh, Katy, Katy! How lovely! But," she says, "I hope it will never come to that, that we'll have to let you go."

"Well, I wouldn't go if you sent me. Nothing could drive me away," I says. "I'll never leave you, no matter what happens."

You know, I really think that when that old typesetting machine busted itself finally, in his heart Mr. Clemens was really glad of it because he was getting awful sick of business. He used to say he was tired of it—tired to death. He warn't suited to a business life—he wanted to get out and never touch it again.

'Twas just about the time the publishing house was going to pieces that he met Mr. Rogers, who was such a wonderful friend to him all his life.

Yes, it was when Mr. Clemens lost his money that he first met Mr. Rogers, right after that. You see so many things come out in the newspapers then, how he was so poor and so many people wanted to help him. Everybody knew Mark Twain then and loved him. They were going to take up a five-cent collection all over the world for him (that was in the newspapers). Mrs. Clemens heard that and put a stop to all that newspaper talk. She had some money of her own, you know, and she didn't want them to take up a collection from all over the world. Then Mr. Rogers came forward to help Mr. Clemens—but he didn't offer Mr. Clemens any money. He thought Mr. Clemens was too fine a man to offer him anything like that, but he did offer to help him take care of what he had—and invest it good, and so he done that for him. He invested it and advised him and took care of it for a good many years. He was a kind friend to them and a wonderful, lovely man all his life.

So they went to Europe, as I said before, because they could live cheaper there. We all went. That was the end of the Hartford days. They closed the house, but they didn't know then it was forever. It was a sad time. They found a place for Patrick, the coachman, and

Brown Brothers, N. Y.

GENERAL ULYSSES S. GRANT

© Rockwood, N. Y.

ANDREW CARNEGIE

MARK TWAIN WRITING IN BED

George, too. He went to the Players Club in New York later on. I was the only one of the servants that went with them. First they thought they'd just take that German nurse for the children, but Mrs. Clemens really thought I could pack and do things better than this German girl, so finally it was settled I should go. I was glad of it. Mrs. Clemens said, "Katy, you'd like to go to Europe, wouldn't you?" I said, "Yes, I'd be delighted." Then she says: "We was talking it over last night, Mr. Clemens and I, and decided it would be best to take you. You would be a great help to the children and me and tend to the packing and everything." You see there was twenty-five trunks to pack and remember what was in every one of them! That was no small job, I'll tell you.

It was at that time (when the family first went to Europe) I had a real beau, and I told him that I was going away with the family, going to leave America.

"What!" he says. "You think more of that family than you do of anybody else. Well," he says, "you're not going if I can help it!" But I didn't take him very serious then, because I was so crazy to go to Europe. And then later, just before we sailed, I broke it to him, and I says, "Well, I'm going to Europe, I'm really going, and I'm glad!"

"What," he says, "you are?" he says. "Why, I was making all the plans for us to get married! I bought a lot up on Farmington Avenue and I was going to build a nice little house there for you, that you would like."

"Well," I says, "you're too late" (you could have knocked me down with a feather, though!) "Why didn't you tell me that before?"

"Well," he says, "I thought I'd kind of surprise you. I didn't really think you would go with that family, way over there to them foreign countries," he says. He felt pretty bad, but I really didn't care. So you can see how much I loved the family, 'cause even a husband and a little house of my own didn't make me want to leave them.

You see in them days, as a young girl, I didn't think much about life; it just drifted on. I had everything I wanted and didn't have to worry about a single thing. 'Twas just like living in a bed of roses. The family was so good to me. Everywhere they went, I went along, and I was in on about everything, and what I didn't see I heard all about. It seemed like my own house, you know, and they like my own family. I spent all my time thinking about what would be best for them. I didn't think of the money I was earning, ever.

So we all went to Europe, Jean, Susy, Clara, Mr. and Mrs. Clemens, and Mrs. Crane, Mrs. Clemens' sister. She wanted her to go, too. We sailed on a French boat and landed in Havre and went right up to Paris. Mr. Clemens was having kind of paralysis in his arm then, and thought some baths would be a good thing and Mrs.

Clemens wanted to take the baths too, so we went to Aix-les-Bains, and Mr. Clemens took the baths there. He was suffering a great deal of pain and he liked those big men that used to rub him. They put him in a sheet and brought him home in a chair and he was very patient about them baths. They'd cover him all up with a blanket and bring him straight down to the hotel.

We stayed six weeks taking the cure, and then they planned to go to hear the Wagner Opera in Bayreuth. We went back to Geneva where the girls was studying French in some French family—and then we all started for Bayreuth and the Wagner Opera. It was all the rage then. We bought our tickets in America a year before (and our dinners too!) and we started then for Bayreuth. That's the way the thing was managed. You had to get your tickets the year before, because everybody in the world was just crazy to go to that Wagner Music Festival. Well, when we got there, oh, my! It was something awful! Why, we couldn't even get a room in a hotel, it was so full, so full of Royalty. Mr. Clemens used to say, "The damned Royalty gets ahead of me every time! They get ahead of everything!" It used to make him so mad—he couldn't stand it. Bayreuth was just a little place—a little German village way up in the Barbarian Mountains. It was a real pretty little place, too—but nobody'd ever gone there, I guess, except for them Wagner operas.

Yes, 'twas a little insignificant village and nobody'd

think anything of it if it had been in this country. But it was kind of a "shrine," as they called it, over there, for them Wagner operas. The opera house was way up in the mountains and was beautiful. It looked like a low building when you first seen it, but when you got inside you found it was sunk way down in the ground so it was a very, very deep building. You looked way, way down, like you'd been looking into a cellar, and that was where the orchestra was. And then the stage, it raised up, you know, and then went down, when they wanted to change the scenery. It shoved up and down. There warn't no curtain at all to it, and all the boxes where the Royalty set was all around the back of the theater. It was rounding in shape (this theater), different from any other I'd ever seen. I'll tell you more about it later.

You see, Bayreuth was so full of people then that it was impossible to set down hardly. But we finally got into a Pension (that's a boarding-house) because we couldn't get into a hotel. The "damned Royalty" had got all the places, as Mr. Clemens said. Why, you couldn't hardly get anything to eat—even in a restaurant. All we could get was hot dogs! We used to get 'em on the way up to the opera. They was selling them there on the street—oh, plenty of them—and biscuits with them, you know; and if you was very hungry you'd have to eat them, or nothing! Mr. Clemens, when he looked out of the window and saw a cart coming up from the station piled high with great trunks, he'd say, "There goes some more Royalty—getting their trunks off from the train first and getting ahead of everybody else!"

We had a hard time of it sometimes just to get the frankfurters. But Mr. Clemens somehow used to get plenty. I don't know how he managed it—but he'd go somewhere and get a dinner—something like cabbage and corned beef, which the rest of the family wouldn't look at, and then Mrs. Clemens and Mrs. Crane and the children and I would go and try to hunt for some other place to eat. We'd look in the windows and see something nice that we'd like, and sometimes we'd get it, that is, if we was able to get in ahead of the Royalty! They got everything first. But Mr. Clemens was contented with corned beef and cabbage and he used to fill himself up good with that. Then, he said, he could stand anything—even Wagner operas.

Yes, we had a terrible time anyway, in that place, to live at all. It was just a struggle every day; but we did get to the opera—we had our tickets for that. We went to *Parsifal.* They took me to that, too, you know. I don't understand music anyway, but honest and true! When we went into that opera house (you could hear a pin drop almost the audience was so quiet); it was so wonderful to me—I just held my breath.

As I said, I don't understand music, but when the singing began I just took right hold of the seat in front of me to see if I was alive—it was so heavenly. Oh, it was wonderful! We used to go to the opera every day.

They would all go, the family and Mr. Clemens. He used to go and select the places to eat, you know, during the intermission (six o'clock they had the intermission). The curtain never dropped, but there would be an intermission of about an hour to get your dinner, and Mr. Clemens would always hurry out first, and get some guide that knew everything about the place, to find their dinner places for them (you see they bought their dinner tickets, too, in America). So the guide would find those chairs and get a place for the family to set down and we'd come out and have dinner—about the only meal we did get! They give us a wonderful dinner in that place—roast chicken and lots of vegetables and then we had a kind of goulash—all stuff mixed up together, and some of them German noodles. They served beer, too, of course—great steins of beer. I never took that, but I think the rest of the family drank it. That would be a good thing to hold you for a week, most. Mr. Clemens thought it ought to satisfy anybody. It would be enough, really, to last them a week—he used to say.

It seems that opera house was different from any other in the world. It was just as deep in the ground as it was high in the air and you looked way down in the center. They didn't have any curtain on that stage—no curtain at all, and the scenery shifted up and down—going down in the cellar, then upstairs, you know. You couldn't see the orchestra either. That was hid away out of sight, but you could hear it good. It was wonderful, really, for anybody that could understand music.

We stayed there ten days and we seen everything, I think, and heard all them operas. That old Frau Wagner (she was Wagner's wife) she used to run it—the opera. I seen her coming there once in a carriage. They told me that that was Mrs. Wagner. She had an old dress on that was trailing in the mud. They didn't wear trails then, but hers was trailing along and she looked just like a peasant woman. You never'd thought she was a musician. Well, she just hopped out of the carriage and sort of sneaked in the side door without any fuss.

And there was the Royalty, too. The opera house was full of Royalty, and they always set up in their boxes. We had to set in the tier below, but we could look back at them, you know—just see the curtains, that was all. The Royalty sat up in the top of the house, their boxes were up there and they was always covered up with curtains so you could only see the top of their heads. They used to keep the curtains drawn all the time. You couldn't see their faces. I don't blame them much, they're such a homely lot! They're about the homeliest lot I ever seen. Of course, I never seen them in Court with their jewels on. Maybe they looked better then! I think there was a bunch of every kind of Royalty there was, when you got them all together. Oh! if you could see their carriages coming, with the wonderful horses, all gold harness and everything—dashing up to that opera house, and see those people alighting. Oh, my! It was wonderful to see them gold harnesses and then those footmen, with gold breeches on, to help out the Royalty and bow them into the opera house. They was always in plain clothes and muffled right up to the tip of their noses. You couldn't see their dresses at all. It was just the footmen that was in fine clothes. Of course the crowd just stood there and looked at them—they got a kind of peep show for nothing.

The family was just crazy about the opera—especially Clara. They liked *Parsifal* and they thought Parsifal himself was good and that old Kundry—she was wonderful! Clara was mad about Parsifal. She went and shook hands with him once. Mr. Clemens went to all them operas, but I don't think he really liked it very much. I heard him say once that old Kundry was good "if she'd only get up more and walk around." She was really an old woman but she had a wonderful voice just the same. Her costume was good enough but, as I said before, she was half stretched out—lying down most of the time, and her feet was the most you could see of her from where we sat. They was pretty big, her feet, but the music was so beautiful you didn't notice her much anyway. Mr. Clemens used to say she was all right, if she'd only get up and show herself a little more; but he didn't blame her, he said, because he supposed she got tired of standing around! She didn't have much to do

(Parsifal done all the work in that opera)—she was kind of fat, too; but Parsifal was charming. He looked like a regular lover. Oh, he was grand! He was quite a boy, too. He had a beautiful shape and he dressed nice. The family went to every one of them operas. I never heard Mr. Clemens say he was tired, but he'd be getting ready all the morning, dressing himself up—trying to beat the Royalty, I guess, as far as looks went.

Mr. Clemens always used to say he only attended the opera when he couldn't help himself! He didn't like opera that he didn't know or understand—he liked them old operas that he was familiar with and could sing the tunes himself. Once when he was in Germany, and some band began to play a very pretty piece, Mr. Clemens said he knew right away that must be very *low* music, because he really enjoyed it! He said it couldn't be really good music, because it pleased him so much! And I heard him say one time that whenever he heard a big crowd applauding the band's playing, he knew for sure 'twas very bad music, because it was only a few that could ever be educated up to the point where high-class music would give them any pleasure! I guess there's considerable truth in that, and lots of people besides Mr. Clemens feel that way—only they won't own it.

Mr. Clemens was pretty busy on that trip because we couldn't locate Joseph then, the guide—couldn't find him anywheres. Mr. Clemens had had him the first year he ever went abroad; then he met him whenever he'd gone over again. We was kind of waiting round for him to see if we couldn't hear from him, and then Mr. Clemens made up his mind he'd have to be his own guide. He was awful mad—he was almost crazy. He came in one morning when I was packing and was going to leave on the afternoon train. I had all the things spread around the room. All them trunks wide open when he came hurrying into the room and he says, terrible excited:

"Well, Katy, you'll never get through that packing there, never! It'll take two days before them trunks will be ready."

"Now, Youth, dear, never you mind," said Mrs. Clemens. "You run right along," she says, "and if you got anything to do, go and do it now, for those trunks will be ready and waiting when the man comes for them." And they was, because I was never late. Of course Mr. Clemens thought that was wonderful because he really didn't think I'd be ready and would be the cause of not catching the train that day. It used to fuss him terrible. He was on a terrible rampage that time because we had to go without the guide. He was afraid he'd have to buy the tickets and do all the fussing with the luggage, and it was a great mountain on him to have to take Mrs. Clemens and Mrs. Crane and all us six in the party and get car seats and everything. You know, it was really a great burden to him. The trains then were bad, but he'd always get a car for nine people. He used to buy seats for the whole car, nine, so then he wouldn't have to let anybody else in.

Right after going to Bayreuth, we went to take some of them mud baths, as they called them, at some place in Germany—regular mud, it was. People used to kind of cure themselves of the troubles they had with it. Miss Clara took them mud baths, too, although I don't know what for. 'Twas kind of a ceremony, the way you took 'em. All the people would go to that mud-bath house very serious and march in a regular procession every morning. You had to get up very early and then begin marching around under the trees, and then they'd have kind of a little cake or biscuit that they'd eat, and then they'd march up to a fountain where they'd drink the water, and eat that tough old cake, and then march along to the mud-bath place. They used to march half an hour to very beautiful music, 'cause there was a nice band there that used to play for them. Kind o' kept them going, I guess, the music. I liked that part of it myself. Then after drinking the water and eating the cake, they'd march up to the bathroom and jump right into the mud! There was three baths in the room. The first one was solid mud. They'd set in that for a while, then pull themselves out, dripping all over, and step into another one that warn't quite so thick. Then the last one was pure water. That'd clean them off good, and they had towels to rub themselves dry—and then they'd start back home again. It's what you call a "cure," you know. I didn't think so much of it myself, but everybody that went there thought they got better—maybe they did—but I guess their thinking so helped them as much as the mud!

We went to Switzerland that summer. We went to all the beautiful places there. We had a cottage near the hotel down by the water. I don't remember the name of the place. Clara had a piano and she practiced, and Mr. Clemens wrote during that time, but I don't remember what he was writing. And then they used to go up the mountains. He used to think he'd walk up, but he never did—they used to go in the train; but he used to take long walks every day that wasn't climbing. He was very happy there. He used to get all the things he liked to eat at that hotel, because after the chef got acquainted with him and he seen him a couple of times and Mr. Clemens greased his hand, he used to fix special things for Mr. Clemens which was very nice, and of course we always had a private dining-room, too. We had a suite generally, bedroom, sitting-room, and dining-room. Always just like Royalty. It was in Switzerland that Joseph, the lost guide, turned up at last, which was a relief to Mr. Clemens. They called him Joseph Very. But that really wasn't his own name. It was some awful Russian name—nobody could pronounce it, but he named himself "Very," because he said all the Americans were always saying "very" to everything—it was "*very* nice, *very* good, *very* beautiful, *very* big," so he thought as long as that was a word they all liked so much, he'd just take it himself for his own name, and he did—called himself Joseph Very—which was kind of sensible of him, I think.

Well, after Switzerland, the family went to Berlin for the winter, and I came back to America—the first time I ever left them. They didn't want me to come home but I felt they could get along without me and it would save money. Mrs. Clemens thought maybe the girls were getting so big they could pack for themselves, and as they didn't have much money then, I thought they could get along without me. They were going to live in one place all winter and I told Mrs. Clemens I'd come back any time they wanted me. Mrs. Clemens thought it would be a good thing if the girls took care of themselves—get used to packing twenty-five trunks! We had to have lots of trunks because we carried all our bed linen and table linen, too. You didn't rent that there on the other side, then; you had to take your own in them days.

So I went home to America, and they went to Berlin. I went back to Elmira and begun to work as I used to before I went to Hartford. I began sewing again by the day for Mrs. Fassett. I knew her husband, J. Sloat Fassett, when he was a young fellow in Elmira, before he was married; and he married that rich Miss Crocker from California. He met her when she was attending the wedding of some friend of hers. Well, young Sloat fell in love with her then and there and they was married. They lived in Elmira and had a great beautiful place they built there. Years after, he went into politics and he went to Washington and to Congress, I hear, and had his finger in lots of pies. I used to sew for Mrs. Fassett in the early days, you know, before I went to Mrs. Clemens—made all her baby clothes for her. They was in very high society in Washington—I heard—but he was an Elmira boy—started in Elmira all the same, like some other folks—myself for instance!

But, oh! Elmira looked pretty small—after all of Europe. It struck me as being very shabby and dirty and yet there was places in Europe that was pretty dirty, too. In fact, I never seen a dirtier place than Naples, never. But even so, Elmira was a great change after Europe.

Mr. Clemens made all the arrangements for me to go home—he got my stateroom and tickets, and gave me tickets to the captain, too, for fear I'd get lost. I got to America safe and sound and landed back in the old place, and then I was sorry that I left Europe. Oh, I was lonesome for the family! I missed them so—missed just hearing their voices around, and, oh! Elmira was so dead! I had plenty of time for thinking, and it came over me in a great flood, what a wonderful life I'd been leadin' with them all them years. How it had opened up a kind of new world to me that I'd never had if I hadn't gone to them; and all their kindness and the care they took of me! Just like one of their very own. I seemed to take it in then really for the first time—how much they was always doin' for me; that they was just as considerate of me as they was of one of themselves—and I'll tell you a story to prove it.

Mrs. Clemens once said that when she hired me to go and live with her that first time (she told me afterwards) she was impressed by me asking her only two questions and that was, could I have a room to myself, and could I go to mass every Sunday?

Well, she saw that I had a room to myself (she always managed to have the girls have rooms by themselves) and she always arranged time so that we could go to mass regular.

The family always took such good care of me when I was sick, too, just like one of themselves. One time I had pneumonia and they had to send me to the hospital and Mr. Clemens arranged for me to have a nice room by myself and the very best treatment and doctors, and he would settle the bill. They even was going to give me a special nurse. They was very much impressed by this, the Sisters was, at that hospital, and one day the Head Sister come to me and said, "Why, are you working for Mark Twain?" And I says "Yes," and she says, "Well, they're certainly wonderful people to work for, for they have been telephoning every morning to know how you was getting on." Miss Clara, she used to telephone and send me flowers, and then they sent me extra things to eat if I needed them. The Sister who took care of me never could understand it.

"Well," she'd say, "do you *work* for this family, or

are you *adopted* by them, or what? I can't make it out!"

"Why," I says, "Sister, I work there."

"Then," the Sister says, "they certainly must think a great deal of you."

"Well," I says, "I guess they do." Then she said, "You must love them very much, it must be mutual, for a family couldn't care for their own children more than they care for you."

"Yes," I says, "that's true"—and it was true, all the days of my life that I lived with them.

Yes, they always looked after me in every way. That guide we had over in Europe used to get so mad because they'd always get an extra carriage or place—"For *Katy*," he'd say, "for *Katy!*" And when we got into a hotel, Mrs. Clemens always wanted me to have a nice room right near hers, so that I could help her if she was sick or anything. Most of the maids that was traveling over there'd have to sleep in an awful little hole up in the rear shed in the servants' quarters. One hotel we was at, there was a maid standing outside as I was going into Mrs. Clemens' room one time, and she heard her say "Good night" to me, and when I come out, this maid said, "Why, you know, I would think that the heavens would fall if my lady ever said 'Good night' to me like that, in that tone!"

"Why," I says, "don't you say 'Good night' and 'Good morning' to your lady?"

"No," this maid says, "no, not like that! She never

MARK TWAIN WITH SUSY AND CLARA

Bundy, Hartford

JEAN AS A SMALL CHILD

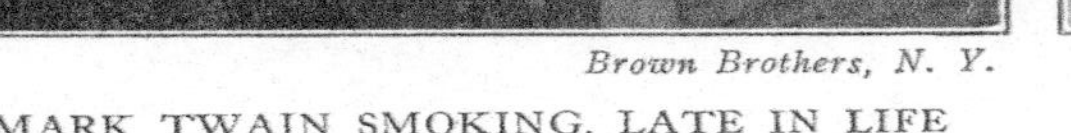

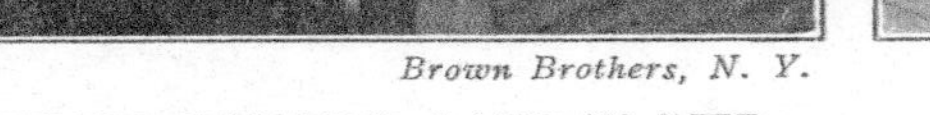

Brown Brothers, N. Y.

MARK TWAIN SMOKING, LATE IN LIFE

MARK TWAIN AT DUBLIN, N. H.
(Courtesy Harper & Brothers)

looks at me unless to tell me to do something—give me some order. Oh, I think your lady is a perfectly lovely, wonderful woman. How I wish I could work for some one like that! You must love her," she says. "You don't realize, then, that you're living among strangers all the time, do you?"

"Oh, no!" I says. "Never—and I'm not living among strangers. They're my family," I says.

I felt sorry for that maid, poor thing, to be treated that way, but lots of people treated their servants like that. But, you know, on the other hand, you couldn't really blame them, because their servants was kind of nasty to them, too, and wouldn't do anything that they wasn't compelled to do. I guess there's good and bad on both sides of the question.

Well, to go back to Elmira. There I was again, at my old job and missing the family more and more every single day. Elmira seemed so dead. Of course, I had lots of friends there, but it wasn't the same—they wasn't like Royalty! I had got used to Royalty then, you know. I couldn't see anything good in Elmira. I'd left it eleven years before and that's a long while to be away. I had a pretty lonesome time of it.

I used to go to dances once in a while, but it wasn't much of a life. Everything seemed so tame after the Clemens family. I tried to cheer myself up with a party now and then, and I remember going to a surprise party once that I wasn't invited to. I peeked in the window of the house where it was going on, and I was so lonesome, I just felt I must go in. I had only an old calico dress on and a red ribbon in my hair, so I wasn't dressed up much; but anyway a man that was there seen me through the window and he come out and says: "What's the matter? Why don't you come in and dance?" I says, "Well, I wasn't invited, but I'd like to come."

"Oh," he says, "that don't make no difference. Come on in."

Well, there was a dance just forming on the floor, so we began to dance. He was swinging me round pretty lively when he just whispered in my ear (oh, I didn't know any better than to think he was telling the truth), "Dance light, for my heart lies under your feet, dear!"

Well, I fell madly in love with him right then and there on the spot, and I thought he certainly had fell in love with me, to say that.

Of course that was stupid of me to believe the first thing he said, but I thought he meant it, and just that whispering in my ear made me feel faint all over. I didn't know any better, for all my traveling and seeing Royalty and high society! Well, he got married, it seems, a few weeks after that—which shows you what a hit I made! It made a terrible impression on me, though, that night, and I felt sure he'd come and see me next day and say it all over again. I don't know how I could be so stupid as to fall for that, but I did. Some girls are like that. Yes, it went down deep in my heart—deep through. That proves you can't believe everything that's told you, don't it? and that there's men flirts as well as women!

Years afterwards, though, I seen him again, and he was a grandfather then. So it just occurred to me I'd ask him what he meant that time when he said, "Dance light, for my heart lies under your feet, dear"—and he says: "Why," he says, "I didn't mean a thing by it! It just happened to come into my head, that's all. It was just for fun."

"Well," I said, " 'twasn't any fun for me, at the time. I really believed you. I didn't know any better in those days, you see—but, thank God, I know better now—now that I'm an old woman—and my knowledge isn't any use to me!"

As I said before, it was a pretty dull, lonesome time, just sewing and living at home, and every day I was hoping and praying that a letter would come from the Clemens family asking me to come back. I just longed and prayed for that!

Well, one day the letter came and it said,

"We're making up our minds to go around the world and we are coming to America in July and want you to be ready to join us."

That was the happiest day I had seen for three years. I just sung for joy. Well, they come back and went up to Quarry Farm, and when I went up there to join them I was beside myself with delight to see the family again.

I didn't cry, I just laughed and laughed, I was so glad! I really felt like screaming—with joy. I felt as though I'd been dead a thousand years and had just come to life again!

I was with them while they was making all their plans to go around the world, and it was then that Susy decided not to go with them. Madame Marchesi, the great singing teacher in Paris, had told her she could be a fine singer if she would only get a little stronger. She advised her to go on a farm for a year and drink lots of milk, live outdoors and everything like that, to get her chest stronger, because if she could do that, she'd have more volume to sing with. Of course Susy took in everything old Marchesi said and believed every word, so she wanted to live on a farm while the family was going round the world. So they had to give up Susy. Then when Susy backed out, Mr. and Mrs. Clemens said they'd let Jean stay in America, too. She was going to a preparatory school in Elmira. So I was to live with them and take care of Susy and Jean. I had a little horse and wagon and used to drive down to the college to get Jean every night.

Then the family got everything ready to start on this great lecture tour, so Mr. Clemens could make money and pay back all his debts. He was going to write another book. You know, when the publishing house failed, he took all the debts on his own shoulders to pay, and it was very hard for him then, 'cause they'd lost so much money with that old typesettin' machine. So when the publishing house failed, poor Mr. Clemens had all them terrible debts on his hands, and he said then and there he'd pay everybody back—not fifty cents on the dollar, but one hundred cents on the dollar! There's very few would have felt the way he did about owing that money. So that's what the lecture tour was for. Mr. Clemens was going on this great long tour round the world, to earn money for what he owed.

Major Pond was the one that proposed that lecture tour. He said they could make a fortune for Mr. Clemens by going all around the world lecturing. Major Pond was going with him out to California, and then a man by the name of Smythe, I think it was—he used to be manager for Charles Dickens—he was going to take him the rest of the way. He was going to Australia and everywhere. The family dreaded starting out again after all their travels, but they had to go; and of course Mrs. Clemens, she wouldn't let Mr. Clemens go all alone, although it was going to be awful hard on her, but she said she must go just the same.

Well, they started off, and, oh, it was hard to let them go! We all felt terrible at parting again. They went to Vancouver and to California and lectured; then sailed from California to Australia, where they started their grand tour. He lectured all around in these different places and it was a great success—a triumph, you might call it; and then they came back to London and was going to take a house and settle down there, and I was to meet them in London with the girls later on.

By this time Susy got kind of lonesome staying up on the farm so she decided to go to New York for a little change. She visited Dr. Rice and she stayed with the Howells, too, for a little visit; then she come back to Hartford. She didn't want to go back to Elmira again, as we was going to join the family so soon. The Hartford house was closed and she couldn't go there; so she went to Mrs. Charles Dudley Warner's, and I took a little apartment on Spring Street. I lived in it and Susy'd come over every day to do her practicing. People used to listen to her from the street and I remember one boy that used to come every day to listen. He was a little boy, then, Max Smith was his name. He's quite famous now, and a well known critic.

Yes, I knew Max Smith. I remember him very well. He lived right there on Forest Street in Hartford—right across from Harriet Beecher Stowe. He was an awful nice boy, but he was quite a fat little boy in them days—and very good-looking and pleasant. He used to play with Susy and Clara when he was little. He liked to hear Susy sing, and he used to stand right outside the window and listen to her, there at the Warners' that time, just before she was taken sick in Hartford. Well, he's a music critic now in New York—one of the best, they say, but I never seen him since he was a little boy.

Well, there was always a crowd outside in the street

listening to Susy sing, for she had a wonderful voice and really we had a concert every afternoon.

We lived that way till Susy got word from the family to sail, and then she was taken sick. We was having good news from the family all the while. They was having a splendid time traveling, and Mr. Clemens was having grand success with his lectures, so they decided to take that house in London and were making great plans for Susy to go to Paris to study with old Marchesi. I was looking forward to that, too—going to Paris again.

I'd seen Marchesi's daughter, Blanche, once. She taught a good many pupils for her mother, old Madame Marchesi. She always come forward in the drawing-room to greet the pupils. I seen her at her house in Paris. It was a lovely house in the Latin quarter. She had Susy sing then and told her she had really a wonderful voice, only that she must get stronger. I heard this Blanche Marchesi sing once myself at a concert. I don't think she sounded very good for a woman with such a wonderful reputation. Anyway, her singing didn't sound good to me. It wasn't good, either. The people that was setting right behind me all said she "had considerable nerve to get up and sing like that!" She tried to get the high notes—tried pretty hard too, but she couldn't reach 'em! She cracked right in the middle. You know, when you hear a lot about a person being so famous, and having such a wonderful person as her mother for a teacher, you'd think she ought to drill her into something fine; but then, you can't make a silk purse out of a sow's ear—and I guess that's true with voices, too!

When Susy got back to Hartford from visiting in New York, just before we was to sail for London, she didn't seem very well. It seems she met some Christian Scientists and Spiritualists in New York and got terrible interested in them; and she got very much excited and carried away. She used to have "absent treatments" from Miss B— every day. "Absent treatment," they called it, and when she got that treatment she'd have to be all alone by herself for about an hour. She'd just "concentrate" her mind on Miss B— and they would do the praying for her and the thinking at the other end. Yes! And she used to go to the Beechers' a good deal and met some Spiritualists there, but I can't remember the names.

There was one Spiritualist—a kind of healer—a woman, and Susy, she used to go to her, and she made passes over Susy's throat—to make it strong so she could sing good, you know. I used to go and set in the back room while Susy was in the parlor getting the treatment. One time they thought I was asleep, but I heard that Spiritualist woman tell Susy how there was a wonderful concert the night before and asked if Susy was there; then she said:

"My husband was there, too, with me, and he enjoyed it so much!"

Now her husband had been dead twenty-five years,

and I knew it! When I heard that I just called right out, "Rats!" and Susy said:

"Oh, Katy, Katy!"

"Susy," I says, "don't you come into this house again! That woman's crazy and the worst kind of a Spiritualist!"

"Yes, maybe," says Susy, "but she's a good healer."

"There's nothing to her," I said. "She's a pirate, a regular pirate! Don't you go near her again. She told you her husband was with her last night," I says, "and you know that *her husband has been dead for twenty-five years!* It's all a darn lie, and if you go there, you'll go alone, 'cause I won't come into this house ever again," I says. Why, I had the awfullest feelings while I was sitting there! I wouldn't go under that roof again for anything—not for any money. I said to Susy: "No, no. You can't go again; that's settled!"

By then we were getting letters that the family was nearing Europe, and the next thing we got a cable to come at once, to sail for London the following Saturday, Susy, Jean, and I. Well, I hurried up to Elmira to get Jean ready. I left Susy at Mr. Warner's. My! it was the hottest day we had that summer. Mr. and Mrs. Crane, Mr. Langdon, and Jean and myself went to New York the day before sailing, then I went back to Hartford to bring Susy down and all the trunks. Mr. Langdon had the tickets and everything was ready. I went up to the Warners' and I found Susy wasn't feeling very well. She looked very bad and says:

"Oh, Katy, did you come for me?"

"I said, "Yes." Then she says: "Oh, have I got to leave now?" She was really in an awful state and I said: "Yes, Susy. We are sailing to-morrow, you know."

"Oh!" she says, "I don't think I can start now. Couldn't we wait till evening, when it's cooler?"

"Well," I said, "that's all right. It's pretty hot now and we can go in the evening when it's cooler." This was in the morning, and then I went to our own house to get a few things we needed, and when I got back in the afternoon, Susy was in a pitiful state, so sick and full of fever. I took hold of her hand and I said:

"Oh, Susy! You got a fever! What shall we do? I am going to send for the doctor."

"Oh, I can't have any doctor, Katy," she said.

"You will have a doctor," I said. But she said: "No, no! I don't want any doctor or any medicine. Miss B— will treat me." I said: "No! Nobody will treat you but the doctor. I'll get him now, myself."

So I hurried right off and I got Dr. Porter right away, and he said she was coming down with spinal meningitis. That evening she got very bad. I saw then she couldn't travel. There was no chance of our sailing the next day, so I telephoned to Mr. Langdon to New York, where he was waiting for us, and told him Susy was sick. He cabled right away to her mother "Unavoidably delayed," and that we would leave on the next steamer.

But poor Susy got worse and worse. Mr. Langdon come to Hartford in the morning and we took her over to the old home. She was very sick and she wouldn't take a bit of medicine from anybody but me. She wouldn't let the nurses touch her or come near her, so I sat by her night and day—night and day, I sat! Oh, it was a terrible time! My heart aches even now when I think of it, after all these years. Poor little Susy! She died before we ever could sail. She died a few days after. We dressed her nice and then brought her little body to Elmira, to the Langdon house to wait for her mother, who was on the ocean. Mrs. Clemens and Clara had sailed for America right after getting our cable. They didn't know how sick Susy was, but they hurried right off and Mr. Clemens was going to take the next steamer after them. We was all waiting in New York for them to land. Mr. Howells and Mr. Twitchell was there too, to meet Mrs. Clemens. I'll never forget how bad Mr. Twitchell felt. He said to me that day: "Oh, Katy! I don't know how I'm ever going to tell Mrs. Clemens! I don't know how I can ever talk to her about Susy!"

He felt then as though he couldn't see her, but I urged him to stay; and he did and he talked to her, and I think she was better after that, if anything in this world could make her better. I'll never forget Mrs. Clemens when she landed, the way she looked, and Clara, too. Oh, Clara! She was a pitiful object. I was afraid for Clara. All the time I watched her like a cat would a mouse.

Such grief is terrible to see. I could hardly bear to look at Mrs. Clemens just at first. It was something awful when she turned to me and held out her hands and said, "Katy," she said, "Katy, Susy's gone—Life has killed her!"

I said: "Oh, Mrs. Clemens, no! No, she just died. God wanted her—and so she died. Everything in the world was done for her and she was talking of you all the time and thinking of you when she died; and the last words she ever said was that she wanted to see her mother."

That seemed to be some little comfort to Mrs. Clemens. I had to repeat it over and over again. The anguish of her heart was terrible. I told her how that last night I was lifting Susy in her bed, how she put her arms around my neck and rubbed down my face with her two little hot hands, and she laid her cheek against mine and said, "Mamma, mamma, mamma!" She thought I was her mother then. When I told this, Mrs. Clemens was sitting in a big chair in the Waldorf, leaning back, just crushed with her grief, but when she heard this, she just stretched out her two hands and held mine hard. I was crying then, I was crying so I couldn't speak; so I just held her hands and she held mine, and I tried to brace her up that way. It was the only thing we could do for each other. We talked a long while that morning and then got ready to go to Elmira and we went up in the train together. We cried together, then we'd talk again, and she wanted to know, over and over, all the things about Susy, the little things that anybody else would have forgot. And I told her everything—every single thing, how I gave her the medicine, how she wouldn't take it from anybody else—that she wouldn't let the nurse do anything for her, and how I lay on that couch day and night, right in front of her bed where I could see her every second, and how I jumped up every time she wanted anything.

"Oh, Katy!" said Mrs. Clemens. "Oh, Katy, if it could only have been *me* instead of you! But how glad I am that you were able to do for her when I wasn't there!"

I didn't think Mrs. Clemens could live then. Her heart almost broke in front of our eyes. You know Mr. Clemens, he wasn't there to help her, either, so she was very much alone. I believe it was that, thinking about him, that kept her up and alive.

When we got to Elmira I went with her to the drawing-room where Susy lay. I was afraid to leave her alone. I hurried in after her and seen her standing there looking at Susy. Such anguish! She didn't speak, only she moaned a little bit, just like a child. Then I said, "Oh, Mrs. Clemens, come away." But she says, "Oh, Katy, can't we stay here just a little longer and look at my Susy? See how beautiful she is." And she did look beautiful. So quiet and peaceful-like, and so fair. The very sight of her was lovely. It seemed to calm Mrs. Clemens a little, and somehow or other she lived through that awful time; and two weeks later we got ready to go back to Europe, without our Susy.

That was the first death in the family since the first little baby—the first break that had ever come, and they never got over the loss. I don't think Mrs. Clemens ever stopped grieving for Susy. She was a beautiful character. She wouldn't hurt anybody's feelings—not for the world. She was always so tender and sweet. Why, I can't tell you how many wonderful qualities she had. She was so pretty, too, and her voice was lovely. She had what they called a perfect soprano, and her notes was wonderful—high—without a break. I think back at that time and know she was in a very nervous condition. She was trying so hard to be a singer. I think it preyed on her mind, her efforts to get strong and well, for whatever she did, she was very serious about. They were such wonderful companions, Susy and her mother. There wasn't ever a secret between them. Susy would pour her heart out to her mother and all her thoughts. After she died—some time after—Mrs. Clemens said to me one day (she was talking about Clara), she says, "Clara is a dear little thing, such a sweet little thing. She's such a comfort to me now," she says. Susy's death had brought them even closer together. But she never really got over losing Susy. It was always on her heart. She was not the kind of a woman to resent it, though. She felt God knew best what to do. That was her faith and her comfort.

Susy was buried in Elmira long ago. They found a little poem once that her father liked and put it on her headstone. It was lovely, I think. I copied it one time on a piece of paper. I never forgot it:

> Warm summer sun, shine brightly here,
> Warm Southern wind, blow softly here,
> Green sod above, lie light, lie light,
> Good night, dear heart; good night, good night.

Ain't that beautiful? And just what it should be for little Susy. Everything soft and kind. 'Twas just like saying good night to her, wasn't it? Perhaps that's all it was, anyway.

We went back to Europe, Mrs. Clemens and Clara and me, just as quick as we could after this. Mr. Clemens was waiting there for us. Mr. Rogers arranged everything about our sailing. He was so kind. He got a wonderful stateroom for Mrs. Clemens and everything to make her comfortable on the voyage back.

Mr. Clemens rented a house in Tedworth Square, No. 23. It was a very nice house and there they stayed all that winter. They stayed very much to themselves, didn't let many people know they was there. We lived in London two years and lots of things happened during that time. They'd fill a big book. I'll tell you some of them, and one is about going and settin' in the Queen's box—when they took me for the Queen! Oh! that was a funny thing! Well, Henry Irving (he was *Sir* Henry then) sent Mr. Clemens tickets to his theater to see him in one of his plays. Irving had sent his own box to Mr. Clemens as a special treat. Mr. and Mrs. Clemens wasn't going out then, so Jean and I went to all the theaters and Mr. Clemens said we could take those tickets too. Well, we started off and took the penny bus to the theater (we usually did that)—that's the way we went; but the way we come back—oh, my! that was quite a different affair!

When we got to the theater Jean presented her tickets to the doorman, and he looked at them and says, "Just wait a minute, please," and went away. Then he come back and says:

"There's some mistake, miss. There isn't any box for you, since Sir Henry Irving's box is given away."

"Oh," Jean says, "that's strange!"

"Well," says the man, "what's your name?" And she told him "Clemens." So he went off and found Ellen Terry this time and took us to her dressing-room, and then Irving appeared, too, and Irving says: "Why, what's the matter with my box? I didn't give my box to anybody but *Mark Twain.*"

"Oh, well," Ellen says, "*I* give it away, Henry!"

"What!" he says. "Gave away my box? Well, then, open your own box, Ellen."

"Oh," she says, "I gave that away, too!"

My! Irving was pretty mad then, but he thought for a

minute, then he says to the man: "Well, open the *Queen's* box! Her Majesty's not coming this afternoon. I have word from her. Open the *Queen's* box!"

So Irving sent us up with one of them page boys with gold breeches on, and everything gold hanging to him, you know. He sent us up the stairs, and one of them gold-mounted boys opened the Queen's box and let us in! Of course there was no light then as the play had begun. It was awful dark and we stepped in very quiet and sat down; but after the first act all the lights was turned up in the theater, and there I was settin' right in front of the Queen's box, and suddenly all them opera glasses in the theater was turned straight at *our* box, at me! They thought I was the Queen! I got frightened and drew the little curtains quick. I felt—well—I'll tell you it was funny. I felt like a rat in a strange garret; but I must say I felt pretty set up, too. It seemed like a dream, don't you know, to be setting in the Queen's box and to be taken for the Queen!

At the intermission we was invited to a little room and had tea. Yes, we had tea in the "Green Room." That's what they call it, though there wasn't anything green in it that I could see. This was a little room where they'd have their tea—the Queen I mean, when she come to the theater. They gave us tea out of solid gold cups. What do you think of that? Out of gold cups—the Queen of England's cups! I suppose if she knew I drank out of them she'd never drink out of them gold cups again; but she didn't know it—which was lucky for her! We enjoyed the box and the tea and the people looking at us, too. We enjoyed everything, the tea and the gold-spangled boys with their gold clothes on. Their knee breeches was gold, they was all gold, them page boys—gold garters, gold all over, gold everything. They was what you might call gold-mounted.

When the play was over we came down the Royal stairs where the Queen comes down, and there was a carpet already laid for the Royal party. It was red velvet. It was laid for us to walk on down them stairs like the Queen; and Jean and I walked right on the Royal carpet. But when we come to the door we didn't know exactly what to do. We didn't want to take a penny bus in front of the theater after sitting in the Queen's box, so we thought we'd just sneak over to the next street and take the bus there. But no indeed! Nothing like that! Irving had his carriage right there at the front entrance, at the end of the Royal carpet, and we was ushered straight into the carriage by them gold-spangled boys, and got in and drove away as though we never seen a bus in all our lives!

Oh, my! We roared after we got home, and I told the story to Mr. and Mrs. Clemens, and Mr. Clemens just was in spasms. He laughed and laughed and jumped around and said, "Well, Katy, Katy, what do you think?"

"Well," I said, "I was just feeling all the time like I *was* the Queen."

"Well," he says, "well, I'm glad that you was able to do that for *once!*"

And of course that really was a wonderful thing to happen to any one, wasn't it? Mr. Clemens and Mrs. Clemens they had spasms about it. They thought it was the funniest thing that had ever happened to the family. He said if Henry Irving hadn't given us a box after sending it to him, that he'd just raised hell with Henry the next time he seen him. I was glad myself that they gave away their own boxes, so we could set in the Queen's box. Of course Irving was pretty mad that afternoon about the mistake in his box. He didn't say anything before all them gold boys, but he was really mad enough to give Ellen Terry a crack over the head. Ellen Terry used to live down there in Chelsea somewhere, not far from us. We used to pass her house very often. I liked Irving, he was very nice. I remembered him from the Hartford days.

I didn't care very much for Ellen Terry's acting. She seemed just kind of ordinary. I don't know just what —she wasn't dainty and exciting like Bernhardt, you know. I seen her in quite a few things, but I can't remember 'em very good. One play, though, I liked her in very much. Irving—he was with her in that too, where she was a washwoman and hanging up the clothes.

She had three clothespins in her mouth, I remember. And, yes, she was doing Henry Irving's washing—no, it was Napoleon's washing she was doing—but Irving was Napoleon in the play. He was a fine Napoleon, too—looked like Napoleon. Yes, he made a good Napoleon—stuffed himself out good to make Napoleon, for he had to be fat, a little round fat stomach and legs. Napoleon always had good calves, judging from his pictures. Irving had good calves, too. Yes, Ellen Terry played in that play and I liked her in that better than anything I ever seen. Napoleon was a wonderful man—and this play was all about him. Of course, I never seen Napoleon himself, only once I remember seeing a picture of him somewheres. It was called "The Last Look at France." He was on a boat leaving for his exile—and it was awful sad. Oh, to see him all alone on that steamer. Standing up on the deck all alone, after all he'd done, fighting the world with his grand army. Yes, 'twas a pretty bad finish for him; but I kept thinking—the worst was being alone. That's always the worst of anything. Well, he looked the way we all look, I guess, when we're seeing the thing we love most for the last time.

We was very comfortable there in London. We had the Hatfield house, it was called, at 23 Tedworth Square. Oh, a beautiful house it was, with big rooms and a lovely porch and a fine billiard room, which Mr. Clemens rented the house for, I guess. Yes, it was a fine house, and we had some of the servants that belonged to the house. They rented the servants when they rented the house.

We didn't have any parties that winter because we lived very quiet. People used to come there to dinner, though, a lot, and Mr. and Mrs. Clemens was invited everywhere. They was flooded with invitations and everybody wanted them.

When we was living at Tedworth Square there was a man there that was trying to get us out of that house all the time, on account of Miss Clara's practicing on the piano. Well, this man (he used to work nights) was a writer, and he was home all day, and Miss Clara had the piano up against the wall of what was his bedroom next door, and it used to set him crazy to listen to her. He said she begun practicing at eight o'clock in the morning, and kept it up until ten o'clock at night. He said her playing was awful bad and her practicing got on his nerves so that he couldn't write. Then he asked if she wouldn't please move her piano over to the other side of the wall, and maybe he wouldn't hear her quite so plain then.

Well, Clara said she was willing to do that, so she did and Mr. Clemens wrote him a letter after that piano was moved and asked him if it was any better, and he said yes, he didn't hear the sound quite so plain and thanked him, but still, he said, we was a "terrible nuisance"—all on account of Miss Clara's playing. Of course that made Mr. Clemens pretty mad, but it didn't amount to much except that they kept writing letters back and forth, fussing about it.

I didn't like London at first. I thought it was the dirtiest city I ever seen—nothing but smoke and fog. The fog was something awful. But when spring come, and the sun came out and everything was gay, and it was the "Season," then London was wonderful. Of course, everything was very different there and the food was quite different, too. Can't say I liked it very much. Of course we cooked our own meals because the English, they didn't half cook the things through, specially the vegetables. I got our cook, though, so she would cook things through after a fashion. But Sunday nights I always used to get the supper myself.

I'll tell this because it takes in Poultney Bigelow and his wife. He was a very famous man in those days. Well, he was great friends with Mr. Clemens and they was coming one night to supper and Mrs. Clemens asked me if I wouldn't make some of them creamed potatoes, because I could make creamed potatoes perfectly luscious, and she thought that would be very nice to have. And my goodness! The Bigelows were so startled when they seen them creamed potatoes! They said:

"Why—why, you've surely got some one from *America* in your kitchen, because there's no cook in England that could cream potatoes!" And that was true.

They liked them so much they just gobbled them down in no time.

Poultney Bigelow used to come there a good deal and tell funny stories. He was in public life—he was Ambassador to some place—and wrote a book—but I don't know what. He lived in London, too, and Sunday night was his favorite night to come. He was a funny-looking man. It seemed as if he had a beard all over his face. He is divorced now, though he and his wife seemed to be on good terms and very nice to each other then. They was very happy, anyway, at our Sunday night suppers.

I don't think the English cooks thought much of our American dishes. They used to say that creamed potatoes ("Who ever heard of such a thing—creaming potatoes!") was extravagant and ridiculous.

There was another funny thing happened in London. Mr. Clemens had a nephew there. He was a doctor, I think, and when he heard about Mr. Clemens losing all his money (that came out in the papers the time he went around the world), there was a story that his family had deserted him, and he was living alone in some garret in London. I don't know whether he was the man that sent the letter addressed, "Mark Twain, 'God knows where'"—but there was such a letter sent him, and he got it, too! Well, this nephew wrote Mr. Clemens and said he had plenty of money himself, and he'd love to help him any way he could, and not to worry and that he could have recourse to his bank book, because he didn't want him living alone in a garret in London; then he asked if he could see him. So Mr. Clemens thought this was a great joke and wrote and told him to come to 23 Tedworth Square. He come, of course, and when he seen Mr. Clemens and the lovely house he was living in, and all his beautiful family surrounding him, why, he almost fainted, and no wonder! And we had creamed potatoes that night, too, I remember. So you see we always had creamed potatoes on great occasions.

I did a good deal of the cooking that winter. Whenever our cook was sick the girls would say:

"Oh, that's fine! Now we'll have the things that Katy can make so good! We'll have an om'let and apple sauce and Johnny cake and—oh! baked potatoes! For Katy always washes the potatoes so clean that we can eat the skins; and in her apple sauce you never find any of the core!"

I used to make very fine Johnny cake, too. I used to make that in Hartford, and even Mr. Clemens would eat lunch the day I made Johnny cake. He loved it so. We could never get enough for him. "Hoe cake," he called it—like they did down South. We could never get enough for the family. George used to rush out to the kitchen the days I'd make it and say: "Katy, begin another Johnny cake quick! They're going fast in the dining-room, and I want some myself." Then I'd have to make a drippin' pan full just for George!

It was when we was in London there was a newspaper report going round one time that Mark Twain was dying. The reporters all come chasin' up to the house at Tedworth Square to find out about it. There was one young fellow come and he was kind of a green reporter, I guess, for instead of asking about Mr. Clemens, he just showed his orders from the newspaper, which said if Mark Twain was very sick to give a few words, but if he was *dead*—well! to send—oh, two or three thousand words—all they could get—or something like that.

Well, this reporter went in to see Mr. Clemens, and when he seen that order from the newspaper, he just looked at that cub reporter and says,

"Well, young man, you can just say to your newspaper that the report of my death is greatly exaggerated." And that shows you, don't it, the way newspapers do things!

When I first went to Europe I didn't know how to act with the servants, because they called them "upper" and "under" servants. The maid and the butler, they seemed to be the highest in the house. They was not supposed to associate with the kitchen maids—scullery maids. But the cook, she was pretty high, too. She ruled a good deal and the under servants had to take orders from her. Then the housekeeper, she was way up at the very top. All the English servants have their coffee, after dinner, in what is called the housekeeper's room. I used to go, too, myself, sometimes, but I never enjoyed it. But I always got along with all the maids, though. I never could be on my dignity; I would speak even to the scullery maid. Yes, I'd be as friendly with her as I would with the butler. Upper housemaid, under housemaid; upper chambermaid, under chambermaid; upper and under everything! It made me laugh, for I didn't take my position very lofty, you know. I acted more like a nursegirl, went out with the children (they weren't really children then, but I always thought of them that way). I spent most of my time with them.

They have what they call the "Season" in London. That's the high time for society. It begins in June. They have special names for everything over there—for all their holidays, too, like Bank Holiday and Boxing Day. I don't know when that was—Boxing Day; I think 'twas the day after Christmas. I used to wonder what "Boxing Day" was; I never did find out—whether that was the day they boxed their presents and took them away, or whether they boxed each other!

I like the English people. I haven't any prejudices against them like some of the Irish. Everybody treated me very nice—always very polite and nice. But I never cared much for them Bobbies (that's the policemen). They was very handsome, most of them, but all the time flirting. There was one very grand Bobby used to come round every evening to see Mary, the housemaid. She was in love with him, I guess. He come every evening—come by the back door and walked right in. We always had beer on tap. He came for that, I think, as much as Mary. You have to have beer for all the servants. So much a month and their "findings." I used to wonder what their "findings" were. I asked one of the maids what "findings" were and she said, "Why, that's what we have to drink—either beer or whisky. Don't you have that in America?" Oh, yes! We had to keep beer on tap all the time and one cook had to have a quart of whisky every week! I used to see Mary put the beer on the back porch for the Bobby. He'd drink it right down at one gulp, and then set with her for a while as a reward. One night I said, "I guess I'll come out and set with you myself for a change." Then he wanted me to tell him something about New York. So I says: "Were you ever in New York? Do you know what Americans are?"

"Oh, yes," he says, "I know what Americans are. They're not really civilized, you know. They're half Indians, most of them! But *you* don't seem like an Indian," he says, looking at me kind of sly.

"Well, I am," I says, "I'm half Irish and half Indian! That's a dangerous breed," I says. Then he laughed and sort of put his arm round me, but I says: "Look here! Keep your hands off or the wild Indian in me will take that billy you've got there, and use it!" Well, that finished his flirting, for he kind of believed me! They was pretty bold, them policemen, and very ignorant—especially about Americans. In those days almost everybody over there thought the Americans was half Indians.

They thought all the Americans was illiterate and half Indian—which shows they don't know much about our country, nor care either. I suppose, though, they know more about us now since the old war.

Of course, Royalty makes for high society. But then, there's all kinds of Royalty, and we've got some of our own kind, over here. Mr. Clemens was never much in awe of Royalty, as he called them. He used to think all men was equal if their hearts was right, and he said so in one of his books.

I must tell you, now, about the time he wrote a letter to Queen Victoria. They was trying to tax him on his books published there. There was some report in the newspapers that he'd taken a house and was going to live in England, so Mr. Clemens thought he'd have some fun, and he up and wrote a letter to the Queen—addressed it to her anyway, but of course he never sent it to her herself; just had it published in some magazine, telling her how he didn't want to pay a tax; that he didn't think it was fair; and that he wasn't going to take no place in England, and that he was a poor author with a large family to support, and that the lecturing business was pretty bad, too. And he was sure, he said, that when the Queen heard about his real circumstances, she'd let him off. And—oh! I mustn't forget to tell you—he was very sorry that he didn't know her, but that he had met her son, anyway—(that was the Prince of Wales); that he seen him from the top of a bus where he was a-riding, while the Prince was marching down the street at the head of his army! Of course everybody read that letter and it made a great to-do. Everybody thought 'twas a wonderful joke. They say the Queen seen it herself, too, after a while, and that the Prince of Wales heard about it and thought it was very funny, and told Mr. Clemens so when he met him afterwards. And the Queen laughed hearty, they said, and fixed things up so Mr. Clemens didn't have to pay the tax. I believe she wrote and asked ("commanded," they call it) him to come and call on her. But the Royalty was always doing that—he was used to it—and I must say, he liked it!

I saw Queen Victoria several times when I was in London. I was there for her Diamond Jubilee. That was a great sight. Of course the Queen had all her soldiers from all her countries there—soldiers from all over the world. Well, the procession was wonderful! They had all their glitterin' royal carriages out that day, and there was four generations of them setting in one carriage. Queen Victoria, the Empress of Germany, Princess Alexandria, and the Duke of York's child was with them; and the old Queen looked very quiet and very subdued. Her outriders was her three sons, and then there was the Royal Guards. They was wonderful-looking men—just the very grandest. They wore beautiful uniforms and great big muffs on their heads—fur muffs like drum majors. The carriage the Queens rode in was wonderful, too. All lined with satin and gold-trimmed, and the trappings of the horses was gold, too. I think there was two white horses and two black horses hitched to that carriage. It was all turned back (the carriage) and you could see the whole thing, the whole show, very plain.

The Queens was all very wonderfully fixed up and dressed, but Queen Victoria looked pretty old and feeble. She didn't do much saluting. She kind of held her umbrella over her face. She didn't do anything with her fan, either. The others did the saluting. Yes, Queen Victoria set there like a little mummy in the back of her carriage. The Empress of Germany, her daughter, rode in the carriage with her. She did all the bowing and scraping and making all kinds of salutes with her fan. She looked as if she was having a good time and enjoying herself. She did flash round that day, I tell you, and oh, how she did bow! Broke her neck, almost, bowing to all them people. She was a fine-looking woman, I remember. She looked like a Queen ought to look. She was an Empress, though—but of course you can't tell a Queen from an Empress. One is as good as the other. But she was Empress enough for that old Kaiser, anyway. He rode on horseback with the Prince of Wales.

Princess Alexandria was there, too, of course. She looked beautiful. The King always said he was afraid to touch her for fear she'd break! She was always so enameled and fixed up, you know. But Queen Victoria was pretty old then, and 'twas a pretty hard trial on her, I guess, to have to even ride out in the carriage—even if it was her Jubilee. Her people loved her very much—they really adored her, and she was a good Queen.

That was a wonderful Jubilee show they gave her and we, Clara and Jean and I, seen every bit of the procession. We set right there in Trafalgar Square, right where I could look up at the statue of Nelson with his one arm. The procession marched right by there and some of it dismounted right in front of us and we saw all the maneuvers. We paid ten dollars apiece for our seats—and that was a lot of money. But it was worth it.

There was all kinds of celebrations going on that week. Every night the streets was illuminated and there was a great benefit at one of the theaters and that great French actress, Sarah Bernhardt, she played a part in it. Oh, she hit me as being wonderful, really! She was all dressed in white and looked lovely, and I thought she had the most wonderful figger and was a regular actress—not a made one—a regular *borned* actress. She seemed like the real thing to me, though I couldn't understand a word she said, as it was all in French.

We saw a great many noted people while we stayed in London. Everybody wanted to know Mr. Clemens. I can't remember the names of all of them, but I do remember some of the most famous ones.

Whistler lived in a little house right near us, right back of us. It was a long rambling old house in Cheyne Walk. That's a funny name, ain't it, for a street? Well, Whistler was an American. He was a famous painter and very smart. He said very bright, sharp things, and people was always repeating funny stories and things he said. I used to hear about him sometimes from the family.

And then Oscar Wilde, he lived right there behind us. He was the one they put in jail. He was a very bad man, Oscar Wilde was, so bad you couldn't talk about what he done. Everybody used to come down to get a good look at his house. He wrote lots of books and plays, and then when he was in jail he wrote a very wonderful poem, they said; but that wasn't strong enough to whitewash him though. He always used to wear a sunflower in his buttonhole and dressed in velvet clothes and had long hair. Everybody read his books and went to see his plays, and he was very much talked about. He lectured over here in America once, and the women was crazy about him. He lectured about what he called *"Beauty"*—whatever that meant! And I guess, from what I heard, that Beauty come first with him, before anything else. He was what you call eccentric in his dressing, and always had a lily or sunflower in his buttonhole, and a flower stuck in a tumbler of water on the table when he was on the lecture platform.

There was one great man that Mr. Clemens seen quite a lot of, and that was Kipling. I must tell you about the first time they met. That was in America, way back in the old Hartford days.

It seems that Mr. Kipling came to America from India,

and was looking for Mr. Clemens. He wanted to see him so much 'cause he had heard a great deal about him. Of course nobody knew who Kipling was or what he had written—or his name, hardly. He warn't famous then. Mr. Clemens hadn't even heard of him.

Well, Kipling went up to Hartford to find Mr. Clemens, but the Clemens family never stayed there summers, you know, so when he got to Hartford, Mr. Clemens was in Elmira, and Kipling, he hurried up to Elmira; and when he got to Elmira, they told him that Mr. Clemens was up at Quarry Farm. Well! Poor Kipling, he hired a horse and wagon and got somebody to drive him up to Quarry Farm. But that day Mr. Clemens happened to be down in Elmira, at Mrs. Langdon's! Well, that was pretty discouraging after all his chasin' around, 'cause Quarry Farm was quite a ways out from Elmira, but there was no help for it, so he had to climb back into his one-horse shay, and cantered right back to Elmira and to the Langdon house, and there, sure enough, he found Mr. Clemens. It was lunch time when he got there. He sent his card in. Mr. Clemens didn't know him—but Susy said: "That's a funny name, papa, Rudyard Kipling. I think you must see him." So he went into the drawing-room and there was Kipling, and they set down together and talked for a while and smoked their big cigars and swapped stories and had a wonderful time, 'cause they both liked each other very much the minute they seen each other. Mr. Clemens said he was a stranger, but was wonderful; and Mr. Kipling thought that Mr. Clemens was about the grandest man he'd ever seen. So they was well satisfied with each other. The only trouble was that Kipling heard the sound of the dishes in the dining-room and knew it was lunch time and there was something to eat, and I suppose it made him hungry as a bear to hear them. But the lunch kept going right on in the dining-room and Mr. Clemens never made any sign. You see Mr. Clemens never eat any lunch himself. Mr. Kipling, of course, didn't know that and so Mr. Clemens, he never thought about asking him to stay. Of course he enjoyed the talk very much but he was pretty hungry, and finally got up to go and started back down to the station.

Well, the next day he had an interview in some of the newspapers (I heard) which was republished and republished. He said he had just come back from India and had heard about Mark Twain so much that he wanted to see him, and he done all this runnin' around and chased all the way up to Elmira to see him—but never got a single thing to eat. But anyway, he'd had the pleasure of seeing Mr. Clemens although they didn't ask him to stay to lunch.

Of course Mr. Clemens answered the letter in the newspaper and said he was very sorry, but to tell the truth, he didn't know who Kipling was; he didn't know where he'd come from nor how hungry he was. If he'd known, Mr. Clemens said, that he'd come from *India* without having anything to eat, why, he said, he'd of invited him to lunch for a week! "But," he says, "Mr. Kipling, the next time we meet, wherever it be, on land or sea, we'll have the very best the place can afford. We'll have the best meal together that money can buy—and I'll buy it, too!"

Well, that was really a funny ending to the visit, and the next time they met—I think it was in London—they did have a wonderful dinner, I suppose, and everything that anybody could want, to make up for that other meeting. They certainly was great friends and admired each other so much. Mr. Clemens wrote all about it in his Diary, telling just what he thought about Kipling, and I guess Kipling did the same. 'Twarn't so very long after that—about a year—that Kipling become very famous and everybody was reading his books all over the world. He was a wonderful writer and Mr. Clemens used to love to read him; he used to read aloud from Kipling and right up to the end, just before he died, he had a book of Kipling's that he read from. So you see them books of Kipling's meant a great deal to him.

I mustn't forget to tell you that Susy always kept that little visiting card of Kipling's, as a kind of momento of his visit. She thought then that he must be somebody that would turn out wonderful, so she kept that card 'cause he had written something on it—his address in India—and she liked that. It was kind of what you might call a souvenir.

We stayed in London two years that time and then went on to Vienna. They spent the winter there. Clara wanted to study piano with Leschetizky. That's where she met Mr. Gabrilowitsch. She studied quite a while with Leschetizky and then gave up the piano. I didn't know for some time that Miss Clara turned from piano to voice. It seems after she'd been studying the piano for quite a while her hands were so small she didn't have any stretch—couldn't reach an octave. I told you about that, when she was a little mite of a thing, and used to give us piano lessons—George and me. Leschetizky, they said he felt terrible bad to lose her for a pupil, because he thought she was very talented musically.

Mr. Clemens planned to do a lot of writing there that winter, and they stayed at the Hotel Metropole, one of the most beautiful hotels in Vienna. They had a wonderful suite of rooms there, and Mr. Clemens and the whole family, in fact, was just the idols of Vienna. They had a grand time and was invited everywhere by Royalty and everybody else. They did a great deal of entertaining themselves, too. Everybody went mad over Mark Twain. I never knew anything like it. They was just falling over each other to know him. He gave a lecture one night and the house was just jammed. He spoke in English, of course, and the whole audience was in spasms of laughter the minute he began. All the celebrated singers and people were at that lecture and all the people from the Court, too.

They was very hospitable, the people of Vienna, and gave lots of fine parties, and Mrs. Clemens gave lots of grand parties, too.

They was a sofa right by the fireplace in the drawing-room and it was the rule that the highest-ranked person in the room was to sit on this sofa. Well, one night Löie Fuller, the dancer, she come in and set right down on the top seat of that sofa when the Princess was there! Oh, my! How Mrs. Clemens had to work to manage to get her off that seat and not let her know, and hurt her feelings.

When they went to them Royal entertainments, of course Mr. Clemens had to back out of the room and he hated that! He didn't know how to back out. It used to make him swear—to have to back out for the Royalty. He'd always try to get out of it, somehow.

Miss Clara had lots of officers for beaux that winter. They used to call every day for tea and was very musical. I don't remember who they was, but some of them was Royalty, though not very deep in the Royal blood.

The Newcomb girls was there that winter—Ethel and her sister Mary. Ethel Newcomb was a pianist. She was studying with Leschetizky, too. She was a great friend of Miss Clara's. They used to study the piano together and they had a picture taken once that Leschetizky admired very much and called "Day and Night," 'cause Ethel was very fair and Clara was very dark.

There was lots of music that winter, and all these elegant military men used to come in for music and tea every afternoon. It was a wonderful sight to see them coming up the hall. You'd think it was a whole regiment, the way they walked and clicked their swords against their heels—and oh, the wonderful uniforms they wore! They'd come in the room with such style. They was very fond of music and Miss Clara would always play for them. Oh, my! They'd make such a low bow, such a wonderful bow, and click their heels together when they come into the room. It was so different from anything we ever seen in this country. If I knew they was coming, I'd be on the watch because they was so interesting to look at. Just to see them standing there at the door, march in and take off their coats and hats and hand them to the butler—all in military style! It used to hit me as though I'd like to live there forever and see that style all the time. I liked that much of war, anyway—the dressing part; but I didn't want Miss Clara to marry one of those officers.

Yes, all the celebrated people in the world used to come together to see Mark Twain. The King and the Kaiser and that old Austrian Emperor, and lots of princes and poets and all kinds of writers and of course lots and lots of musicians—most everybody you ever heard of, wanted to know Mark Twain. There was Leschetizky and Mark Hambourg and Paderewski; then there was that little Bohemian composer—Dvork—and lots of famous painters, too. And then that Queen—the

Queen of Roumania—Carmen Sylva was her real name. She was a kind of poetess, too, and used to send some of her writings to Mr. Clemens and was crazy about him.

Princess Metternich come, too, and there was a story about her that I'll tell you. And then there was some grand Archduchess, too. She was a wonderful person—a regular Princess, and she asked Mr. and Mrs. Clemens out there to tea one time—and they went and enjoyed themselves very much, they said.

The Clemens always had tea parties every single Sunday night, and as I told you, Leschetizky and lots of famous men came to them. Leschetizky was a funny man. I remember the way he laughed. He used to grin and show his teeth, like a gorilla. I never really liked him, but most people liked him because he was such a celebrated man, I guess. He was the greatest piano teacher in the world, you know. Almost all the women fell for him. He made wives of most of his pupils.

As I told you, he used to give student concerts—weekly entertainments, and all his best pupils would play. I went to one of them once. My, but Leschetizky used to be nervous! He would be rushing all round the room, fit to kill himself, if they didn't play right. He walked around all the time they was playing, and if they made one single little mistake, he almost had a fit! There was very few he let play until they'd gone a long ways in his methods. He was a very severe teacher. He almost killed Mark Hambourg for playing bad at a concert. One thing he couldn't stand was to have the students play wrong notes. He used to give them "down the banks" for that! Well, this night at class meeting, Mark Hambourg was playing his piece and he made a mistake and it upset Leschetizky something terrible, so he got up and took Mark Hambourg by the collar and walked him down, right off the stage, and told him to set down and not play any more, and scolded him because he made such a mistake. He talked so loud and he scolded him so, and his eyes looked so wild, he looked as though he'd kill you, with his eyes! He was mad through and through. He was a very great teacher, though—the greatest in the world, as you can see from his pupils. Paderewski was his greatest pupil, and Mr. Gabrilowitsch studied with him, too, and lots of others. But his pupils always stood in great awe of him. I heard one time (I don't remember the little American girl's name) one day when she was waiting for her lesson, she was so frightened she went right into Leschetizky's garden and began scrubbing the face of Beethoven's statue. She was so nervous waiting for her turn to play she didn't know what she was doing hardly.

We had great times that season in Vienna. We settled down there to live very happy and comfortable. That was the time Mr. Clemens told me about closing the door. He had a little study right off the dining-room and when I left the door open one time and he told me to shut it, I asked him was he cold; and he said:

"Oh, no, Katy, no, I'm not cold. It isn't that the open door lets the cold *in*, but it lets the coziness *out!*"

It was after that great lecture tour around the world that Mr. Clemens wrote that book about his travels. It was called *Following the Equator;* and it was soon after that that Mr. Clemens paid off all his debts. That's what he went around the world for—to get money and pay everybody dollar for dollar. He'd allowed himself five years to do it in, but it seems he done it in about three years. I guess there's few men living in this world that would have undertaken to do what he did. 'Twas pretty hard on him, but Mr. Clemens warn't the man to go on living and enjoying himself when he owed anybody anything. He was so happy when all them debts was paid that he said he felt just like a boy again—free and out of school.

It was in Vienna that winter that we was there that the Kaiser's sister came there with her train of servants and everything grand. Her daughter was with her and she was engaged, and her sweetheart was in the party, and they came to the hotel in Vienna where we was to spend some time. When Mr. Clemens heard that, he said he knew the Princess would send for him soon to have a talk. The girls laughed and said: "Oh, papa, you think that all the Royalty are crazy about you! We don't think the Princess will ever send for you at all! Why, she don't even know you're here!" Clara said.

"Oh, yes, yes indeed, she knows I'm here," he said. "They always look to see who's registered! The Royalty wouldn't stay in a hotel unless there was some *celebrity* there! So they know I'm here," he says.

There was a window from the balcony of our room where you could look down into all the different little dining-rooms and see who was there. We spotted the Royal Family at once—and I had the honor of eating with the Royal dogs, two of them. They brought those dogs into the room where I had my dinner. Mr. Clemens said that was quite an honor—to be able to eat with Royalty's dogs. The men that had the care of them dogs eat in this dining-room where all the maids of the Royal Family ate, and the dogs were fed just like Christians. That night I come up and said that anyway I'd had the Royalty first! I told Mr. Clemens that I'd beat him, because I'd had the Royal dogs with me for supper that night. They was nice little Pekinese dogs. They had nice manners, too. The men that took care of them was very lively and jolly and had a demitasse every night with a big bottle of brandy. They said to me, one night:

"Why, don't you drink brandy with your coffee?"

Of course I never did. We used to look down at them, the girls and myself, from our window, and sometimes you could hardly see them for the clouds of smoke.

They smoked cigarettes—all the maids, too. I thought it was terrible in those days, but they did smoke nice. I was like John Magee, watching the way they held their cigarettes. John Magee married Florence Seely. He fell in love with her because he seen her smoke a cigarette. He thought it was the most fascinating thing he ever seen—the *way* she smoked it. So he married her. She's in high society now in New York.

Well, the Princess seemed to have a wonderful time. She was a beautiful woman and she was always beautifully dressed and so was her daughter.

The time went on and the girls kept saying to their father, "The Princess hasn't sent for you yet, papa—not yet!"

"Well, she will," he says, "she will!" Then one night I seen 'em getting the dogs all ready to depart the next day. The dogs was the first to get ready! So I went right upstairs and told them the Princess was leaving the next day.

"Now, papa," Clara said, "your hopes are all gone. The Royal Family is going to leave to-morrow and the Princess hasn't sent for you! So you needn't expect it any more!"

This was about noon, and at two o'clock a man in great military style, gold breeches, gold headdress and everything, come and knocked very loud at the door and asked for Mr. Clemens, and sent in a note from the Princess that she would be pleased to see Mr. Clemens any time it was convenient for him that day. Well, he wrote right back, saying he would be delighted to see her at half-past two; that he would come to her quarters then, or she could come to him—whichever would be most pleasing to her. Then he decided to go to her. So he dressed himself up, though he didn't have anything gold to put on. He had his shoes cleaned and his clothes brushed and we made him look nice and tidy, and then he went down to see the Princess, and she was just delighted with him. And she asked him then for one of his books—his last book, *Following the Equator*. She'd love to have that, she said, so he said he'd be delighted, and would have a special one made.

He wrote to Harper Brothers in New York and told them to make a book of the very finest they could procure, gold-edged leaves and a wonderful cover, and have this Princess's name stuck right on the cover in gold letters. And it was done. I saw it before he sent it to her, and it was a wonderful book. He wrote a grand autograph in it and sent it to her. He did it up brown, I tell you! Of course, after that, the girls didn't say another word. He had the laugh on them that time! He was generally right about most things, I found out.

While we are talking of Royalty, we mustn't forget to speak about the Kaiser. He was Royalty then—though there ain't much left of him now—much Royalty. He was very anxious to meet Mr. Clemens, too, and he had a dinner for him, and just the right people come to that. Mr. Clemens, it seems, had a cousin, Frau von Versen. She was married to a German officer in high society there. She was way up, and when the Kaiser wanted to have a dinner and special people, he always had her get it up and invite those he wanted to meet, and he wanted to meet Mark Twain terrible bad, so the Kaiser had her get up this wonderful dinner and invite some of the men he thought would be congenial to Mr. Clemens. They had a grand time and Mr. Clemens told us all about it afterwards. He said the Kaiser talked a great deal—he spoke English very good, too. Of course, the Kaiser, he done most of the talking, because in Royal circles the guests can't speak unless they're spoken to—that is, they can't start a subject, I guess. The Kaiser would have to sort of start it off, and then they answered when they was spoken to.

Mr. Clemens didn't like that very well, because he was used to running the whole show wherever he went—used to being the host, as you might say. But I suppose he had to put up with it this time, although there was a story about his bursting out and doing quite considerable talking on his own hook at that dinner, and they said the Kaiser didn't like it very well—but I don't know whether that's true or not. Anyway, 'twarn't very long after that the Empress invited him to breakfast, and the old Empress (the one they called the Dowager) she asked him to something, too; so I guess he must have made a good impression—just as he always did.

Well, the Kaiser! He looked to be about the biggest thing in the world in them days. He was a handsome-looking man, and his uniform was wonderful. I used to see him every morning riding out, comin' up the Plaza. His Palace was down in Potsdam, and he used to ride every morning on a wonderful-looking horse, with a long sweeping tail and trappings of gold and silver. Oh! He was a fine-looking fellow. I seen him a good many times. I remember his mustaches very well. I used to think they looked like a pigeon's wing, stuck on his face like a sharp lance, and they went up around his nose and was waxed so stiff they looked as though they was made out of cardboard.

I seen the Emperor of Austria, too, very often. But he was an old, crusty-looking thing. I didn't care so much for him, you know. He was a pretty old man, and pretty hard, and tried to get all he could out of life, I guess. 'Twas awful sad that time when the Empress Elizabeth was assassinated in that hotel in Geneva. I was there just two days before, and I crossed right over the very place where she was shot. The old Emperor was a gay bird, and had so many pleasures and people chasing after him, he didn't care much for her, I suppose.

They said the Empress wasn't very happy with him—and they lived their lives quite separate. Of course, every one knows about that actress Katrina Schratt, that the Emperor was so devoted to. She was a very nice woman, I believe,—kind of simple and sort of like a housekeeper, they said, when she wasn't on the stage; and the story is that the Empress Elizabeth selected her herself, as a sort of companion and to cheer the Emperor up, one time, when she was goin' off on one of her gay visits. At any rate, the Empress didn't bother much about it and she used to "receive" Katrina Schratt and sometimes go with the Emperor, they said, to lunch at Katrina Schratt's house. She had a beautiful house there in Vienna, full of all kinds of wonderful things, and then she had a villa, too, at Ischl—that's the summer home of the Emperor; and whenever he was there, she was at Ischl, too. She'd kind of go along to be near him. 'Twas quite a well known affair, romance—whatever they call it, in Royal circles. At least, that's the story and it seems to be history. At any rate, I used to hear a good deal about it at the time we was in Vienna. She come to New York once, a great many years ago, they said, with some German company, and acted in the old Irving Place Theatre, and they said she was a very fine actress, too.

Well, of course, like all the rest of the Royalty, the Emperor of Austria (Francis Joseph was his name), he wanted to meet Mr. Clemens, too, so that was arranged and Mr. Clemens was to have an "audience" with him (that's what they call a visit in Royal circles). Well, Mr. Clemens fixed himself all up and was working hard over a little speech that he could make in German, but when he got to the Palace the Emperor was so kind and nice and cozy, and began talking in English right away, that Mr. Clemens forgot all about his German speech. Mr. Clemens, when he come home, said he thought the Emperor was a very nice kind of a man—pleasant and natural. Mr. Clemens, of course, cracked some jokes with him, I suppose—just the same as he did with all the Royalty—which they liked.

Yes, that was a terrible time when the Empress was assassinated. She was a fine-looking woman with an elegant figure. She had beautiful hair—bright brown, it was. She wore it in a great big braid on the top of her head, just like a crown. She was a great walker, they said—used to walk for hours and hours in the forests. She sort of lived in retirement after her only son, Rudolph, was murdered in his hunting lodge. They never knew just who did it—whether it was that woman he was with and so in love with him, or whether he just killed himself, 'Twas a terrible tragedy and a kind of a mystery and 'twarn't never cleared up—and the whole world was talking about it.

I remember the funeral of the Empress. 'Twas when we was in Vienna, and oh, it was a wonderful sight, but very sad. The whole city was draped in black. We saw the funeral procession and ceremony right from the windows in the hotel. All the soldiers of the Austrian Empire was there on horseback, and all kinds of flags—black flags, too, hung down from all the buildings and there was a great cavalcade, they called it, that marched

SUSY CLEMENS AS A YOUNG LADY

W. C. Rowley, Elmira, N. Y.

JEAN CLEMENS AS A YOUNG GIRL

© Marceau

CLARA CLEMENS AS A YOUNG WOMAN

Georg Brokesch, Leipzig

OSSIP GABRILOWITSCH TAKEN IN HIS STUDENT DAYS IN VIENNA

down the street—and all the pavements was covered with sand so everything was very quiet and solemn. It made a great impression on me. I shall never forget it.

The Royalty ain't very much in the way of happy marriages! I never seen the Kaiserin, but once, at Queen Victoria's Jubilee—she was her daughter, you know—but the Kaiser I seen often—generally dashing around on horseback. He struck me then as a wonderful man—a great man—a real nobleman. He never struck me as being the man he turned out to be. I thought he was too big a man to act as he did at the finish. I really thought, when the war broke out, and when it was nearing the end, and I said to everybody: "Why, he'll kill himself. If he's captured, he'll never be taken alive. He's too brave a man for that!" I didn't never think he would give up the throne alive and let himself be imprisoned. Yes, he struck me in those days as a handsome, courageous, wonderful nobleman—the type of a King you would read about. Every bit of that feeling is lost in me now, though. He's shown himself for what he really was. He's a great coward.

There's a funny kind of a little story told about the time Roosevelt went over to see him. The Kaiser and Roosevelt was very friendly and the Emperor wanted to show off everything he had, and so he showed Roosevelt his army and everything, and his military things and all, and when he seen that, Roosevelt says, "Why, man, you could whip the world!"—which shows how much impressed Roosevelt was. And then they said that when the Crown Prince was talking one morning with his father, the Kaiser, he said:

"Why, father, what made you think of having the war?" And the Kaiser said, "Well, Roosevelt kind of gave me the idea." But of course, that's all a story, and like a good many stories, there ain't a word of truth in it, I suppose. It's just gossip. It went the rounds, though, that story, and I heard it lots of times. I suppose he and Roosevelt must have had a wonderful time there with all their military doings, and the Kaiser probably showed off everything he had in the best kind of style to impress Roosevelt with his power and glory, and I guess that great army he'd got together was worth looking at, too! They probably had a high old time of it together, for Roosevelt was always very interested in military things —and they do say that if Roosevelt had been President when the war started, he'd of put the "kibosh" on it in the beginning; and I guess he would have, maybe. Well, the Kaiser's end is pretty bad. I guess there ain't anything worse in this life than imprisonment, and that's what it amounts to, when you have to stay in one place all the time. As I said before, he really didn't have enough courage to kill himself, and this is the end of it all, and the world knows the whole thing now.

I think I told you that I'd never tasted beer until I went to Germany. I used to go to the beer gardens with

Jean and sit out there under the trees and listen to the music, and Jean used to scold me every time, 'cause when our glasses was filled, I just used to pour it out under the table. I didn't like the smell of it, even; but of course, everybody there in Germany drinks beer. The children are weaned on it, I guess.

The German people are awful clumsy kind o' people and they dress awful—but they were kind of nice, and the waiters was very kind and gentlemanly at our hotel. Now, the French are so much more refined. They are always very neat and nice, especially the French women. They have very good figures and dress beautiful and always wore very fine petticoats and dainty stockings. The Italians, though, always struck me as being pretty dirty, but it didn't seem to matter so much with them, because they was what you call "picturesque."

The customs in Europe was so different from ours; although Mr. and Mrs. Clemens loved to live in Europe they couldn't help noticing these things. I remember one time Mr. Clemens said he wondered if he wouldn't even have to tip the *proprietor* of the hotel because you had to tip everybody in the place, everybody, whether they'd done anything for you or not. From the man that blacked the boots, to the man that stood at the door when we would leave the hotel—they was all standin' in a long row just waiting, with their palms stretched out. Mr. Clemens used to have to go down the line, and he always gave very big tips, too. He was very generous. But I only used to give a twopence when we was in England or a few pennies—and I always kind of begrudged that!

When we kept house in Italy and had that villa with the fifty rooms, all those Italian servants used to sleep way upstairs, and I remember one night having to go up for something and when I got there I thought I'd stifle! Not a darn window open, where all those people slept! Their doors was closed, too. I don't know how they could stand it—they was afraid of the night air, you know, afraid it would give them consumption. They are funny about their children, too. They take them out in the morning, take all their clothes off—right on the curbing—and rub them down a little mite—(that's all the washing they'd give 'em), then put their clothes on again! If they have a new dress for their children they make it right over the old one and sew it on to that.

The servants we had in the Villa used to make a terrible noise hammering bones in the kitchen to make gravies and soups. It was to get the inside out of the bone—the marrow, they called it. They put that in the soup, it was considered quite a delicacy but I didn't think much of it myself—which proves that people in different countries have different ideas about things. I found that out after I left Elmira and began traveling in Europe and seeing the world.

I didn't have much trouble with the German language

while we was in Vienna. I used to speak a little before I went to Germany. Mr. Clemens used to write a whole page every day for me in German—questions and the answers to them—and that's how I picked up a great deal more. I really studied it that way. I could speak it very good then. I used to tell him about lots of things he wanted to know, and they used to wonder how I got on so well. But I understood quite a little before I went to Europe, because in Hartford, the children never spoke English in the nursery—they always spoke German, 'cause Mrs. Clemens wanted them to be able to talk it good before they got over there; and once little Jean undertook to give me lessons in German. I really learned a good deal from her, but it certainly is a jaw-breaking language! I'm glad I don't have to speak it all the time.

But Germany is a very pretty country. We went to lots of places there and we went to Heidelberg, too. That's a pretty little town on the Rhine—the river Rhine. It was Mrs. Clemens that said I must go there and see it, and it come about in this way.

I remember one time (there was a beautiful picture of Heidelberg in her room) and I was always looking at it and one day I says to her:

"Oh, that's a wonderful-looking place. Was you ever there, Mrs. Clemens? I'd like to see it myself."

"Oh, yes, Katy," she says, "I've been there, right there, on top of that beautiful hill!" And then she looked at me kind of funny, and says: "And Katy, I hope before I die, that I shall be able to take you right up there on that mountain so you'll see it too, just as I have."

Well, that first year we went to Europe, the morning we were starting for Geneva, she said to Mr. Clemens: "Youth, dear, I want to take Katy to Heidelberg along with the children on this trip. You know, she's always talking about that picture of Heidelberg in my room being so wonderful, and I promised her some day to let her see the real thing. So I want to take her up there to that lovely Castle and to see the great barrel there that's so big wagons can turn around on it, and to see them pretty gardens and the river."

And Mr. Clemens says, "Oh, yes, we must do that, Livy." So we went and they took me up to the Castle and then we stopped at that wonderful Schloss Hotel, and the first thing Mr. Clemens did he took me out to the front of the hotel ('twas built way up on a hill, you know). "Because," he says, "Katy, I want to show you a string of diamonds—the most beautiful string of diamonds in the whole world," he says. And so he took me out there to the open, and looking down there was rows and rows of these pretty little gas lights—all down that hill—two rows of them—glittering and sparkling and flashing in the night. And, oh! it did look just like a string of diamonds. It was a great sight, and Mr. Clemens he loved that. It struck him as looking so real—them rows of twinkling little lights—just like diamonds, as he said. And they was really more beautiful than anything I'd ever seen before.

It was when we was in Heidelberg that we seen them students with their faces all cut up. My! They was awful-looking things! Why, I didn't want the girls to even look at them, 'cause they was so battered up, I thought they'd be kind of sensitive and not want folks to see them.

It seems that the students go there to Heidelberg to study, and the great sport was fencing; and it was considered a great mark of honor to be all scratched up.

Well, one young fellow come out in the garden one morning, walking around where we was, and I said to Miss Clara: "Oh, don't look at him, don't look at him! He's the awfullest sight!" And she just laughed and laughed and says:

"Why, Katy, he's delighted to have you look at him, because he's proud to have his face all slashed open! He's studying there in that college," says Clara, "and he's glad to be one of them with his face all cut up, 'cause that's a mark of honor!"

It seems when they're all cut open (their faces) them students just go and pour beer into the wounds, to make them uglier—to make them look worse yet! Why, some of their faces was all out of shape! Sometimes the whole face would be all pulled down to one side. I thought that looked fierce—really terrible! I couldn't bear to look at 'em; but the girls seemed to think it was wonderful. Well, that shows you again, don't it, that all the world don't think alike.

I think I'll tell you now about the time Mr. Clemens went to see a famous palmist in London. Well, Mr. Clemens had this man read his palm, and then he told Mr. Clemens that he didn't want to tell him all he'd seen. He said: "You're a very distinguished man; but there's something in the next year I don't want to tell you. You're going to be a *widower*, and going to have a lot of trouble—you're going to lose your wife!"

I don't know what all he told him, but anyway, Mr. Clemens came home terribly upset, and he met the girls on the doorstep and he says: "You musn't tell your mother. I'll never let her know what that palmist said." So when Mrs. Clemens asked what the man told him, oh, he just made up some wonderful things—the wonderful life they was goin' to have and how everything was going on fine, and then he says, "But I'd like *you* to go to him, Livy."

So Mrs. Clemens went, and then this man read Mrs. Clemens' palm and told her she was going to be a *widow* —that her husband was going to die very soon, and a lot o' stuff like that. Oh, dear! She come home broken-hearted, and when Mr. Clemens asked what the palmist said to her, well, she just up and told him. When Mr. Clemens heard that, he says:

"Well, now damn that man! I'm going up and knock his head off! He don't know a damn thing! He told me that *you* were going to die, and I was going to be a widower! Now he tells you that *I'm* going to die and you're going to be a widow! Why," Mr. Clemens says, "he's a regular pirate!"

Well, of course he didn't go and knock his head off; he just scolded and stormed around and told Mrs. Clemens not to believe a word of it. But Miss Clara went to him, anyway, in spite of all this. And I went too, but I didn't have any faith in him. Miss Clara sent me and paid the five dollars—a guinea. 'Twas worth five dollars just to hear him talk, and it was worth a couple o' dollars at least to see his rooms. He had lovely rooms, with all those things from the East. It seems he was in the East for years, studyin'—at least that's what they said. His rooms, at any rate, was lovely, and he had 'em all dadoed with them Eastern things. He was a handsome-looking man, a big fine fellow. I wanted to tell him I didn't believe in him, but I was kind of afraid, afraid he might get his Indian blood up and kill me. I don't suppose, though, he was really Indian—but that's what he pretended. He come from India, they said, and he'd set up this place in London and he charged a guinea—that's $5.25—for people to have their palms read—that was his fare. I suppose if he'd charged any less people wouldn't go to him; they would think he was no good! Really, I thought it was a grand thing just to be able to see him. I thought if he read my palm I'd know everything about myself to the end of time. But

I don't remember anything very good or great that he said. I tried to fool him and I guess I did, 'cause I put a new wedding ring on and pretended I had a husband; but my fortune didn't amount to much, so far as he was concerned. Of course all this happened in London, while we was livin' there.

There's something else happened that I must tell you about. That was the time I went to see all them wonderful jewels in the Tower of London, in the Jewel Room where all the Crown Jewels were, and oh, my! weren't they wonderful! All the jewels that kings and queens wear. That was quite a jump from anything you'd see in the place I come from—Elmira! We had a guide the day we went there, and he showed us all around—showed us everything; told us just where all King Henry's wives had their heads cut off. I was mighty glad then that I wasn't born a queen. You're in more danger of your head with a crown than a bonnet—on!

Speaking of Queens, I told you that story about Mr. Clemens writing to Queen Victoria and telling her he couldn't pay the tax, and how he seen her son, the Prince of Wales, one time from the top of a bus while the Prince was marching down Piccadilly at the head of his army. Well, Mr. Clemens *did* really meet the Prince of Wales—spoke to him and they got quite friendly—slapped each other on the back, they say, and had long talks together.

The first time it was in one of them bath places in Germany—Hamburg, where the Prince was taking the baths, I guess, and he wanted to meet Mr. Clemens and he said so, and so it was fixed up. They had a nice talk together, I heard, and when they parted they both swapped compliments, and Mr. Clemens says what a pleasure it was to meet his grand Royal Highness, and then the Prince, he says:

"Oh, but I met you before, Mr. Clemens. Don't you remember?" Mr. Clemens says no, and he wondered where. Then the Prince of Wales says:

"Why, when you was a-ridin' on top of that bus, and I was marching down Piccadilly with my army!"

Of course, they both roared at that, 'cause that's what Mr. Clemens had said in his letter to old Queen Victoria. It showed 'twas quite a compliment to Mr. Clemens, 'cause the Prince of Wales had remembered all about it. They got to be real good friends, I believe, and then he got invited to one of their garden parties—but that was in London, after Queen Victoria died. I don't remember exactly when. But he went, anyway, and then the Prince of Wales was King Edward, and Princess Alexandria was the Queen.

And there is a story about how some one introduced him to Queen Alexandria, and it was kind of a chilly day and Mr. Clemens had a cold and was very hoarse, and when the Queen noticed that, she says:

"Why, Mr. Clemens, you talk as though you had a

cold. You must put your hat right on." (Of course he was standing with his hat *off* when he was talking with the Queen.) But Mr. Clemens says:

"Oh, no, no! I couldn't keep my hat on when talkin to a Queen!"

"Well, then," she says, "if I am the Queen, I *command* you to put your hat right on!" So of course, after that, he put his hat on pretty quick—and was glad of it, I guess.

While he stood there talkin' with her, quite a good many people passed and looked very cross to see him talkin' with the Queen with his hat on, and one man, they say, went up to Mr. Clemens and says:

"Don't you know you're talkin' to the Queen? Remove your hat, sir!" The King heard that and he put his hand on Mr. Clemens' shoulder and says, "What did that man say?" "Well," says Mr. Clemens, "he told me to remove my hat but you know, your Majesty, that I was just commanded by the Queen *not* to remove my hat, so I couldn't take it off, could I?"

"No," the King said, "that's all right. Don't you remove your hat." So Mr. Clemens didn't take his hat off; he kept it right on, and stood there talkin' with all the Royalty just the same.

I don't remember just when it was, but I was in London when the Prince of Wales was born—that is, the present Prince of Wales, and so I've always been kind of interested in him since he's grown up. I just loved him and thought he was a darling, I was in hopes it could have been arranged that he'd marry some nice American girl, maybe. Of course, that's all newspaper talk that they thought he was interested in some one over here, for it couldn't be done, I guess. Royal blood's got to marry Royal blood—whether or no. They couldn't just put up with a plain American.

Of course all these things—that is, the garden party for the King and Queen and all—happened in London; but it was just the same wherever we went. Royalty was always chasing after Mr. Clemens. The name *Mark Twain* was just like magic. People was always crazy to see him wherever he went, and nothin' could ever have been more wonderful than them two winters in Vienna that I told you about. It was just one wonderful thing after another that was happening. Mr. Clemens, he wrote a lot while we was there, too, for magazines and newspapers, I think it was. You see, everything had all smoothed out then. It wasn't such hard times with him any more, and they was very prosperous again; and although they never got over the death of Susy (it was always a shadow in the background somehow), still, everything was very gay and pleasant and they was all happy and enjoyed themselves. And Mr. Clemens, he just reveled in every bit of it—and it was right that he should.

While Mr. Clemens was in Europe that time, he saw a lot of the people that he'd seen years before in

America when they used to come out to Hartford to see him. There was Kipling, for one, and Henry Stanley, too—and I must tell you a little something about him while I think of it, quite a pretty story, too.

He was that famous explorer. He explored out in Africa—the Free States, they called it. Well, at any rate, he was some kind of a famous explorer, and he wrote a book—*In Darkest Africa*, it was called; and he come to this country to give a lecture tour years ago. They come to Hartford to see Mr. Clemens, and Stanley's wife stayed about ten days at our house, to rest herself—and he went off to lecture. Her name was Dorothy Tennant. She was a very interesting and beautiful woman. She could draw quite good, too, and she made a little pen-and-ink drawing of some children—("waifs," she called them) in London. It was a very attractive little picture, and I've got it now.

Well, they tell a story about Stanley's bein' in love with her before he went off to explore the first time, and that when he come back and asked her to marry him, she said, Well, she'd never marry a man that would dye his mustache (or hair), and that, it seems, is what he used to do, a little. Well, then he went off a second time and when he come back after that trip he had white hair and mustache, and then he asked her to marry him again; and she said "Yes." She accepted him. Anyway, I guess she loved him from what I seen of them—whether he dyed his mustache or not. And while we are on the subject—I never could see why anybody would want to let their hair grow gray, that is, if it is unbecoming. Of course, some people's gray hair—like Mr. Clemens'—is perfectly beautiful, for it just suited him; but most people, especially women, don't look so good when they begin to turn gray; and I never could see any disgrace in dyeing your hair if you wanted to. I believe in keeping up a good appearance to the very end.

Stanley—he got to be Sir Henry Stanley after a while. The English people give him a title, as a reward, I guess, for what he did in Africa. The English people are great on that—rewarding people with titles—and I guess it's a pretty good idea. It keeps them contented and it shows, too, that they're appreciated, which is the main thing. We don't have anything like that in this country. It's only Royalty that can bestow titles. There seems to be a good many advantages, I found out, to live in a country where there's Royalty.

Well, to go back to the family: of course they was beginning to think after a while about coming home to America again. But there was one sad thing, though, that was just beginning to trouble them—and that was Jean. She had begun to be sick. You know, she had quite a serious trouble and the doctors thought it was something like epilepsy. It was really a most terrible thing, because Jean was so lovely and it seemed wicked and cruel to have anything like that come upon her, for it made her almost an invalid at times. So this was one terrible grief, right in the midst of all the gayety.

One of Mr. Clemens' friends (I think it was Poultney Bigelow) told about a cure he'd been havin' for something some place in Sweden that helped him a great deal —an osteopath, they called him, this doctor. Mrs. Clemens thought it might help Jean, and they got awfully excited about it and decided to go there and try this treatment for Jean. So they went that summer to Sweden and stayed until the fall, and Jean was greatly benefited, and they had great hopes she would get well from it. Mr. Clemens got so interested he took this treatment himself, too, and said it helped him, and they was all very enthusiastic about it. Then they come back to London and took an apartment to be near a branch of this Swedish institute, where they could get the same treatment for Jean in London.

They kept plannin' to return to America that spring, but they always postponed it. They didn't know where they was going to live, when they got to America. They dreaded the thought of going back to the Hartford house —they couldn't never go back to it again, now that Susy was dead. No, they couldn't bear the thought of that! So they kind of stayed on in London and finally took a place outside in the country—an awful pretty place. It was called Dollis House. I've got a nice picture of Mr. Clemens, taken right there under a tree. There was a

HER MAJESTY QUEEN VICTORIA

KING EDWARD AS THE PRINCE OF WALES

Bundy, Hartford

MARK TWAIN'S FAMILY IN EARLY HARTFORD DAYS
(Courtesy Harper & Brothers)

little pond in that place, and the lawns and trees (oak trees, they was) were lovely. They said Gladstone come there quite a good deal when he was alive, as he was a friend of the man that owned the place. 'Twas very peaceful and sweet, and Mr. Clemens, he really loved it. Mrs. Clemens adored it too, and they spent a lot of time that summer settin' out under them beautiful trees, and enjoying themselves.

Of course there was always a lot of company on hand. Everybody used to come from London, and all the Americans that was in London come along, too. Brander Matthews come out there once with his family, and they talked and talked and had a grand time. 'Twas a little Paradise, that place was; but even so, nothing could keep them much longer from America.

So in October we sailed for America. And, oh, my! How glad Mr. Clemens was to get home! Of course, all the reporters was there to meet him on the dock and he joked with them, and told them how glad he was to be home and said if he ever got ashore he thought he'd *break* both his legs (or something terrible like that) so's he could never leave home any more!

Well, it was wonderful how glad everybody was in America to have Mark Twain back again. The newspapers was just full of it. They couldn't say enough. They admired him so for all the fine things he'd done, goin' round the world on that lecture tour and payin' back all his debts and everything like that. My! He was a real hero, I tell you. And they couldn't do enough for him—the people as well as the newspapers. They couldn't have done more if he'd been Royalty—if he'd been a king! And he was a king—in his own way. And he didn't need any crown on his head to prove it. Men don't come any better in this world than Mr. Clemens.

Of course the family began hunting right away for a furnished house to live in and they got one pretty soon through Mr. Doubleday. He was some kind of a publisher. It was a nice, big, spacious house, and they was lucky to find such a fine place.

Yes, 'twas Mr. Frank Doubleday that got Mr. Clemens that house in Tenth Street (14 West Tenth Street). 'Twas all furnished, too. It seems Mr. Clemens told Doubleday that he'd have to get a house for him somehow or other, so Mr. Doubleday went to an agent and got the lease all fixed up good, and told Mr. Clemens it was all ready to sign, and then he could consider the house his.

Well, you know Mr. Clemens was always so funny about everything, and when he heard that, he didn't bother to sign no lease, but we all went and just moved right into the house! Mr. Doubleday was away for a few days, it seems, and when he come back and went to hunt up Mr. Clemens at the hotel and found that he'd moved over to this new house without even signing the lease or seeing the agent, why, poor Mr. Doubleday, he nearly fainted!

"Why," he says, "Mr. Clemens, why you haven't even signed the lease yet! You can't move into a house until you've signed the lease!"

"Well," Mr. Clemens says, "I *have* moved in, haven't I? and that's all there is to it. But bring along your lease, Doubleday. I'll sign it *now*." I guess Mr. Clemens thought possession was nine points of the law, as they say. But of course, nobody else could have done a thing like that, except Mr. Clemens. They wouldn't be allowed. He could do anything, and one of the reasons was, I think, that he was so kind of unconscious of what he was doing.

Well, as I told you, everybody was crazy about Mr. Clemens, and as soon as it got into the papers where he was living, that house in Tenth Street become a regular landmark. The street was always full of people just walking by to see where Mark Twain lived, 'cause he was very famous then and all his books was read by everybody, and everybody knew what a grand time he'd had in Europe with Royalty and all the wonderful things that happened to him. Everybody, great and small, was proud of Mr. Clemens. He's what you would call a leadin' American. He could just have and do anything he wanted to. Every kind of honor, as they called it, was heaped on him. Everybody wanted him for everything; he had to speak at all the grand dinners that was given in New York or Boston or any of the big cities, and all the famous people that come to America was just chasin' right after him. So we had a pretty lively household, I can tell you.

Oh! I could fill a book with just the doings that winter. It was like a fairy story, and it was just as exciting to me to hear about them things as it was to the rest of the family. I couldn't help feelin' as though I had some share in it, too. Everybody was so glad to have Mark Twain back again, they was just chasin' him everywhere. He was flooded with invitations from the highest and grandest in the town. I heard one of them men there at the Players Club call him "the Belle of New York"—which was a kind of a joke, I suppose. But no "belle" ever was run after more than he was. You see, people was crazier about him than ever, and every magazine and newspaper in the world was after him to write for 'em. They'd pay him anything he wanted. Why, I heard that one time he was offered as much as a dollar a word from one magazine if he'd give them an article. Of course, I don't know whether he did it or not—but I guess he did. He was under contract to the Harper Brothers—they was his publishers, and they was to have everything he wrote, and they paid him a good, big price for it, too—for his articles and for the publishing of all his books.

It was right after Mr. Clemens returned from Europe with the family, only a few days afterwards, that Mr. Warner died—Charles Dudley Warner—his old friend that used to live next to him in Hartford and that he loved so much. Mr. Clemens felt terrible. It affected him very deeply. He went up to Hartford to the funeral and was one of the pallbearers. That was the only sad thing that happened then, that I remember.

Oh! There was something very funny happened at the Tenth Street house. It was while everybody in New York was chasin' down to see Mr. Clemens. The number of our house was 14 West Tenth Street and there was a woman, it appears, living at 10 West Fourteenth Street; and people kept comin' to her house to ask for Mark Twain, to know if he lived there. They'd get the addresses mixed (they was so much alike—14 West Tenth Street, and 10 West Fourteenth Street).

Well, this kept up for a long time, all these strangers asking for Mr. Clemens, or Mark Twain, and finally she got so sick of it, she called the police and said she wanted to inform them of a man living at 14 West Tenth Street—that he ought to be looked after, because he was really living under *two* names! Well, that was such a good joke (on her)—that she didn't know who Mark Twain was—that the policeman laughed very hearty and thought it was so funny he come right down and told Mr. Clemens. And Mr. Clemens when he heard that, says: "Thank God! Thank God! There's *one* woman in New York don't know me! That's *something* to be grateful for!"

This woman was really terrible disturbed about this. She thought he was some kind of a tough character and that the police ought to look him up. But it shows how ignorant she was, don't it?

It was about this time that I had trouble with a cabman. I'd been up to Hartford to get some things, and when I got back into the Grand Central Station, I didn't know enough to take a cab inside (they used to have cabs on the inside then); I went outside and called the first cab I seen. I didn't have no baggage—just a little satchel in my hand. I told the cabman to take me down quick to 14 West Tenth Street. Well, he just took me all over New York instead! I didn't know the city very well then, but I did know that I shouldn't be ridin' all through Central Park! Up and down he took me, all over Central Park! Finally, after I hollered to him, he took me down to Tenth Street.

I was pretty mad, but I only said, "How much it is?" Then he said, very sharp, "Seven dollars!" Well, I nearly fainted! I didn't have only two dollars in my purse, so I says: "Just you wait a minute. I'll go and get the money for you." I rang and the butler let me in, but Mr. Clemens, it happened, was standin' right there in the hall when I opened the door, so I just burst out and says:

"Oh, Mr. Clemens! That cabman outside wants to charge seven dollars for bringing me down here."

"What?" said Mr. Clemens. "Bring him right inside, Katy." Then he put his head out the front door and shouted to the man, "Bring in your tariff!"

Well, the cabman brought it in and Mr. Clemens looked at it and says, "Young man, you're entitled to exactly seventy-five cents—for bringing this woman down here—just seventy-five cents," he says.

"Yes," I said, "and you told me it would be *seven dollars!*"

The cabman was pretty scared by that time, for he said: "Oh, you didn't understand me! I only said *five* dollars."

"Well," says Mr. Clemens, "we can't hear no more about it," he says. "You can just take this dollar and be off! But," he says, "I think I'd better know who you work for." The cabman was mad, but he told him, of course. Then Mr. Clemens says, "Is this your own cab?"

"No," says the man, "I'm working for my boss."

"Well," says Mr. Clemens, "you take this dollar and if your boss ain't satisfied with that, report to me in the morning." And then Mr. Clemens added, "If you don't report to me, I'll report *you*, for the way you've acted."

The man started to go and he kind of muttered to himself, "The damned old fool!"

Oh! Then Mr. Clemens said, "I heard you, I heard you, and you'll hear more in the morning from me!"

Of course the man never came back, but Mr. Clemens was pretty mad at his ridin' me all over the park and trying to cheat me; so he had the cabman arrested and his license taken away. Oh, we had a great time! The trial was down at the City Hall and the judge was a friend of Mr. Clemens, and they said I'd have to appear, too. But they didn't ask me a word, so I didn't have to say anything. Of course, by that time everybody heard about it and the room was just crowded. Lots and lots of reporters. They was even settin' up on the windows and on everything, these reporters was, while the trial was going on. The cabman told his story—Bock was his name—how I'd engaged him and that the regular fare was five dollars; and then Mr. Clemens spoke right up and says: "He's a regular pirate! A pirate and no mistake!"

I can't remember all the trial, but they pointed me out and says the man was guilty; that they would take his license away; how he'd insulted Mr. Clemens at his door, and the whole thing. Then the cabman says: "Well, I have to stand outside the station while them cabs inside get all the first jobs, the best ones; and sometimes I have to stand outside for hours and don't get anything; so when I do get a job, I have to make it pay!"

"That's enough," said Mr. Clemens. "That's all I want to know. That's all you need to say. Didn't I tell you that they was regular pirates? Here is this poor woman," says Mr. Clemens, "that he tried to cheat out of all that money. She's workin' for me and I pay the bills; but I wasn't goin' to pay such a pirate bill as *that!* I paid that man one dollar and he was only entitled to seventy-five cents."

Well, Mr. Clemens read the riot act after that, said

what pirates these cab drivers was, how they robbed people, and it made a great impression in New York. There was a lot in the papers about it, and it really made the cab drivers look out a little bit and behave themselves after that.

When the trial was over, Mrs. Clemens and Miss Clara came down there, and I says: "Well, it's over and it's all beautiful and I didn't have to say a word! Mr. Clemens, he done all the talking." So we all got into a cab and they brought me home in triumph!

A little while after that, I was going down the street and a man who had been watching me come out of the house, stepped up, and says, "Is your name Leary, and are you the woman who had trouble with the cab driver?"

I says, "Yes, and Mr. Clemens took his license away from him."

"Well," this man says, "that cab driver is really a nice young man but his boss is a rascal, and he has to turn in just so much money or else lose his job. And his mother is a widow and he's her only support."

Oh, that made me feel awful, thinkin' I was the cause of it! "He hasn't any work now," this man says, "and don't know where to get any work, because he's a cabman and can't do anything else."

Of course, I went right home and told Mr. Clemens.

"Why, I'll get his address," said Mr. Clemens. "I'll fix that up all right, Katy." So Mr. Clemens sent for the man and paid him for the time he'd been idle since he was arrested, and had the judge or whoever it was took the license away, give it back, and he got a new job. Now, wasn't that lovely of Mr. Clemens? He gave him good advice and talked to him for about an hour, Mr. Clemens did—had the cabman up in the Billiard Room, talking to him, and I guess he made a real good man of Mr. Bock. But that was always Mr. Clemens' way. He never could bear to see anybody in trouble.

Yes, that was certainly a wonderful winter we spent in the Tenth Street house, and all Mr. Clemens' old friends was there a great deal—which made him very happy. Mr. Howells, of course, and then Mr. Rogers and Mr. Gilder (he had that *Century Magazine*, you know) and Mr. Aldrich, and then Chauncey Depew—mustn't forget him. He was a very famous kind of a public man. He was a Senator, too, and a great joker. Well, all them great clubs in New York—I can't remember all the names—they was always askin' Mr. Clemens to speak at all the great dinners they'd give. There was no end to the things he was into. Why, somebody even said he ought to be the next President. But he never took that seriously, of course. I think myself he might of made a wonderful President. He'd been an honest one, anyway! But I guess honesty ain't the main quality that is wanted in a President.

Of course, Mr. Clemens was writin' all the time, stories and pieces in the newspapers and I don't know what not, and he was always interested in some new invention or things like that. I think it was about that time he got interested in a kind of a food—Plasmon—a health food that you mixed up with water, and the idea was that it was goin' to make you strong. He believed in that Plasmon stuff—used to take it himself, drink it—or whatever it was they did to it. And I believe he put quite a bit of money into it, too. But that never come to much—that Plasmon venture.

Of course, I could keep on forever with the doin's of Mr. Clemens and the family. They was all very happy there and Mrs. Clemens was enjoying herself, too, and Miss Clara had lots of parties and lots of beaux. There was a young man used to come there quite a lot, he was a poet or something like that. His name was Bynner—Witter Bynner—which is kind of a funny name for a poet. He wrote lots of poetry and he wrote one piece to Miss Clara. He was very good-looking, too—tall and dark—a nice, handsome-looking fellow. He was really very charming, I believe. I used to see him quite often and liked him myself, and so did Mr. Clemens; and of course, Mr. Gabrilowitsch comes in again about this period. I think I'll tell you a little more about him now. I used to carry the notes back and forth between them, so I guess I had a hand in that courtship. That's a long story and it's very pretty, too, I think. It began way back in Vienna, as I told you, where Miss Clara, of course, had lots of beaux as she was very much admired, but none of them cared very much about me, because you see I had to be with Miss Clara everywhere she went. I was right there on the spot, escorting her. I was right at her heels all the time and they couldn't say I warn't a good chaperon and a good watchdog—because that's what I was; and some of them, I guess, would have been glad if I'd got lost and hadn't stuck around so much.

In Vienna one time, Clara was at a party and Mr. Gabrilowitsch was there, too (to be with her, I guess), and they gave me the directions how to get to the place to bring her home, as I'd never been there before. I almost got lost—couldn't find the way, and when I did finally arrive, I says to Mr. Gabrilowitsch:

"Oh, my goodness! I thought I'd never get here, I've wandered all over Vienna. I almost lost my way," I says.

"Well," he said, "Katy, I wish you had lost your way for once! That'd be a good thing," he says, "—the very best thing that could happen!" And he laughed and laughed at me.

You know, I told you how much I liked Mr. Gabrilowitsch—he was always my favorite, and I think I helped that match along a good deal carrying them love letters back and forth. Yes, I liked him from the very first time I seen him, and I always wanted Miss Clara to marry him. I really think I helped the thing along as much as anybody.

When he first come to America to play, he was stopping there at the Hoffman House, I think it was, and he left that address so's we'd know where he was. So one Sunday afternoon, I was going up to vespers at St. Patrick's Cathedral, and Clara, she gave me a note and she says: "Now, Katy, please take that note for me. It's very important, and leave it at the hotel for Mr. Gabrilowitsch."

Well, I left the note at the hotel but he warn't in then, so I told the clerk at the desk to be sure and give him that note the minute he got back. Then I went off to vespers, but thought I'd just drop into the hotel on my way home, to be sure he got that note safe, and my goodness! when I got there and see that clerk behind the desk glaring at me (he wore spectacles), for the life of me I couldn't remember Mr. Gabrilowitsch's name! I was sort of dazed—I don't know *what* happened to me! But I *forgot* his name, can you believe that, as much as I liked him? I don't know whether the church knocked it out of me or not, but for the moment I couldn't remember his name—it just went from me. The clerk was looking at me and I was looking at the clerk, and then I says, very embarrassed:

"Well, I brought a letter here this afternoon for a young foreign man that's in this hotel and I want to know if he got it, as 'twas very important." Then the clerk said: "I don't know. I'll see,—and what's his name?" And I says, "Well, I can't think for the minute, but," I says, "he only arrived this morning from Europe and he's a wonderful pianist and musician, you know, and he's got a terrible queer foreign name."

"Oh, yes, yes—I know him," he says, "I know who you mean *now!*"

"Well," I says, "if you do, I want an answer to that note I left." So then the clerk, he went up and seen Mr. Gabrilowitsch and got me the answer to take home, and when I told Miss Clara what I'd done, why, she almost had a fit to think I'd forgot that name! 'Twas kind of funny, too, when you come to think of it, but I guess I was always what you call "absent-minded"—even in them days.

I've told you that Mr. Clemens was awful funny and fussy about his food; he always had lots of fads, as they call it, about food. Sometimes he would just leave off eating everything except one thing, and would live on that all the time. Then there was a certain kind of bread he would have to have; and he took it into his head once to live just on breakfast food, and ran all about with it. Why, he would even go to dinners and parties and carry that old breakfast food with him! But Mrs. Clemens, when she was alive, used to kind of head him off; and then he got very interested in what you call—well, not exactly religion, but what's called a cult, and would follow it up to the very end.

Of course, people always said Mr. Clemens didn't have any faith in God. But I know that warn't so, because everything he did showed he had faith in something, anyway. He wasn't ever religious, the way most people was, but he *did* believe—I know it. Of course he got terrible interested in Christian Science—he was down on it in a way, tore it all to pieces and wrote a book about it, too, in which he argued it all out; but he believed there was something in it, although he didn't give them a leg to stand on, in his book. But I can't tell much about that. It's beyond me! You can read about it in his book. But he certainly loved Mr. Twitchell very much. Mr. Twitchell, you know, was the pastor in the old church in Hartford. I told you about him in the beginning—how Mrs. Clemens and the children all loved him, and Mrs. Twitchell, too. And how the children all called him "Uncle Joe."

Mr. Twitchell and Mr. Clemens was just devoted to each other, and Mr. Twitchell used to influence him a great deal, I think—more than anybody else, except Mrs. Clemens. They used to have the grandest times together, tellin' stories and laughing, and every fall when Mr. Clemens got back from Elmira, he and Mr. Twitchell (Joe and Sam, they called themselves) used to take a long walk together. They'd walk right up Talcott Mountain. 'Twas a ten-mile walk and they'd rig themselves all up good and walk out there and back to that old mountain every fall. Mr. Clemens said they'd have to take that long walk at least once a year, just to see if they was holdin' their own! Of course, they enjoyed it and they talked all the way, I'll bet!

Mr. Twitchell used to preach at the Congregational Church in Hartford, and at first Mr. Clemens went to church every Sunday—never missed. But after a while he kind of dropped off a little bit and Mr. Twitchell, of course, he noticed that, so he come in one evening and says, "I didn't see you in church this morning, Sam." Then Mr. Clemens says:

"Well, Joe, if you weren't so long-winded, I would go more regular," he says, "but I do get so weary, so tired, with them long, long sermons of yours!"

Well, Mr. Twitchell, he just laughed and laughed, and said: "Well, Sam, I'll cut them sermons short the next time I see you settin' in church. I promise you!"

Mr. Clemens used to tell a funny story about Mr. Twitchell. You see Mr. Twitchell was very much loved by everybody. His parishioners liked him so well they gave him a big salary to live on, to take care of his children. He had so many—I think there was nine or ten. Well, it seems that Mr. Twitchell had a friend—a man that was married at the same time he was, and that man was always telegraphing whenever there was a baby born in his house, the same as Mr. Twitchell did. He lived in Albany and Mr. Twitchell lived in Hartford, you know. And Mr. Clemens said if it warn't for them two men—Twitchell and the other—I don't remember his name—well, anyway, Mr. Clemens said that the Western Union would certainly go under if it warn't for them two men sending telegrams to each other about their babies being born. A telegram would come from Albany, "There was a boy born last night"; and next day they'd shoot up a telegram from Hartford, "Girl born this mornin'!" They kept them wires hot, telegraphin' about the babies that was born, and Mr. Clemens says, really and truly, the telegraph would go under at that time except there was so many births in them two families —they actually kept the Western Union going!

Well, speaking of birth control, people talk a lot about that nowadays, and there is a woman goes around lecturing on it. Of course in them days, when I was young, I didn't think much about it, but the way I look at it now, is this way: that perhaps there is some good in it; that is, that after a time it will better the whole human race. Maybe. But in our church, the Catholic Church, you know, it is against it, and if you are a Catholic, they would give you a terrible penance for anything like that. Oh, of course that's a pretty deep question—another thing I can't answer.

Yes, Mr. Twitchell and Mr. Clemens was always together in the old days. Mr. Twitchell was a tall man, not too fat, just right. Nice-looking. Told jolly stories and used to talk a lot everywhere; and they were a very happy family, too, the Twitchells. He and his wife was always together. As long as either Mr. Clemens or Mr. Twitchell lived they was really very close friends.

I mustn't forget to tell you how Mr. Clemens and Mr. Twitchell decided one time that they would walk all the way to Boston, too. Everybody thought it was a joke, but they was quite serious about it and said they was going to do it anyway and show the world! So they started off and took to the road. Mr. Twitchell had a bag and Mr. Clemens, he had some lunch, I guess. Of course, by that time the newspapers got hold of it, for everything that Mark Twain did always got into the newspapers even then, in the old days.

Well, they walked along the first day or two all right, and walked about twenty-five miles or so and got into a town of some kind where there was a hotel—where they could get a good dinner and stay overnight. They planned to go on the next morning, but by that time Mr. Clemens was terrible mad, and he was limping 'cause his feet was sore (and swearing, too, I guess); so they gave it up and drove to the nearest railway station and Mr. Clemens sent a telegram to somebody: "We walked about thirty miles already, and we've done it in three days, which shows the world that we *can* walk, if we want to, so now we'll be comfortable and finish by train!! We'll take another one of these walking trips maybe next year to show that we enjoy walking." It was something like that. That's an old story.

Well, of course, that was one of his best jokes. He was always doing that kind of thing. He did it later on when we went to Switzerland. He was always talking about Alpine climbing, too, but as I told you, he did most of his climbing by the railroad as a rule. But Mr. Clemens and Mr. Twitchell did take a long walking tour once in Switzerland and they went through the Black Forest, too. They had a wonderful time together. Of course they didn't walk all the time—they stole a good many rides, I guess, in a train or wagon or anything they could get into. But Mr. Clemens just loved Switzerland—he loved them great snow mountains, the Alps, and he and Mr. Twitchell had a glorious time of it on that trip. I used to hear him telling about it and what wonderful talks they had, and how happy they was together.

About the Twitchells, I want to say that was a very loving family. Mr. Twitchell was devoted to his wife and children. 'Twas about as nice as the Clemens household, although I suppose no household could be quite as nice as ours. I used to like Mr. Twitchell very much and he used to talk to me quite a good deal, and I remember years afterwards when his wife died and almost all the children was gone, and all our family was gone, too, he said to me:

"Oh," he said, "oh, Katy, we're about the last, you and I! They're all gone, our loved ones, yours and mine. All our family are gone but you and me. We went through some mighty hard times, didn't we, Katy? You lost all your family" (meaning the Clemens family), "and you were with every one of them to the end—and I've lost a good many of my family and my dear wife. It's about the end," he says, "and we'll go next, Katy—we'll go next." Oh, that was a sad thing, but it was true.

We seen 'em all go, and 'twas hard, I tell you. But in the days I'm tellin' you about now, it didn't seem to me there ever could be any unhappiness come to us.

Mr. Clemens was interested in everything under the sun. I told you how he wrote about Christian Science, and then he got kind of interested in Spiritualism at one time. It was this way:

In the old Hartford days there was a man by the name of Hooker. He was married to Henry Ward Beecher's sister. They was friends of Mr. Clemens and Mr. Clemens admired her very much, I guess, 'cause he always listened to everything she said—quiet as a lamb. Mr. Hooker was a Spiritualist, and it was funny to see Mr. Clemens with them, 'cause he listened to everything they said and sort o' believed it—even Spiritualism! I remember how Mr. Hooker told about seein' his daughter who had died. It must have been at a séance he seen her. He said her spirit come to him and she held in her hands two little blue worsted shoes, which was the little shoes that had belonged to her. Mr. Hooker said his daughter just held up them little blue shoes and says, "Father, don't you know me?"

Now, Mr. Clemens when he heard Mr. Hooker say that, seemed greatly impressed and he says:

"Well, I've never seen anybody who come back from the other world, but I believe so much in John Hooker that I'd take his word for anything, and if he says he saw his daughter carryin' them two little blue worsted shoes, then it must be so, because I'd take John Hooker's word for it!"

This shows, doesn't it, that Mr. Clemens had a great deal of confidence in that man? But he was just like that always. When he believed in any one, he believed in them thorough, and— Oh! I must tell you something about a little photograph he bought at that time.

It was a very strange photograph. It was in one of the guest chambers in the house. 'Twas a picture of a little girl—just an ordinary-looking little girl—don't know who it was, and I remember a lady visiting at the Warners' come over and said to Mr. Clemens: "Whose picture is that in the guest chamber? Whose little girl is that?" He said: "I don't know who it is; I haven't any idea. I just bought it in an old photograph shop one time, because it looked so *human*, and I go in there very often and look at it, and I say to it: '*What* has become of you? *What* has become of you, little girl?' "

Then the lady said to Mr. Clemens, "Did you ever find out who it was and what had become of her?" And he says, very quick: "Oh, no! No, I wouldn't find out for anything—not for anything! That would spoil it all!"

I think all this kind o' proves, no matter what people say, that Mr. Clemens was interested in the hereafter. Yes, Mr. Clemens was really a good Christian man, but people really never understood that. I think he was one of the purest men that I ever knew. I mean by that—

well, I don't know how you would put it exactly, but pure and clean and true—and just devoted to his home and family; but, oh, my! He'd joke about anything. He'd joke even at a funeral! I remember when Mrs. Clemens' mother was dying. She was sick a long time, and Mrs. Clemens was in Elmira and kept telegraphing Mr. Clemens every morning to come that day. Finally he said he'd go, but the children all began to cry and hung on to him and begged him not to, so he hadn't the heart to leave 'em and he got terrible upset. So he went over to Mr. Warner and says: "Warner, I've written a letter to everybody who has a single drop of my blood in their veins and whose funeral I may ever have to go to, and I have asked them *all* to come and settle right down here within a radius of two blocks and just *stay* until they all die, so I won't ever have to go out of town to attend their funerals!" Yes, he'd joke about anything.

I remember one time Mr. Clemens went to Mr. Twitchell's church and there was some negro singers there—the Hampton Singers—and they sang all them negro airs they called Spirituals, and Mr. Clemens loved it and begun to sing with 'em, too—he had a lovely voice and was very dramatic in his singing, and he sung with them Hampton Singers under his breath. He used to sing negro Spirituals himself. I heard about one night when there was company at the Warners' and Mr. Clemens was there, and it was a perfectly lovely night and there was a full moon outside and no lights in the house. They was just settin' there in the music room, looking out at the moonlight. And suddenly Mr. Clemens got right up without any warning and begun to sing one of them negro Spirituals. A lady that was there told me he just stood up with both his eyes shut and begun to sing kind of soft like—a faint sound, just as if there was wind in the trees, she said; and he kept right on singin' kind o' low and sweet, and it was beautiful and made your heart ache somehow. And he kept on singin' and singin' and became kind of lost in it, and he was all lit up—his face was. 'Twas somethin' from another world, she said, and when he got through, he put his two hands up to his head, just as though all the sorrow of them negroes was upon him; and then he begun to sing, "Nobody Knows the Trouble I Got, Nobody Knows but Jesus." That was one of them negro spirituals songs, and when he come to the end, to the Glory Halleluiah, he gave a great shout—just like the negroes do—he shouted out the Glory, Glory, Halleluiah! They said it was wonderful and none of them would forget it as long as they lived.

No, nothin' can ever make me think that Mr. Clemens didn't believe in a God—some kind of a God. I can't say it too often! I've heard that he said one time, "Pretty poor materials went into the making of man." He said, "God must have made him at the end of the week when He was tired." Yes, pretty poor stuff went into the makings of the human race—"the damned human race," he used to call it. He used to say all the race had an axe to grind, and always askin' somebody else to whet it!

Mr. Clemens was always saying funny things that there was a lot of truth in. I remember one thing he said once—a kind of a motto, and it certainly appealed to me, and that was:

"When you're mad, count four; when you're very mad, swear!" But most of us don't wait to count four! at least I don't!

After all the grand doin's that winter in New York, the family went to spend the summer at Saranac Lake—way up in the Adirondack Mountains. They rented a nice little log-cabin cottage up there. It was called "The Lair"—which is kind of funny, 'cause if you twist them letters a bit, you would make it the liar! That's one of my jokes, but it don't sound so very good—not like one of Mr. Clemens'. Very quiet and peaceful it was, after all that gay city life, and they just lived there right on the edge of the lake in the woods and didn't have any company and didn't bother about newspapers nor letters nor nothing—they just lived out-of-doors all the time and enjoyed themselves. They was so glad to get away from the doings in New York. Mr. Clemens was doing his writin', of course, just as usual, so there wasn't very much to tell about that time. Then they decided not to go back to New York the next winter but go somewheres near New York and they heard about the Appleton house up on the Hudson at Riverdale. So they went and seen that and liked it and rented it. It proved to be very convenient for them 'cause they could go back and forth to New York easy, and Miss Clara was studyin' singing and went for her lessons two or three times a week, and of course there was just a stream of company chasin' up to see them, all the time, and Mr. Clemens, he used to chase down to New York, too, for dinners and things. They liked that Riverdale house 'cause it was in the country and better for Mrs. Clemens, who wasn't very well then. And they lived really a pretty quiet life—for them!—after all they'd gone through with the Royalty!

Of course, Mr. Clemens seen a lot of Mr. Rogers at this time, and went off on his yacht with him. They had several trips on that yacht—I forget its name. And once they took a long trip—quite a party of celebrated men. Dr. Rice was there, too, and they went way off to the West Indies and had a grand old time.

And I must tell you about another trip when they played a terrible joke on Mr. Clemens about his umbrella.

Dr. Rice was on that trip, too, and some Senator; and Mr. Rogers invited a lot of them—six or seven men—to go on this elegant yachting trip with him. Well, they had that yacht pretty well filled up with everything good to eat (and drink), I can tell you! And it sailed right up the Hudson and anchored right at the foot of the

Appleton house, so all Mr. Clemens had to do was to step on board.

Well, after Mr. Clemens had been on that yacht for a few days, he began lookin' around for his things. He said he didn't know if they was *all* real nice honest men like himself or not! So he thought he'd better get his things together and lock 'em up to make sure! And he couldn't find his umbrella! He said he brought a beautiful new umbrella on board—('cause you always needed an umbrella on a boat!) a very expensive one, and he couldn't find it! That he had his suspicions, but wasn't quite sure *who'd* took it! Then he told 'em he was going to watch 'em *all*, and when they landed and were getting off, he'd find out who had his umbrella and he'd nab it and get it back. But, my goodness! he never found it. Of course then, all them elegant gentlemen got interested in it, too, and Mr. Clemens searched them all on the pier, under their overcoats and through all their baggage, but he couldn't find his umbrella. Mr. Rogers and Dr. Rice, they kind o' kept it up and fell in with it as a joke, and Mr. Rogers, he advertised for the lost umbrella. They advertised the whole thing, givin' a full description; said it was Mark Twain's umbrella and of course very valuable, and that they'd like to find it and give it back to him and Mr. Rogers, he advertised where the umbrella could be returned. Oh, Lord! You should have seen the kinds of umbrellas that was sent! The awfullest-lookin' things you ever seen! Dozens and dozens of them! So Mr. Rogers had a big box made to put 'em in. A great big box, it was, and crammed full of them awful-lookin' old umbrellas. Such things! Well, when that bix box was crammed full, they sent it up to Mr. Clemens to Riverdale and the express not paid! When Mr. Clemens seen that great box and the express not paid, he thought it must be somethin' wonderful, so he paid all the charges on it quick, and then he got Claude to open the box; but when he seen that great box full of them terrible umbrellas! Well, he gave just one look—and Claude (he was the butler then; French, he was—and very good) told me he couldn't really bear to repeat what Mr. Clemens said when he saw them umbrellas! I guess he did some talking that time!

Of course, they all had the joke on him then, and was all hangin' around (Mr. Rogers and the rest) to hear what Mr. Clemens would say, but Mr. Clemens was pretty smart and turned the joke back on them again. He fooled 'em all over again! He didn't even let on he got the box, so Mr. Rogers, he had to come way out to Riverdale to find out; and there that awful box was, a-standin' open on the porch. He pretended to be surprised when he seen it and said, "Why, where did that box come from?"

Mr. Clemens says, "Well, Rogers, that box come from *your* house, that's where it come from, with all them damned old umbrellas," he says, "that you and those other idiots contributed!"

Of course, Mr. Rogers just roared at that and said, "Well, that's so, but we had to do *somethin'* to you, 'cause you accused everybody on my yacht of bein' a thief, so we had to get even with you somehow," he said.

"Well," says Mr. Clemens, "that's all right, but I never intend to have another umbrella again—never!"

"Oh, yes, you will," says Mr. Rogers, " 'cause I'll buy you one, the handsomest I can find." So he sent him an elegant umbrella—a beautiful silk one with a gold handle, and then Mr. Clemens had printed all over the inside of it, "Stolen from Samuel L. Clemens"—and that ended that joke.

Of course Mr. Clemens was writing all the time, wherever he was, and there is an awful lot to tell about the different things he wrote. I used to hear a great deal about some of them, and I haven't said anything yet about one of Mr. Clemens' most wonderful books: that was the book about Joan of Arc. Mr. Clemens liked *Joan* the best of all his books, and he said it was the best, too, his whole life, she was his favorite character in history—he was always talkin' about her. She was kind of sacred to him. It took him a long time to write that book. He'd been thinkin' about it for years, he said, but he didn't finish it until he was nearly sixty years old.

Yes, he first got the idea way back when he was a little boy, about Joan of Arc, from some book that he found, tellin' about her. He got awfully interested in her and he begun readin' everything about her and thinkin' of her, and he kept it up all his life—readin' and studyin' about Joan for years and years, before he even begun his book. I heard him say he loved writin' it so ('twas so kind of a part of him) that 'twarn't no trouble at all—it just kind of wrote itself. He begun that Joan book in Europe, but he didn't finish until a long time afterwards, and it was published in *Harper's Magazine*, I think, and 'twas anonymous. He was afraid, you see, if he put the name "Mark Twain" on it that nobody'd take it serious, because he used to say that people always wanted to laugh at everything he wrote; so that's why he had it published under another name first. The public always thought he joked about everything, but that warn't so; he was really very serious about lots of things, but it took people a long while to find this out. Susy used to say, though, very often, that her father was what you might call a philosopher (which means a deep thinker), as well as a humorist. Susy always realized and saw things very clear—even when she was quite a little girl—and she was very proud of her father and said there warn't anything he couldn't do or be.

Well, about Joan of Arc, although she was a saint—as everybody knows—Mr. Clemens in his book, he made her sort of *human*, too—which added to the thing. I guess almost everybody in the world read that book and liked it. I know I did. He dedicated it to Mrs. Clemens and that was the only book he ever did dedicate to her—because it was his very best. He gave me a copy of Joan with his autograph in it that time when he gave me copies of all his books.

Well, to get back to the Riverdale house: we spent the winter there and then went up to York Harbor in Maine the next summer. They thought that would be cool and bracing for Mrs. Clemens and they took a nice little cottage up there, called "The Pines." They all liked it very much and Mrs. Clemens felt a little better at first. Mr. Clemens, he enjoyed it 'cause Mr. Howells and his family was spending the summer near there, and they was visitin' back and forth all the time and swapping stories. They used to read to each other the pieces they wrote—their manuscripts—all the time. Of course they enjoyed that and laughed and talked by the hour. But after a while Mrs. Clemens got very sick and Mrs. Crane, her sister, come up from Elmira, because Mrs. Clemens was really very sick, and couldn't see anybody or hear the slightest noise—hardly could see Mr. Clemens except a few minutes at a time. Miss Clara, she took entire charge of the house then—managed everything so as nothing could disturb her mother. Even the slightest noise they was afraid might upset her 'cause she was so very weak.

Mr. Clemens used to say that, even the birds would please not sing loud near the house; so that was a sad endin' to that summer, and we all had anxious hearts for Mrs. Clemens.

Well, then they thought they'd go back to Riverdale again—to the Appleton house, and they went back in

October. Oh! it was a terrible hard winter, for Mrs. Clemens was sick all the time, and Mr. Clemens was nearly frantic. It seemed as though half his life had stopped, and he was all the time wishin' and prayin' he could take her sickness on himself.

Mrs. Clemens grew worse and they could only see her a few minutes at a time. Mr. Clemens could only see her two minutes at a time every day, and oh! he was always waiting at her door long, long before he could get in. He just stood there waitin'! And sometimes when he couldn't stand it any longer, he used to write little notes and push them under her door. That seemed to comfort him a little. He couldn't write his stories that winter; he was like a lost soul, really, and Miss Clara, it was terrible for her. All the burdens fell on her shoulders; and then Miss Jean had pneumonia and was very sick, too, and they had to keep it from Mrs. Clemens so she'd never know; and poor Miss Clara used to have to go to her mother every day and make up all kinds of stories (yarns) about Jean—how well she was and what she was doin' and what a lovely time she was having—so as to deceive Mrs. Clemens and never let her even suspect how sick Jean was. Clara used to have to go every morning and afternoon to lie about Jean. She had to make up all kinds of things every day to tell her mother. That's the time Mr. Clemens wrote that story "Heaven and Hell"—and it seems all the details of the story was identical with what was happenin' to us in the house.

Of course, Jean got well after a time, but it was a long winter, I'll tell you, and a hard one! That house was just like a hospital, and it seems as though every one was holding their breath, almost—waitin' and wonderin' what was goin' to happen next.

We dragged along somehow, but Mrs. Clemens didn't get any better, and then they decided they'd go up to Elmira for the summer—up to old Quarry Farm. Mrs. Clemens wanted to go there again, 'cause the old Hartford house was sold then. They never could go back to that after Susy died. You see, they was beginnin' to talk then about going to Italy the comin' winter. They thought that warm sunny climate would make Mrs. Clemens well again.

So we went to Elmira for the summer, and stayed there at Quarry Farm and Mrs. Clemens seemed to get a little better; she just lay on the porch all day long, enjoying the scenery, lookin' out at the view—at them pretty hills in the sunshine; and some days she was well enough to ride out in the carriage, and she loved that, and it made her happy. And Mr. Clemens, he set with her most of the time, tryin' to cheer her up and plan for the trip, for they'd decided to go to Italy for the winter.

Mr. Clemens was almost happy again because she seemed a little better, and he begun writin' his stories once more, and he wrote a beautiful one about a dog—*A Dog's Tale,* it was called, and it was a very sad story. 'Twas all about how wicked it was to cut up dogs and use them to experiment with—vivisection—they call it, I think. Mr. Clemens always used to rage about that, and he wrote this beautiful little story just to show how wicked it was.

And so the summer drifted by and Mrs. Clemens seemed a little better all the time, and then all the plans was made to start for Italy and we sailed from New York in October. They took a house in Florence—a beautiful villa—the Villa di Quarto. That was rented before we started. It belonged to some American woman who married an Italian Count. She rented it to Mr. Clemens through an agent. This American Countess was very disagreeable, and made everything awful hard for them. She was mad at having to rent her villa, 'cause she had to live in the stable herself; so she done everything she could to make it uncomfortable for us. Mr. Clemens hated her, of course. The family was always looking for another place to move to, but they was never able to find one that they liked. She did an awful mean thing once to the girls. They was having a tea party out on the lawn one day and the Countess' big dog came over. He was very fond of Miss Clara and Miss Jean. He was playin' with them in the garden, snapping round with them, and when the Countess seen him, she called him into the house, and put some grease all over his body and his head and his nose, and then she let him out again! Of course he ran right back to the girls and he began playing and rubbing up against them and rubbed all the grease right off onto their nice dresses! She did that on purpose. I think it was a pretty mean thing to do.

Well! We sailed for Florence in the fall and went right to that villa. Everything was all ready for us. Yes, it was a lovely villa with beautiful grounds. All around the grounds was a great big iron fence so high you couldn't look over it; and there was a lovely olive grove right across the road from there. There was great big fireplaces in every room and they used to burn bricks (they called them) made out of olive pulp. They took the skins and refuse that was left from the olive and made them into these bricks and burned them in the fireplace. They lasted a long time and made a red-hot fire. It was a palace, really (there was fifty rooms in it); and we had horses and a carriage and everything else. It was very somber and quiet but had very nice furniture in it. But the garden was wonderful. A great beautiful garden with roses trailing all over it. It was enchanting. You could cut the roses by the bushel; even in December we had beautiful bouquets, and all along the walk there was rows of orange trees growing, and oh! they smelled so sweet.

Mrs. Clemens got better at first, but it didn't last long. She was very weak. We had a nurse, of course. The nurse was with her daytimes and Miss Clara sat with her every afternoon, too, but I stayed with her nights. And oh! it was glorious! The nights and the roses! Every window was open during the night, and the smell of the roses and the scented laurel (there was hedges of it all around the house) and the orange blossoms—and all those mingling in together while the nightingales was singing. Oh, it was perfectly beautiful! The nightingales, they sung so sweet; but 'twas kind of forlorn, too, and lonesome. It used to make me sad and lonesome just to hear the tones they made, them nightingales.

How happy we could have been if only Mrs. Clemens was well enough to enjoy it! She was too sick then to talk much, but one night she spoke about Mr. Clemens and her sister, Mrs. Crane. She said, "Oh, Katy, how I'd love to be in America and have my sister Sue walk in!" And then another time she said, when we was talking together, "Katy," she says, "I don't think I can live much longer."

Yes, I think she knew she was going to die then, for she told me what she wanted me to put on her when she was dead. She'd had some dresses made in New York—a lavender one made into kind of a robe—a flowing dress. Lavender satin, it was, beautifully trimmed with lace, and she said she'd like to have that put on her. It was a week before she died she told me this. She was in bed and I slept on a bed right near her, and she was telling me what I should do when she was gone. "Oh," I said, "Mrs. Clemens! *Don't* talk about death. It's too awful. You're not going to die." But she never answered me at all.

"I know," I says, "I realize everything you're telling

me, and what you want done—and I'll make everything just as you'd like it."

That night there was some owls come along and they was hootin' outside the house and she said:

"Do you hear those owls, Katy? I know that's a sign of death."

"Well," I said, "that's what they say; but those owls have been there a long time. The priest says" (the priest lived next door) "they come every year. They have a nest here, and they come back to visit it." She didn't say anything more, but she kept thinking to herself, I know, and that's what brought up the conversation about her dress.

That was a nice priest that told us about the owls. His church was close to our house. He come to see Mr. Clemens very often and always had a candle burning on the altar for Mrs. Clemens. He used to light one every morning for her. The church bells rang there all the time—they had so many Holy days and Feast days, and sometimes they rang right in the middle of the night, too. When the Father found that it disturbed Mrs. Clemens, he had them stopped right away. Oh! I'm sure Mrs. Clemens knew she was going to die, but she didn't let the family know how she felt.

Miss Clara used to set with her every afternoon. She did that from the beginning of her illness in Riverdale. And Mr. Clemens was always right in the next room. He only could see her once a day, and it almost killed him. His room was right next to hers, and he could hear any little sound she made. He wanted to be near her day and night. He was only allowed to come in every night to bid her good night, but he broke the rules pretty often and he'd slip in sometimes during the day, just for a glimpse of her. She'd put her arms around his neck the first thing, and he'd hold her soft, and give her one of them tender kisses. Oh, it was lovely! It was a great love, I tell you. It was a love that was more than earthly love—it was heavenly.

She seemed better for a few days before she died, and they was all so hopeful again, and Mr. Clemens had gone out to look for another villa—one that would be more comfortable for her, and one night he felt so encouraged about Mrs. Clemens, after he'd seen her, that he went into the parlor and set down at the piano, just as he used to do in the old Hartford days, and begun singing them old negro Spirituals, the ones Mrs. Clemens loved so much. She heard him singing them, and it made her happy to have him do that again.

The night she died, there was some great doings going on at the church and I went out to them. It's what they call the Forty Hours' Adoration. A grand procession with boys carrying lighted candles and the priests going around to the different churches and then marching back to their own. I went round in that procession to all the different churches. I'd walked for miles that day, and I was dead beat, but when I got back to the house I went right up to the nurse and said, "How is Mrs. Clemens?" She said: "She is not so well, she's having a bad spell. I am going to give her some oxygen." I hurried to her room on the ground floor, to get it ready, and when she saw me she whispered: "Oh! I've been awful sick all the afternoon, Katy."

"Well," I says, "you'll be all right now." And I held her up, held her in my arms, and I was fanning her and then—then she fell right over on my shoulder. She died right then in my arms. She drew a little short breath, you know, just once, and was gone! She died so peaceful and a smile was on her face. I looked at her—and I knew that was the end. I knew she'd gone. I couldn't hear her breathe any more. I lay her back on the pillow and ran out to get the family. They had all been right around her only a few minutes before, and had left because the nurse thought it best for her to be alone.

Miss Clara was in the parlor and Mr. Clemens was in the dining-room, waiting. Oh! I don't know how I told them. I guess I didn't have to—they knew. They really felt that she was dying all that day. Clara told me afterward that she felt her mother was going to die that very day. She did not rouse up like she did some days.

They came into the room and oh, God! it was pitiful. Mr. Clemens ran right up to the bed and took her in his arms like he always did and held her for the longest time, and then he laid her back and he said, "How beautiful she is—how young and sweet—and look, she's smiling!"

It was a pitiful thing to see her there dead, and him looking at her. Oh, he cried all that time, and Clara and Jean, they put their arms around their father's neck and they cried, the three of them, as though their hearts would break. And then Clara and Jean, they took their father by the hand, one on each side, and led him away. Then the doctor came and we got her ready. I kept my promise, and put on her the dress she wanted, the beautiful lavender silk dress and the stockings and the little slippers that matched. I dressed Susy for her burial and I dressed Mrs. Clemens for hers, and then, later on, I dressed Jean. It fell to me to do it for her, too. But oh! we won't speak of that now. Mrs. Clemens looked so lovely lying there, so calm and fair after all her suffering. We laid her in the parlor, and Mr. Clemens walked back and forth all that long Sunday night from her bedroom to his. I come down to see how things was going with him and there he was walking up and down the floor. Up and down he was walking—not knowing what he was doing! And Clara! Oh! Clara, she was lying under the casket in a little heap, sobbing. I took her up in my arms and she says: "Oh, no. Let me lie here."

"No, Miss Clara. No," I says, "you've got to go to bed." And then she said, "Then I'll lie right here on this bed where mamma was." And she laid down on her mother's bed for a while to comfort herself.

Yes, Mr. Clemens walked all that night long and in the morning he was all used up. He was like a dead man. They took Mrs. Clemens then somewheres to a vault and put the coffin in it. I went with it. The family couldn't go, they was all so sick, so I went alone. I was so broken-hearted, and when I got off by myself and seen her laid in that vault, so still and all alone, I thought I should die, too. Then I began to think that we was coming home. That was the only consolation I had, that we would be in America in a little while.

Just at first Jean and Clara didn't want to go back; but Mr. Clemens says: "Yes, yes. I'm going home where I have friends I can talk to. Where I can see Howells and Gilder and Twitchell and Mr. Rogers—all those dear friends of mine. I'll have somebody to speak to. There's nobody here." He said, "Why, just the sight of a dog from home that I could lay my hand on and speak to now—would help me." He was so lonesome for his friends.

After Mrs. Clemens died we stayed for two weeks until the steamer was ready to sail. Mrs. Clemens' body was put on the steamer at Genoa. Mr. Clemens was terrible to see, but he kept up pretty good on that voyage, though he hardly spoke at all. I knew, though, that he was thinkin' about her—about Mrs. Clemens lying dead and still in the hold of the ship. But Miss Clara was terrible. The captain used to take her on the upper deck to sit there. I used to hate to have her out of my sight a moment. She was so broken-hearted she didn't want to live.

Well, we got to America somehow. Mr. Rogers' yacht came down to meet them with Mr. Rogers and Mr. Langdon, I think. Roosevelt was President then, and he sent word to the customs not to delay Mr. Clemens in any way, but just to pass him right through.

We went right up to Elmira as soon as we landed. The funeral was to be there, from the old Langdon house. There was an immense crowd there that day, 'cause everybody loved Mrs. Clemens. You couldn't see all around the yard, it was so crowded with people, and the services was in the great parlor there, where her body laid, and where she was married more than thirty years ago. Her coffin was right there in the very same place, where she had stood all them years before, as a happy young bride. Mr. Twitchell, who had married her then, he preached the funeral sermon, and Mr. Eastman said the prayers; and then they played "Nearer, My God, to Thee."

Mr. Clemens went to the cemetery, Woodlawn, and when he seen her coffin lowered down, then he made a great vow. He said standing there, that he'd never see another being that he loved lowered in the grave again.

When it was all over, Miss Clara gave a great cry and threw up her hands and her father caught her in his arms and held her. Her cry, it went through everybody. It hit everybody's heart. He didn't say a word. He just held her until the carriage came along and he put her in it, with Jean. Mr. Clemens was just like a dead person. It was all over and our lives was just broken in two. But by and by they had to try to begin life again.

We didn't stay very long in Elmira. We went right to Tyringham, in Massachusetts, after the funeral. We went there to be near the Gilders, and oh! it seemed kind of heavenly to get there with those lovely friends after them awful weeks of suffering. Mrs. Gilder was there and the children, Dorothea, Francesca, and Rosamond, and Mr. Gilder was there too—some of the time. He used to come up from New York every week; and Mr. Rodman Gilder, the son, he used to be there a lot, too. He was very nice. I liked him. He used to come and see Miss Clara and cheer her up. We stayed there all summer and Mr. Clemens got calmer, and went back and forth to New York and busied himself looking for a house for the winter. Miss Clara got sort of depressed while we was there, hearing just cow bells and country things, she couldn't stand it, so she came to New York and went to Dr. Parry's and stayed for a while till she got quieter, but I stayed on in Tyringham with Jean and Mr. Clemens.

Only one funny thing happened that summer. Dr. Parry told me about it. There was some gentleman in Stockbridge (that's right near Tyringham), and he had perfectly magnificent horses; and he was always driving over to ask Mr. Clemens to please take a ride to Stockbridge with him. He come every day to invite him, and finally Mr. Clemens couldn't stand it any longer, so he says to him, "My friend, I don't want to hurt your feelings but, to tell you the truth, I'd just as soon go to hell as go to Stockbridge!" He really didn't want to see people then—he didn't want to go anywheres those first months after Mrs. Clemens' death.

Yes, that was a pretty sad summer after Mrs. Clemens' death. We could never get even a little bit used to the idea that she was gone. It left a great hole in all our lives, and Mr. Clemens, he never got over it; and poor Jean and Clara, it would make your heart ache just to look at 'em! You see, a person like Mrs. Clemens, you keep on missin' more an' more, not less an' less. She'd been so wonderful to everybody all her life, so kind and loving and with so much common sense—always wantin' to help everybody, and so generous, too, with everything she had. There aren't so many people like that in the world, and it makes those that are left behind lonely—as if a great hole had come into your life that you'd fallen into, and never was going to get up again. That's the way we all felt after she'd gone.

There was only one bright spot, and that was being among friends again—that Mr. Clemens could be with his old friends and see and talk with them once more. Of course, I had a lot of time for settin' around and thinkin', and after that terrible break I used to think a lot about Mrs. Clemens, the things she'd done for me and for everybody; how she used to take charge of, and plan everything in the house, and how she used to—as they say—edit everything Mr. Clemens wrote. She was just like the foundation to a house, and now that one of the great props was gone, we had to turn around and fill it up somehow. Yes, Mrs. Clemens always had the management of everything in the old days. She made every plan—looked after everything, and Mr. Clemens always come first—and everything she did was perfect. Mr. Clemens never crossed her in any plan and never upset anything she did. You know, there is men that enjoy breaking up their wives' little plans, and bein' cross and fussy; but he warn't that way. When she told him anything she was going to do, he'd say, "All right, Livy, that's all right"—and he would be ready to do anything she said. If she ever did tell him not to do anything, he'd always say, very sweet and lovely, "Yes, Livy darling, yes." But of course she never did like to upset or cross him in anything. Whatever he wanted to do—no matter what it was, she always wanted him to do it.

There was a plumber in Hartford, one time, I remember, and she called out to Mr. Clemens when the plumber was in the room, "Youth, dear." And Mr. Clemens answered back, "Yes, Livy darling!" Now when this plumber heard that, why, he just was struck dumb! And he says to me afterwards in the kitchen:

"Well, I never! I never heard anything like that talking! I done work in a great many houses all my life, but I never heard a man and wife so loving to each other as Mr. and Mrs. Clemens. I guess they never holler at each other! From what I heard to-day, this place must be pretty near heaven!"

And this plumber kept repeating it over to himself, "Youth, dear," and "Livy, darling!" He kept saying them names over and over. He got them down fine, that plumber did. Then he asked me how long they'd been married and when I told him it was almost twenty years, why, he nearly fainted! "Well," he says, "I never seen such an ideal couple—never!"

Yes, the plumber was right, it was kind of heavenly, really, to see them smiling to each other every time they met, always with such nice manners. And the children was just the same. He was perfectly lovely with the children, Mr. Clemens was. It was kind of a Paradise, that house! There warn't never any quarreling of the children or their mother either. Of course, Mrs. Clemens made them mind, but she'd do it in such a gentle way. She would be very firm with them, but never cross. It was a wonderful place to live in—it was a little bit of heaven on earth!

I know I've said it a good many times, but it keeps coming back to me now it's all over—what a wonderful life I had with them; and my heart is just full of these things about her and always will be.

I guess everybody knows how Mrs. Clemens always edited all them stories of his. He used to bring every bit of his writing to her every night and lay it on a stand by her bed; and she always read it before she went to sleep; and whatever she cut out (swear words, she used to scratch out sometimes), he'd write it over again—always acted as if he'd never said them swear words. He liked it, if she liked it—even if it did make him write a little more—what she'd scratched out.

But, of course, Mr. Clemens' swearing really warn't like most people's cussing—it wasn't what you'd call *profane.* I heard somebody say once that his swear words just rolled off him like perspiration—it was part of the *way* he talked. Nobody that had any sense could take offense at it. I always liked to hear it myself, really, 'twas sort of lively and picturesque—and even Mrs. Clemens, although she didn't approve of it, really didn't mind it so much, way down in her heart, I know.

No, his swearing never seemed like other people's swearing, and that makes me think of a funny story about Jean and her father when Jean was a little girl. It seems Mr. Clemens was terrible mad one day; some man had done something mean and he was cussing very fierce and giving this man "down the banks." Mr. Clemens had little Jean by the hand, and he was walking back and forth in the living-room, just swearing all to himself as hard as he could. Jean had her little hand in his, trying to keep step with him, and looking up at him and hearing them words she'd never heard before, as she was trotting along beside him. She didn't know they was oaths, you know, didn't know what kind of language he was using, of course.

Well, soon after this I was out walking with her one day when a terrible rough-looking man come along, right in front of us, and he was swearing "to beat the band," and she says: "Oh, Katy! Did you hear that man?"

I said: "Oh, yes! I heard him."

"Oh," she says, "he's using awful language. He's swearing!"

"How do you *know* he's swearing?" I says.

"Oh, I know he is," says Jean, "and swearing's terrible!"

"Well," says I, "sometimes your father swears a little mite!"

"Oh, no, Katy!" says Jean. "No, no. Papa never swears."

"Why, yes," I says, "he did some swearing last Sunday in the living-room when you was walking back and forth with him."

But Jean says, very cross: "Oh, no Katy! No! You're mistaken. That wasn't swearing. That was only one of papa's *jokes!*"

So you see, it didn't seem like swearing to her, either; it just didn't seem like *real* swearing to Jean any more than it did to the rest of us, and she wanted me to think it was a joke, so I let her fool me—pretended to, anyway. I didn't say any more. I learned a little every day! But I didn't learn to swear, though, because

I could do that before I went to the Clemens household. I guess everybody has a few private cuss words of their own, to help them over the rough places.

So many things come back to me about the children and Mrs. Clemens, even now after all these years, and I can see Mrs. Clemens just as she used to look in the Hartford days when she was young.

I told you how I used to comb her hair and how beautiful it was and how I loved braiding it every night. She had such lovely eyes, too. They was blue and very clear, and something shone out of them that was different from anybody else. She always wore beautiful clothes, too, but she didn't care much for style herself. Madam Fogarty was a great dressmaker in New York and made all her clothes; she went to Paris once a year, you know, and made the loveliest things for Mrs. Clemens—always about a year in advance of the regular styles.

Yes, Mrs. Clemens always dressed in very nice clothes and pretty colors, too. Only once I remember when Mr. Clemens' mother died and he come back from the funeral, I think it was, Mrs. Clemens had a new dress on—a black dress—a kind of a mourning dress, you know, out of respect to his mother—and Mr. Clemens says:

"Oh, Livy," he says, "no, I don't like to see you dressed in black like that."

"But, Youth dear," she says, "I thought it would please you—on account of your mother."

"Well," he says, "Livy, it was very sweet of you to

Kellogg's, Hartford

Rev. Joe Twichell when he was the handsomest man in America except Joseph H. Choate.

(Courtesy Harper & Brothers)

CLARA CLEMENS GABRILOWITSCH

think of that, but even so I can't see you going around in mourning. Oh, no," he says, "I never want to see you in black clothes." He always hated black, and loved colors all his life.

Mrs. Clemens always wore her hair parted—combed down very smooth and nice, and twisted in a kind of figure eight in the back, and sometimes, in the early days, she wore her hair on the top of her head in a great big braid—right on the top of her head, just like a coronet. You'll see it like that in one of her pictures; and that's the way the Empress of Austria used to wear her hair, and she had beautiful hair, too—just like Mrs. Clemens. The only time Mrs. Clemens ever frizzed her hair, she was going to take part in some play—it was a Dickens play, and they was going as the different characters; and she was going as a very dressed-up lady. Then I says: "Oh, Mrs. Clemens! You can't go to that party with your hair flat and smooth—you ought to have it curled. I'll put it up in hairpins for you." At first she said no, she wouldn't do it, but I finally persuaded her. Well, it didn't seem to curl very good, so I said, "Well, I'll have to iron them curls." Oh, she thought it was the worst thing you could do to anybody, but she finally let me, on account of the play. Anyway, her hair curled nice and looked very pretty. And she had a light green satin dress to wear, all trimmed with white bugle beads. The beads was shiny, like crystal. Oh, it was a lovely dress! But she really never cared much for clothes or fixing herself up, and I don't know of her ever curling her hair but just that once. She never put powder nor cream on her face, either. She was just natural, and everything about her was lovely. She didn't have to fix herself up, the way most people do, to make a good appearance.

I remember Dr. Parry (she knew them in Vienna—she was a woman doctor, a great friend of theirs, and very nice) once said that Mrs. Clemens was the most ideal hostess she ever seen; that she always received a person as if they was the only one in the world—the most loved and honored guest. She'd do this to every single person—even at a big party when the place was crowded—and she'd do it from her heart, too, Dr. Parry said. Nothing put on, nothing pretended! She wasn't thinking of anything but just the person she was talking to. It made everybody happy where she was.

She said once that when she was first married, Mr. Clemens would sometimes be what was called kind of sacrilegious. He'd say hard, severe things about religion, and Mrs. Clemens, although she hated to have him talk that way, said she'd made up her mind when they first married, that her husband was going to be *free* to *say* anything and everything that he wanted to—no matter what it was; that he wasn't ever going to dread her criticizing him—there was never going to be any "curtain lectures" or nothing like that; that his home was going to be a place where he could say and do what he wanted. It struck me as kind of wonderful for her to think all that out when she was just a young wife. It showed how much she loved him and what a lot of common sense she had, and how she never believed in interfering with other people's rights—even if they was her husband's. It showed, I think, that she had a great deal of strength and a great deal of character, to be able to stand up to that, and she did live up to it, that promise she made herself, all her life. So Mr. Clemens was never afraid to say anything he wanted to—and there's very few married men that aren't nagged by their wives some time or other—and a good many of them most of the time!

I guess, perhaps, it was just because she was like this that Mr. Clemens always went to her for advice about everything.

And now I must tell you about the time he was asked to have some city named after him—some place out West, it was; and they wrote and wanted to know if they couldn't please use his name for that place. And I heard him talking to Mrs. Clemens about it and she was delighted and she says, "Oh, Youth dear, I think that's lovely! That's a great honor."

"Well, Livy," he says, "I don't know. I really don't think I'll let 'em do it. You see," he says, "I'm not dead yet, and they might name that place after me, and before I died I might (as likely as not) do something that they'd want to get my name off—I might kind of disgrace 'em—commit a murder or a robbery, or some little thing like that; so I guess I won't let 'em name that place after me—better not take any chances!" he says, laughing. Yes, I heard him say that very thing myself. So he didn't let them name the place after him. He had no conceit, you see, and this kind of proves it, don't it? But he did like compliments. It made him feel good when anybody paid him a real compliment. He was always tickled to death—like all great people. And he was always sayin' things as jokes that had a meaning underneath. He fooled lots of people that way. Why, I heard Mr. Clemens say one day that he couldn't bear to hear anybody talk but himself, but that he could listen to himself talk for hours and hours! Of course, this was one of his jokes, but like most jokes, I suppose there was considerable truth back of it, and I must say that anybody'd rather hear Mark Twain talk for hours than any other person in the world. I guess there was no good reason why he shouldn't realize this himself, as well as other folks.

Mr. Clemens had an awful funny way of speaking, too. He always drawled—drawled his words out. I never knew how he got it, but he used to talk that way always—all the time; but 'twas very interesting, and them pauses and drawls of his made a very deep impression when he talked—sort of emphasized the thing, as you might say—made you remember it better.

Why, I heard him tell once, that that drawl would find him out anywhere—even in the Desert of Sahara. He said even if he was to put on a green wig, and red spectacles, and lose all his front teeth and walk with a cane—as soon as they heard him speak and heard that drawl of his, they'd know who it was! There wouldn't be no escape then!

Of course, by this time I was beginning to understand and appreciate what an author was—that they was very important, and different from ordinary people—that is, if they was great authors. I remember when I was reading that book, *Jane Eyre,* that was written by that girl (Charlotte Brontë that I told you about, that was such a very famous writer), I said to Mrs. Clemens that time,

"Now, did that girl really write that book *herself,*" says I, "just out of her own head?" And when Mrs. Clemens told me that it was just her own writing, original, and that she did not have any help about it, I really couldn't make it out. In early days, when I first went to work for the Clemenses I was dreadful stupid, you see, because I didn't know that there was people who used to actually write books themselves. I thought they was just like the newspapers, you know, that these writers went out and picked up their little stories, just like reporters did, and fixed them up that way. I didn't know what an author really meant. I was so puzzled when I first heard that word "author." I told you, you know, the first time I seen Mr. Clemens, I didn't know he was an author—it didn't mean anything to me, but afterwards I found out. I found out a good many things. Mrs. Clemens was always teaching me things that helped me; and I certainly understood the value of manuscripts after I'd lived with the Clemens family awhile. When I'd been with the family twenty-five years, and knew about books, Mr. Clemens gave me a complete set of his books. I had every single one of them, and he's written a funny little thing in each one on the front page, which makes them very valuable.

I've told you so many stories that I'm forgetting all about Tyringham, but we spent the whole summer there. Mr. Clemens used to go over to Mr. Gilder's in the evenings and they'd sit and smoke and talk—right after Mrs. Clemens' death. And Mr. Clemens went down to New York a great deal—to try to take up the time, I guess. He used to go to the Colliers' very often, too. Oh, I remember the morning Mr. Gilder died—several years afterwards—right after Miss Clara's wedding, it was. Mr. Clemens felt terrible, and he said: "So Gilder is dead—dead. Isn't he a happy man! We'll all be that way pretty soon—we're going fast."

It made him very sad, Mr. Gilder's death. He was all broken up about it. Well, to go back to Tyringham: it was that fall the family decided to go to New York and take a house; so they rented that house at 21 Fifth Avenue. It was a nice big house with lots of rooms—funny windows in it, too; looked sort of like church windows. It was at the corner of Fifth Avenue and Ninth Street—it's still there, but it's turned into an apartment house now.

When they took that house, Clara begun working on it, too, she and her father. She began to select the things for it and that kind of got her mind off herself and her troubles. She picked out the wall paper and lots of things like that herself. She had a beautiful suite right on the corner of Fifth Avenue and Ninth Street—a great big sitting-room where her piano was and then her bedroom and bath off that. The sitting-room was really her music room and 'twas a lovely room—all lavender paper—a real lavender room. I never seen anything like that before—a lavender room—but 'twas very nice and everybody exclaimed over it. Yes, it was a lovely room—all lavender—lavender and gold; and she used to have lots of company in it—when she got well, later on.

Well, Mr. Clemens busied himself fussing with that house and Miss Jean and Miss Clara helped, too, although Miss Clara was still sick and going into a sanitarium for the winter where she could have perfect rest. Jean had an accident that fall in Tyringham—she was crazy about riding horseback, and she used to dash all about the country on very skittish horses; and she tumbled off her horse and scratched her face and did something to her collar bone, so that was kind of an upset, and she stayed up there in Tyringham for some time.

When they got the Fifth Avenue house I went to Hartford to bring down the furniture from the old house, the old Hartford house where we had all them happy, wonderful years together. When I begun to get the stuff out, and see all those things that had been put away so long, I just set right down there and cried! It brought it all back so—it brought Mrs. Clemens back, and I seemed to see her just as she used to be then, so lovely and gentle, moving around among them things—'twas just as if her loving ghost had come and stood by me that day while I was working there all alone.

Well, we got the New York house all fixed up good and put the old Hartford furniture in it. 'Twas a very handsome house, a real elegant residence for Mr. Clemens—everything very nice—just the kind of a place he ought to live in. So they settled down there and tried to call it home, and it was home, as much as any place could be with Mrs. Clemens gone.

Mr. Clemens, he didn't go out much that winter—everything was very quiet, but he seen a lot of his old friends. They was always there, trying to cheer him up, 'cause they knew it was a very sad time for him. And it really made it worse, because Miss Clara was in the sanitarium then. Of course, Mr. Clemens was writing all the time, and he was interested in all kinds of things that was going on in the world, and he got terrible mad about King Leopold of Belgium and some terrible things he'd done in the Congo—murdering all them innocent blacks for his own selfishness, to get more money, I suppose. "Greed! Terrible greed!" Mr. Clemens called it. Mr. Clemens was just raging about that, and he wrote a piece about that old king, tellin' how wicked he was, and that piece was printed all over. I guess you can read it in some magazine or in one of his books, but I'm not sure.

Well, that winter was got through somehow, and oh, I mustn't forget to tell you that Mr. Clemens wrote another book, but it was a little book—a little bit of a one—and it was called *Eve's Diary*—I think he begun that up in Tyringham—kind of started it there. And, oh, it was lovely! It was kind of a momento, I think, to Mrs. Clemens—at least that's the way I took it. The idea was, that where "Eve" was (meanin' Mrs. Clemens), that was heaven—and so it was, for all of us.

Well, when summer come along, they decided to go to Dublin, New Hampshire, in the mountains. A lot of their friends was there, and Mr. Clemens thought that would be nice and not so lonely. There was a good many people Mr. Clemens knew up there—some artists, and a gentleman by the name of Thayer—Abbott Thayer. He was a painter. Then there was another artist, too, by the name of Brush. They was both famous artists and Mr. Clemens liked them. And Mr. Higginson was there, too—Colonel Higginson, they called him—from Boston.

Well, Jean, she selected the house and we went up together in the dead of winter to look it over. Oh, my! That was a funny trip!

Mr. Clemens heard about this Copley house in Dublin; that it was for rent, but he said somebody must see it first—give it the "once over" before he rented it. This was in the winter and we was in New York, but he said,

"Katy, you'll have to go up and look at it anyway." Then Jean said she would go with me, and I thought it would be a good thing for her, so we started for Dublin in the dead of winter.

Mrs. Thayer, it seems, and the Brushes lived there all the year around, and they wrote Mr. Clemens there warn't no hotel there for us to go to, so Mrs. Brush said to come right to them; that she would send her sleigh to the station to meet us.

We got there a bitter cold night and drove nine or ten miles to the Brushes' house. They was all there to meet us and had a great roaring log fire and a nice hot supper all ready, and we were glad of it, for we were nearly frozen to death. We set around and talked to Mrs. Brush and after a while the children and the rest of the family sort of disappeared. There was no noise about the house, but everybody seemed to just fade away. Well, we went up to our rooms, Jean and me, and there was a big fire roaring in the fireplace up there. 'Twas awful warm and comfortable and Mrs. Brush had a lot of big blankets and comfortables piled on the beds to keep us warm. She set awhile and told us stories—how she'd been on that steamer, the *Quaker City*, where she first seen Mr. Clemens, when he was a very young man, and she was a maiden lady, and how Mr. Charles Langdon was on that ship, too (he was Mrs. Clemens' brother). Then the house got so quiet and everybody had disappeared so, I kept wondering where the family was, and come to find out, Mrs. Brush said that *nobody slept in the house!!* They all slept right outdoors—snow or no snow! They'd got great big sleeping blankets and went out into them snowdrifts, dug themselves a place—right out under the Heavens, and slept there! Just stuck themselves down in the snow and covered themselves up good with their blankets! Well—when I heard that! I thought they must all be crazy! It made me actually shiver—right there in that warm room.

The next morning, when we wanted to see that Copley house, they told us the road wasn't even broken through. The snowdrifts was ten feet high! Mr. Brush said it would cost thirty-five dollars maybe (or more) to break through a path to that house. He said we couldn't go to see it unless we went on snowshoes. Oh, Lord!

Well, that was a pretty to-do! I'd never seen a snowshoe myself, but Jean said she had—she could go on snowshoes—skiis, she called them—said she could go all by herself. But I said: "No, *I've* got to see that house. Your father wants me to." Jean said: "Oh, Katy! *You'll* never be able to walk on them snowshoes!" "Well," I says, "maybe not, but I'll try it anyway."

So one of the boys mounted me on them snowshoes (I had on leather moccasins—they wear those, too, you know) and he tied them snowshoes on me good and hard; and Jean got hers on, and we started for that old house. I was beginning to hate it by that time! Oh, I had a terrible time! I fell down twice! And then one of my snowshoes bust off, and we had to sit down in the snow and tie it on again—but somehow or other we got there. I don't see now how we ever did it. It was a terrible task.

We went all over the house, found out everything about it. It was nicely furnished and very comfortable. Nobody had lived in it yet. I thought Mr. Clemens would like it maybe, and he did when I told him about it. So he took it. He was awful glad, he said, that I'd seen that house before he rented it, because then we had some chance then of knowing *what* we was getting, for once!

We moved up there that summer, but it didn't turn out very good, after all. He really didn't like it; it was too lonesome for him. That was where he done the first swearing he'd done since Mrs. Clemens died! And I couldn't blame him much, 'cause I was so darned lonesome myself! I didn't know what to do with myself, neither.

I'll tell you about this time he swore so, 'cause you couldn't help laughing, although it was very sad, too.

You see, Mr. Clemens had promised one time that he wasn't never going to swear any more! And I was so surprised, I says, "Really, Mr. Clemens?"

"No," he says, "never again—that is unless something perfectly *awful* happens, that I just can't get along *without* swearing!"

"Well," I said, "that's a good idea, and now we'll see how long you'll keep to it," I says.

Well, after we come from Florence, for over a year he never used one cuss word until we struck Dublin. One day I was sittin' in my room—which was down the hall from his room where he wrote, when I heard—

"Well! damn this house! Damned old place! Damned old climate! Damnedest room! Not a damn thing here that anybody wants! Can't even find a single pin in the whole place!"

He was walking up and down, swearing to "beat the band!" He was looking for pins, you see, to pin his manuscripts; and he walked right down the hall, talking all the time, saying: "You can never find a thing in this damned old place! Why, I had a new paper of pins only yesterday, and now some old idiot has come and took all my pins away!"

Of course, I was settin' right there with the door open and heard every word, and I was really enjoying myself, I can tell you, 'cause I hated the place as much as he did.

Well, he come down the hall, and when he seen me settin' there, he was kind of startled and he looked a little sheepish. "Why, Katy!" he says. "Are you here?"

"Yes," I says, "I've been here all the time."

"Oh," he says, "I didn't know you was anywheres around."

"No, I know you didn't," I says, "because you've been

swearing to 'beat the band.' I heard every word you said."

"Well," he says, "I have been swearing. There's no mistake about that, but this is the very *first* time I swore since I left Florence."

"Yes, Mr. Clemens," I says, "I know it; but honest, to tell the truth, I was kind of amused," says I, "listenin' to you. I didn't mind it a bit. Bad language is the only thing can take the deadness off *this* place," I says. "It's awful! It would make *anybody* swear!"

"Would it make *you*, Katy?" said Mr. Clemens.

"Yes," I said, "it would, so I don't mind how much you swear. It's *all right!* Go ahead!"

He was kind of relieved, I guess, to know that I felt just as he did. He used to say he could turn the air black and blue and thick with cuss words when he started out! But he certainly was startled that day he seen me settin' there while he was doing all that cussing. He said it made him feel pretty bad and guilty.

Of course, the thing that brought it about was losing his pins. He was very particular about his pins; he never had any of the right things to hold his manuscripts together, so he always depended on pins and never had enough. I got him his pins, of course, after all his fussing; then he calmed down and was quiet as a lamb. But I never liked that place myself—couldn't stand it; and I cleared out back to New York as soon as I could. Jean didn't seem to mind it so much. She used to go horseback-riding every morning and enjoyed herself. There was lots of people up there, but I don't remember them now. They was all alike—all literary people, but that didn't make up for the lonesomeness. If there had only been a dance hall or something lively like that—or maybe even a little bit of moonshine to stir them up! But, oh! that whole country was so quiet! Everybody was always working—I mean writing or painting. It was dull, I tell you, dull!

And another mean thing that happened was that none of the servants had rubber heels to their shoes, so they spoiled Mr. Copley's nice varnished floors—scratched them all up with their heels; and of course Mr. Clemens had to pay for it. They stuck him an enormous price—I don't know the sum, but it was a big check he sent, and he was pretty mad at the time.

No, that summer in Dublin warn't much of a success. The country was pretty enough, but you can't live on country! There was a beautiful lake there and the houses was built so they could look on that lake. It was seven miles round it, and we used to walk around it nearly every night. There wasn't anything else to do! I suppose that was amusement enough for people that's literary. But it wasn't enough for me!

I think 'twas that summer Mr. Clemens wrote that story *A Horse's Tale* that I told you about, and I heard that the actress, Mrs. Fiske, had something to do with it. She was interested in some society against cruelty to animals—or something like that—and she was raging about that, too; and I guess she wrote Mr. Clemens, asking if he wouldn't do something to help her, because she knew that anything he wrote would make a great stir and be read by everybody. Yes, I think that's the way it happened. She sort of started him off, Mrs. Fiske did. Anyway he wrote that story, and it was wonderful! And it was printed in a little book. Mr. Clemens gave me a copy himself, and wrote my name on the flyleaf. Mrs. Fiske was very grateful to him, and wrote him a nice letter of thanks herself, I heard.

After that summer we went back to New York, 21 Fifth Avenue, and it began to be kind of pleasant and gay for Mr. Clemens again, because everybody was chasin' after him again more than ever. He begun to speak at dinners and all them clubs was after him, and everything that happened in the country, people was asking Mr. Clemens to have a finger in the pie. Of course he was writing all the time, and he used to do most of his writing in bed. Everybody knows that.

About this time he got started off on wearing white clothes. That made a terrible sensation, as everybody knows. I'll tell you more later on; how he went to the White House to visit in them. And I mustn't forget about an elegant birthday dinner that was got up for him. It was his seventieth birthday. Colonel Harvey fixed that up. He was a great friend of Mr. Clemens and admired him very much, and all those famous literary

© *Underwood & Underwood, N. Y.*

ONE OF MARK TWAIN'S FAVORITE COMPANIONS
(Courtesy Harper & Brothers)

Brown Brothers, N. Y.

WILLIAM GILLETTE

ON THE PORCH OF LAURENCE HUTTON'S COTTAGE, ONTEORA PARK, CATSKILL MTS.

JAMES W. DODGE MARK TWAIN LAURENCE HUTTON

(Courtesy Mrs. Ossip Gabrilowitsch)

gentlemen thought it would be a fine thing to have this great dinner and show their appreciation of Mr. Clemens. They was to have it in Delmonico's and sent out invitations to every famous writer in America, and a lot that was in Europe, too. A great many people come—everybody that was invited—and they had a wonderful time. Of course there was lots of ladies present—lady writers—and everybody made speeches and read poems and made toasts—they called them—to Mr. Clemens for his seventieth birthday. He made a perfectly wonderful speech in reply to all these compliments, and they said it was terrible funny, and it made them laugh a lot; and then just at the end it made them cry, too, because it was very sad—all that part where he told about being seventy years old—"hitching up to Pier No. 70," he said. Everybody there all got up on their feet and cheered him and drank to his health (they was able to do that in them days, without being poisoned or going to jail for it!), and they made a toast to him and said how much they loved him. Mr. Gilder, he was there, and Mr. Howells, of course, and Brander Matthews and Carnegie, and—oh, everybody that amounted to anything. And Mr. Rogers, Dr. Rice, Dr. Quintard, and Mr. Twitchell, of course. I can't think of any more, except that Mrs. Riggs—she was a writer and wrote by the name of Kate Douglas Wiggins—she was there, too. I've got a photograph of the people that was there.

They sent an invitation to Kipling, too, over in London, I heard; and Helen Keller, she wrote a letter to Mr. Clemens, congratulating him on his birthday. That pleased him very much.

Well, of course this dinner made a great stir and everybody was chasing after him harder than ever. Nobody could believe Mr. Clemens was seventy years old, because he was so young in all his ways. Why, he used to run upstairs three steps at a time. There was no old age around Mr. Clemens. You couldn't never think of him as old. He didn't look or act old, and he never was, either. Right up to the day of his death he was young. He was young in his mind as well as his heart.

Speaking of Helen Keller, I must tell you about how Mr. Clemens got interested in her, how it was really through him that Mr. Rogers helped pay for her education. You know, Helen Keller was a perfectly wonderful girl and she was deaf, dumb, and blind, but she was so smart she learned to do everything, just like other people. She learned by the hand—or whatever it is that they learn them by—and she had a wonderful teacher—a Miss Sullivan, that was with her every minute and taught her everything. Why, she even went through college and took a degree! Mr. Clemens, he seen her first when she was only fourteen years old. It was at dinner and she laughed at everything Mr. Clemens told. She set at the table and Miss Sullivan with her and held her hand all the time. She told her everything by hand, you know; and she understood everything that was going on and enjoyed the jokes that Mr. Clemens made. Oh, it was wonderful how bright and smart she was! Mr. Clemens, he just loved her, and she loved him. And he could talk to her, too, by just putting his hand on the top of her head, and then he'd talk and joke and she understood it just the same as if she could hear and see. That don't seem hardly possible, does it? But it's true. Mr. Clemens enjoyed her very much, and was greatly interested in her case. He said it was wonderful—and that everything ought to be made easy for her and her teacher, so they needn't never worry about money, and he wanted a fund raised so's she could be educated; and Mr. Rogers, he arranged that; and the Huttons, they was interested in it, too. I guess it was at the Huttons' that Mr. Clemens first heard of Helen Keller.

You know, Mr. Hutton was a great friend of Mr. Clemens; he was a writer, too; and there's lots of funny stories about them—for they was often together—and enjoyed each other. Laurence Hutton was his name. He was a tall, nice, slim man, red hair and red mustache—a nice pleasant-looking man. He had a severe black eye. He married after we knew him, and he used to bring his wife up to see us, too. She wasn't the kind of a woman that you'd think such a writer as he would select. I can't seem to remember anything that you'd specially admire her for. But he married her, anyway—quite late in life. Mr. Clemens liked them both, though, very much, so I think she must have been very interesting, too.

But Mr. Clemens warn't the only one that was able to play jokes in them days. His friends was always trying to play them on him, too, though of course none of them was as smart as he was. There is an awful funny story about an April Fool joke that was played on him once. I heard it was Laurence Hutton that done that, too, but I'm not sure. No, I think it was Cable—for he liked to get a rise out of Mr. Clemens. But it don't matter who it was—it was one of his old friends. Well, this man, he wrote a letter. Oh, to lots and lots of people, everybody that Mark Twain knew in Boston, New York, and Hartford, and all over, for them all to be sure and write him a nice letter on April Fool's day *asking for his autograph* and to be sure *not* to enclose any stamped envelope to return it in!

Now you see, it used to make Mr. Clemens terrible mad when people wrote for his autograph and didn't enclose an addressed envelope. He really didn't mind giving them his autograph, you know, but he'd go on a regular rampage if he had to stop and address an envelope. He used to swear "to beat the band" when he'd get them letters for autographs without any stamped envelope. Well, April Fool morning there was about seventy-five letters in the hall for him to open—asking for his autograph! As I said, he didn't mind giving his autograph, if they'd only send an *addressed* envelope, 'cause then all he'd have to do was put in a little slip of paper with his name on it, as he always kept his autograph *ready*. "Mark Twain"—he had that written on a slip of paper all ready to send—always had a lot on hand. Well, when them seventy-five letters was brought up April Fool morning and he seen they was all asking for his autograph, with no addressed envelopes, he got furious; told George to throw them all away. He says: "George, you can throw them all away, I don't care a damn! But I won't open any more of them damned things!"

So Mrs. Clemens said: "Oh, I think you had better open a few more of them, Youth dear, 'cause there might be some there that you'd regret not sending your autograph to." I guess she was kind of on to the joke. After that Mr. Clemens suspected that one of his friends must be at the bottom of it, and so he just sat down and wrote him a very sassy letter, telling what he thought of him, I suppose. Of course, that must have tickled Mr. Cable—if he was the one—getting a rise out of Mr. Clemens like that, 'cause he didn't often do it; and it amused Mrs. Clemens, too, I guess.

Now I must go on and tell you about the swapping of the coats. One night it seems that Mr. Aldrich—T. B. Aldrich, he was that famous literary man—and a great friend, well, he come to dinner and then he and Mr. Clemens wanted to play billiards. It was kind of warm up in the Billiard Room, I suppose, 'cause he took off his dress coat, it seems, and laid it on a chair, and Mr. Clemens he did the same—took off his coat too. Well, the next day Mr. Aldrich wrote Mr. Clemens, saying he'd left his glasses the night before—and would somebody please look around and find them, 'cause of course they was valuable to him.

Oh, we looked high and low, but couldn't find them glasses anywheres! It went on for quite a while, his asking about them, and we hunting for them, but we never found them. Well, the next time Mr. Clemens was going out to dinner and put his dinner coat on, he couldn't understand why the sleeves was so *long!* Why, they hung way over his hands! He got terrible upset and excited, and called George and says, "How in hell does it happen that these sleeves got so *long* to my dress coat, all of a sudden?"

Well, George he examined the coat very carefully and says he couldn't understand it neither. "Well," says Mr. Clemens, "you take that coat to the tailor's the first thing in the morning, and just get them sleeves shortened. Cut them off," he says—and he turned up the cuff to show how much to cut off. So George did take the coat and had 'em cut off, and then brought it to me, 'cause I had to see every time Mr. Clemens put the coat on, that he had a handkerchief in his pocket—not two or three, like he would if I didn't look. Well, I put my hand in the pocket of that coat, and instead of a handkerchief, there was a *spectacle case!* I pulled it out, and there was Mr. Aldrich's glasses that he'd lost! So that was Mr. Aldrich's coat, that's what it was! They'd mixed them up the night they was playing billiards and Mr. Aldrich had took Mr. Clemens' coat and Mr. Clemens had taken Aldrich's coat, and we never found it out until them glasses was found! Now, it seems the same thing happened to Mr. Aldrich that struck Mr. Clemens. When Aldrich put on his coat, he'd found the sleeves was too *short*—his arms stuck way out! He had to go and have a piece put *on* his cuffs to lengthen them—just the same as Mr. Clemens done, when he had a piece taken *off* to make his *shorter!* Oh! When Mr. Clemens found it out, how he roared! Everybody roared, and Mr. Clemens and Mr. Aldrich had spasms over it, and swapped stories—how Aldrich had to have a piece put *on* his coat, and Mr. Clemens having had a piece chopped *off* his! It was a terrible mix-up, and of course both them coats was spoiled, but anyway, they took it as a great joke. I enjoyed it myself, too, because I had hunted every place in the house for those old glasses. So I was kind of in on it, and I must say I enjoyed finding them after all the fuss. Of course this was back in the old days, as I call them. That didn't happen at 21 Fifth Avenue.

But there was never any let-up to the funny things that was happening, and the people that came to see Mr. Clemens about everything under the sun. The Fifth Avenue house was a kind of pilgrimage for people—just as the old Tenth Street house used to be; and that makes me think of the story about Mrs. Stanchfield and Mr. Clemens' picture. It's that beautiful picture done by that great painter—Spiridon, and I've got a copy of the original and I'll tell you how I got it. It was when we was living in Riverdale and Mrs. Stanchfield was visiting there. She's the one that first told Mrs. Clemens about me—got me my position, you know. Well, she seen the copy of that picture, and she said to Mr. Clemens: "Oh, how I'd love to have that picture! It's beautiful!"

"Well," says Mr. Clemens, "you can have it."

So he gave it to her then and there. It was hanging on the door, going into the study, and he told me to give it to her then. But when she went back home to Elmira, it seems she didn't take the picture with her. Maybe she forgot it, or something; anyway, she didn't take it; and when we left Riverdale for good, there was the picture still hanging on the door! So I says to myself: "Well, I'd like that picture, I'd love it. That lovely picture ain't going to be left hanging there, not if I can help it. As long as Mrs. Stanchfield didn't take it or send for it, of course she don't want it. I'll just keep it myself—that's what I'll do." So I put it in the bottom of my trunk and took it off to Europe with me and all over, and then I brought it back home again. When we got back—although I suppose it warn't exactly mine, I still claimed it. My room was next to Jean's and there was a door between with a curtain over it and I hung the picture there. I was secret about it—I didn't want to steal it exactly, but still I couldn't bear to give it up! And I thought I'd had it so many years, it was mine by right, anyway.

But finally one day Mrs. Stanchfield come there again and she called me in and Mr. Clemens says: "Katy, Mrs. Stanchfield has just asked me if I know anything about that picture of mine that I gave her several years ago when we was up in Riverdale. Do you remember it?"

Oh, my heart sank at that! But I says, "Yes, Mr. Clemens, I remember it very well."

"Do you know anything about it?" he says. "Do you know where it is?"

Then I kind of looked at him and says: "Yes, Mr. Clemens, you know that I know where it is, because I know you have seen it yourself hanging on the door under the curtain. But I now claim that picture as my own. Mrs. Stanchfield didn't take it when you gave it to her, and never even sent for it, so," I says, "I took it for myself."

Oh, Mrs. Stanchfield felt terrible then, and said she didn't forget it exactly; she didn't know how it happened, but maybe she was a little careless about it. "But anyway," she says, "you know Mr. Clemens gave me that picture, and I certainly should feel terrible if I couldn't have it now—although this is all my fault."

Well, there warn't nothing more to be said, so I just went and took the picture off the door and brought it down to her. And when I done that, Mr. Clemens he gave me a very funny look, you know. He knew—well—of course he knew—he understood about it—and he was on my side, too, I'll bet. So I handed it to her and says, "Well, I'll give it to you, Mrs. Stanchfield, but I'm sorry that I have to give it up, because I love it more than you do!" Of course, Mr. Clemens didn't say a word then, he kept very quiet; but Mrs. Stanchfield was delighted, and she took it away with her pretty quick that time. 'Twarn't long after that that Mr. Clemens wrote to the photographer's where they was made (struck off) and had a picture done for me, special—and gave it to me.

"There, Katy," he says, "that's yours." And he wrote his autograph on it—"so's nobody can ever take it away from you, Katy," he says. "I felt bad for you that day Mrs. Stanchfield come and took that picture away. I didn't think you cared so much for it," he says, "but now here's one all your own."

Oh, I was delighted to get it, and he was delighted to have me have it. He looked for somewheres to put his autograph that would show good and plain, because the picture was kind of dark, you know, and he looked it all over and then he says, "There, Katy, there's a good place, right here, right on my white hair, so's every one can see it and know it's yours!" So he wrote his autograph right there on his hair over his right ear—and I've got that picture now and treasure it very much—and maybe all the more on account of the time I had gettin' it.

Well, to go back to the Fifth Avenue house: Mr. Clemens, he liked the house at 21 Fifth Avenue, but they had a good deal of trouble about the heat one time, and he was writing letters to the landlord every day, how he had to stay in bed, 'cause the house was so cold.

Mr. Clemens used to have bronchitis a great deal, 'cause he was very careless. I tried to take good care of him, for we was always afraid of pneumonia. When he'd show signs of a cold coming on, I'd say: "Now, Mr. Clemens, you're getting a cold. You go right upstairs and take a foot bath—a very hot one (I'll get it ready) and take some whisky, too." (For of course whisky was the main thing!) Well, one night he had a very bad bronchitis, so I fixed a mustard foot bath for him and it was pretty hot. "Pretty damned hot," he said, "but never mind. I suppose I've got to suffer!" he said.

Well, I got it all ready, and he put his feet into it and I covered him up good with blankets, and give him the whisky so he wouldn't feel the heat too much. Then he got into bed, and after that, of course, I went in to put out the lights. Sometimes he'd call out to me just as I was leaving the room, "Katy, did you take that bottle with you—that whisky bottle?" "Why, no!" I'd say. "No, Mr. Clemens, I put it down on the floor!"

"Now what did you do *that* for?" he'd say. "So's

I'd have a hard time to reach for it? Put it on the table, Katy, where it belongs."

Well, that night I fixed the mustard foot bath. I was very anxious about him 'cause he had a terrible cold, so I went back in about half an hour to see if everything was all right, and oh, my! I opened the door, and there he was settin' right by the window, the window open a little too, his feet up on a chair, smoking just as hard as he could! I nearly fainted! "Oh, Mr. Clemens," I says, "what are you doing?"

"Well, what *am* I doing?" he said.

"Oh," I says, "you're doing just the thing you shouldn't. You'll have pneumonia in the morning."

"Well, of course I don't want pneumonia," he says, "but after all that whisky and mustard foot bath you gave me, did you think I was going to stay in bed and smother?"

Of course he grumbled and fussed, but he went back to bed. In the morning Mr. Rogers he come in to see him. He used to stop in every morning on his way down to business. "Old Hank," Mr. Clemens used to call him. I told Mr. Rogers just how Mr. Clemens had been acting, so he went right upstairs and gave Mr. Clemens a good, hard scolding, I guess; and Mr. Clemens promised he would never do such a thing again. But he made up a terrible yarn about me to "Old Hank" as he called him, saying how I made him put his feet in the hot water in the tub and then, when he was helpless there, I just poured more hot water and mustard right down his knees while he was sittin' there. "That's damned nice treatment to give a poor, sick man!" he said. And he pretended he was mad at me, but of course I knew that was only a joke. I never minded anything he said, 'cause he was always lovely to me about everything, really.

It was while we was living at 21 Fifth Avenue and he was having one of these bad colds that he was trying to get some real Scotch whisky. The whisky we had didn't satisfy him—it warn't very good, and so he happened to think that Andrew Carnegie (being Scotch, I suppose) would have some real good Scotch whisky. So he told me to telephone Mr. Carnegie right away and ask him to send down two good bottles of whisky—of the very best, and to send it in a hurry, too; to get it there before six o'clock that evening, and if he didn't get a move on he'd give him "down the banks"! Something he'd never forget!

Well, I telephoned and the butler at Carnegie's, when he heard what Mr. Clemens said, he was startled and says: "You wait a minute. I want Mr. Carnegie to take this message because coming from Mr. Clemens, he'll understand it better than I do." So Mr. Carnegie, he came trotting right up to the telephone himself and then I repeated all Mr. Clemens said about wanting that whisky. Well, Carnegie, he roared so he almost dropped the receiver; he laughed so loud he could hardly answer me—but he said he'd send it down quick. So old Carnegie, he got them two bottles of whisky there right away—sent them by a messenger boy, and the next week he sent a case of whisky—and then he sent a *barrel* of whisky down to him! Nothing mean about Andrew Carnegie! Then Carnegie came down himself to see Mr. Clemens the morning after he sent the barrel of whisky. I opened the door for him and let him in, and he asked if I was the one that telephoned for the first two bottles. "Yes," I says, "I am; and Mr. Clemens received your barrel of whisky this morning, and he's very glad of it," I says. And Mr. Carnegie, he laughed again, fit to kill himself, and he said, "Well, now, I hope that *barrel* of whisky will keep his mouth shut, at last!" —which was Carnegie's joke.

Of course the whisky was put on tap and it was certainly good! I sampled it myself! It was perfectly delicious, really. "Mellow as honey," Mr. Clemens said, and made a terrible fuss over it.

Mr. Carnegie and Mr. Clemens was always great friends. Carnegie, he was a short thick-set man with whiskers—kind of dry-looking, he was; rather a large, round nose. But he struck me as being very kind and smart and I'm sure he was—he proved it by sending the barrel of whisky. That was kind, wasn't it? I can't think of anything kinder! Well, we finished all that whisky. It was all gone by the time we moved away from the Fifth

Avenue house—the barrel was empty when we went to Redding to live the next year—not a nip left.

Yes, while we was living at Fifth Avenue, Mr. Clemens begun wearing them white clothes I told you about. He always hated black clothes. He used to say that when a man got to be seventy, he was old enough to do what he wanted; so he said he'd wear white. He used to wear white clothes every summer—always wore white linen clothes up on Quarry Farm, but he made up his mind, when he was seventy he could do as he darned pleased and nobody would dare say anything to him. So he was going to wear white for the rest of his life. And what he meant by white was, *everything* white—shoes, stockings, cravats, hats, everything! So he gave the order to his tailor to make him fourteen suits of white clothes, and I guess he ordered about a hundred ties—the way he'd want most things ordered. Why, if we was out of matches even, he'd say, "Now, Katy, go and order a *hundred* boxes of matches sent up here." He always ordered things by the hundred—but he was content with fourteen suits of clothes, though! He said that would be seven for each week—seven at the cleaners and seven fresh ones at home.

Clara thought it was awful when he first started it, and when he ordered a *dress suit* made all in white, she was scandalized! He ordered a purple coat, too—sort of a cape like the sailors wear—all lined with white, to wrap around him when he was cold.

Well, when that dress suit come home, Clara said, "Father, do you ever expect to wear that to a *real* dinner?" "Yes," he says, "that's what it's made for." She says, "Well, you never can go out to a real dinner party with a white dress suit on." "Well," he says, "you'll see. I can go anywhere in it."

He used to go, in the beginning of the summer, and sit on the steps at 21 Fifth Avenue for a little while, in his clean white suit, white shoes, and everything spotless, and he'd have a nice straw hat on his head, too. Then when he'd see one of the busses coming along, he'd just run out and stop it and climb on top and ride to the end of the route to get the fresh air. Everybody used to look at him on top of the bus, but he didn't mind that. He was so used to it. He was a great admirer of Grover Cleveland. It was at the time Mr. Cleveland ran for President that Mr. Clemens turned "Mugwump."

I don't know anything about politics, but I know George, the butler, was terrible upset about this, 'cause he was a Republican, and it made him feel very bad to think Mr. Clemens was going to vote for Cleveland (a Democrat)—and influencing all his friends to vote for him, too. But Mr. Clemens did. He worked hard for Cleveland. He thought he was a great man. He used to go to the White House quite often to visit Mr. Cleveland, and he admired Mrs. Cleveland very much, too. She was very charming, they said, and there was a funny story about his going there for a dinner, and Mrs.

Fred T. Loomis, Elmira, N. Y.

KATY LEARY AS SHE LOOKS NOW
(Spiridon portrait of Mark Twain shows behind Katy Leary)

Brown Brothers, N. Y.

HENRY H. ROGERS

Clemens couldn't go with him that time. She was so afraid he might make some mistake, or forget something, or be careless about what he was wearing, as he generally was, that she put a little note in his pocket—wrote it on a card, I think—saying to be sure not to wear his rubbers to the dinner party. Sometimes he was forgetful, you know, and he'd always forget to take off his rubbers when he had them on. Well! When he found that card, he thought it would be a good joke to have Mrs. Cleveland write on it that he *didn't* wear them rubbers! So she kinder fell in with the joke, and wrote on the card, and they mailed it back to Mrs. Clemens, together, for fun—and a souvenir—I suppose.

Mr. Clemens was always forgetting and doing funny things about his clothes. There was another story about his going to call on some elegant lady one time and he was in kind of a hurry, I guess, and perhaps none of the family seen him before he started. At any rate, he come back from the call very pleased and happy, but when Mrs. Clemens seen him coming in, she says:

"Oh, Youth dear, what have you done!"

And he says, "Why, I don't know, Livy. What *have* I done?"

"Why," she says, "do you know that you've gone out without your necktie? That you've called on that lady, without putting on your cravat?" she says. "Oh, Youth, dear! How could you!"

Well, poor Mr. Clemens, he was just struck dumb!

He put his hand up to his collar, and sure enough—he didn't have his necktie on! So he went right upstairs and fixed up a nice cravat in a little package, and he gave it to George with a note to send over to the lady, and the note said: "Dear Madam: This will complete my call"—meaning the cravat, you see! That always struck me as a very funny thing to happen.

Everything Mr. Clemens did or said always attracted a great deal of attention. I remember Father Hardy said to me one time (when we was living in Hartford years before) after Mr. Clemens wrote *A Yankee at King Arthur's Court*—well, Father Hardy said: "Why, how can you work for such a man as Mark Twain! Why, he's just the biggest atheist," he called it, "that ever was, and he's written an awful book."

I says, "Father Hardy, have you read that book?"

"No," he says, "I haven't, but I've heard enough about it."

"Well," I said, "I'll get it and let you read it, and I'll explain it to you, if you don't know what it means."

Then Father Hardy said, "The way he's written up the Catholic religion is something terrible!"

"Why," I said, "he doesn't say any more about the the Catholic religion than any other. When he wrote that book he was trying to put down 'higher authority,' so one man was just about as good as another. He said the low man (as he called it) was just as good in the sight of God as the King." And I says: "Don't you know about them pictures—the low man being kicked out by the priest, the priest being kicked out by the bishop, and the bishop being kicked out by the cardinal and the cardinal being kicked out by the Pope. All kicking and pushing each other out to see who could be the highest. Well," I says, "he put the low man on one scale and the King on the other, and they was found just about equal. One didn't weigh any more than the other. So Mr. Clemens, he wanted to make the world see it that way—that one would be as good as the other if their hearts was all right. That was the idea he had in mind, I guess, when he wrote that book," I says. "And you haven't read that, or if you have, you read it without understanding."

Well, of course that book was criticized very much, and the Catholics criticized it more than anybody else—but it was sold all over in spite of that, and brought in lots of money. Mrs. Clemens explained it to me herself, and said some parts was very funny. It was what you call a "fairy story" with the meaning underneath. Mr. Clemens said that he could never go to Europe again after writing that book where he told that the man that worked in the fields was just as good, if not better than the King; that one man was about as good as another, if his heart was all right; he was made of the same flesh and blood. But after all was said and done, everybody read the book and liked it, and all the talk didn't amount to a row of pins.

I think I told you that Mr. Clemens didn't have such a very high opinion of Man. He always said we don't any of us make our own traits; we kind of *inherit* them—we really don't have anything to do about it ourselves. He used to say God (or something that means God, to most people) gave us all our good qualities in the beginning; we inherited all we had; the only difference was that some get *more* than others at the start, and it was sort of foolish, I guess he thought, to praise or blame folks for things they done. He was always talking about it and wrote an article on that subject once. It was called, "What Is Man?" It was very deep and created quite a stir. He had it published, sort of private, a long while after he'd written it. Of course, that's a pretty deep subject, and I guess everybody's got to thrash it out for themselves. It's pretty hard to make up your mind why things are the way they are! The more you think about it, the harder it is to know what you believe, 'cause one thing contradicts another. Sometimes it all seems just like an accident, things come out so queer—the sad and the funny get all mixed up and it's hard to tell what it's all about anyway. But I guess if Mr. Clemens couldn't figure it out clear and good for himself, 'tain't much use for me to try.

Speaking of funny things and how people feel differently about things, I guess I'd better tell the story about Gorky—that Russian writer. He come to this country with a friend, a man who was kind of a press agent for him. He had a terrible jaw-breaking name—I can't remember it and couldn't spell it if I did! Anyway, this man was what's called a Revolutionist. He come on some kind of a mission with Gorky, to raise money for Russia (if they could). Well, it made quite a stir. There was a lot about it in the newspapers, 'cause this Gorky, it seems, was a well-known writer—very gloomy, his stories was, but good. I never read any of them, of course, but I used to hear the family talk about them.

Well, Mr. Clemens and Mr. Howells, I think it was, called on Gorky—he being such a famous writer—and was going to get up a grand literary dinner for him and invite all the famous writers in this country when—my goodness! If a piece didn't come out in the paper that very day how Gorky was put out of the hotel for being with that woman he brought to America with him! It seems she warn't really his wife. She was an actress. She was all right in Russia—I mean they didn't care nothing about her living with Gorky there, because she was a kind of a leader, too—a Revolutionist, I guess. But that didn't go down in this country. Nothing like that in America—that is, if it's found out. And so they all dropped Gorky like a hot cake!

Well, Mr. Clemens, when he heard about the dinner they was going to give Gorky (they wanted him to be kind of head of it) he got very enthusiastic and ran all around trying to fix things so as to give him a royal time. They was going to give Gorky a grand spree, but the newspapers just put the kibosh on it. He did the wrong thing when he come to this country with some one that warn't his wife. So he went right back—and pretty quiet, he was, too! I used to hear an awful lot about it, 'cause the reporters was dashing up to the house all that day to see Mr. Clemens. I don't remember all Mr. Clemens said, except that I do remember he said Gorky made a big mistake. I felt kind of sorry for him myself. It was pretty rough on him, 'cause of course he didn't understand our customs over here. I guess he must have been pretty surprised, too. Well, America got *pious,* all at once! I heard some one say once that "morality" was just "geography"—and I guess there's something in it, when you come to think it over. Anyway, Gorky had to pay for his little mistake—like the rest of us do.

It was that winter that Mr. Clemens give a wonderful lecture at Carnegie Hall. It was to be his very last lecture, too. He warn't ever going to speak again on the platform after that, he said, and of course, when people heard it was to be the last one, why Carnegie Hall was just sold out. It was packed jam-full. I went to that lecture, and it was just thrilling to see all them people. Why, that great audience just stood right up on its feet when Mr. Clemens walked on to the platform—and they roared and shouted and waved their handkerchiefs just to welcome him. They couldn't shout loud enough to show what they thought of him. I don't remember all the lecture, but he told lots of funny stories and people laughed and laughed—and cried sometimes—and they was all as quiet as mice, too, so's not to miss one single word he said. Oh, that was a wonderful, wonderful night! And it was sad, too, to think he warn't never going to lecture any more, 'cause there was nobody ever in this world that was such a wonderful lecturer as Mr. Clemens was! Just the sight of him would make anybody feel interested and excited, and when he begun to talk—oh, my! It wasn't like anything you ever heard before, or ever will again, I guess!

I'll tell you another thing about Mr. Clemens, because it was that winter, I think, that Patrick died. Patrick was the coachman, and he'd been with Mr. Clemens about thirty-six years; and he'd driven them while they lived in Hartford. He was like one of the family, as you might say. And then, poor old Patrick, he got sick and died—he died in Hartford. When Mr. Clemens heard how sick he was, he had everything done for him he could think of—had doctors for him and had flowers sent, too. Mr. Clemens always did that when people were sick. When Patrick died, Mr. Clemens went himself, up to the funeral, and was one of the pallbearers, too. There was just two other men (friends of Patrick's) and Mr. Clemens. He wanted to do that, because Patrick was his friend, he said, and because Patrick was always kind and was really a gentleman, Mr. Clemens said; and he told about the time when he first come to them, years and years ago, and drove him and Mrs. Clemens as a bride to their new house, right after they was married.

Mr. Clemens was always like that. Anybody who'd been his friend or served him, loving and faithful like Patrick was, would always have a place in his heart to the very end.

And now I must tell you about Mr. Clemens having his biography written. Mr. Paine was going to do it. I don't know when Mr. Paine met him first. I think it was some time before they really started work, but anyway, Mr. Clemens had read some book Mr. Paine had done—I think it was the book he wrote about Mr. Nast —the man who made that funny picture of Mr. Clemens and the clocks, Mr. Nast being a great friend of Mr. Clemens; and I suppose he was interested in the book that Paine wrote about him. At any rate, they met and Mr. Clemens said he could do his biography if he wanted to. So that was a fine thing for Mr. Paine—a great thing. So they began writing on the biography. Mr. Clemens was writing one of his own then—his autobiography, you call it—but not to be published for fifteen or twenty years after his death, until all the people he wrote about was dead, anyway. Mr. Clemens was telling about his friends and enemies in that—that's why they've got to wait until everybody was dead before publishing it. Yes, Mr. Clemens told all about his friends and enemies in great style and everybody else, too. He polished everything off good, I guess.

Well, Mr. Clemens started the biography with Mr. Paine—that is, he talked, dictated, and they had a very nice stenographer, too, Miss Hobby. Mr. Clemens liked her very much because she was swift and good, and could take dictation from him very easy. He was in bed, of course, when he was dictating. He always used to write in bed, you know. He smoked all the time, too, while he was dictating—that means talking. He always used to lie at the *foot* of the bed so as he could see them beautiful carvings on the head of that wonderful bed—the one that had the fat little cherubs all carved on the four posts that the children used to play with when they was little. We used to pile up lots of pillows for him and he'd kind of rest against them and do his smoking and dictating there. That bed was an awful big one, and he was always losing his scraps of paper and pencils in it and it made him terrible mad where the things would go to! He used to complain how things got lost right while he was lying there—and cuss a little, too!

Well, Miss Hobby, she took everything down and Mr. Clemens talked by the hour and seemed to enjoy it. Mr. Paine had a room off Mr. Clemens' where he done his writing and fixing the things up.

Well, Miss Hobby and Mr. Paine come every day and took dictation. Mr. Paine had access to everything, as I said, all Mr. Clemens' letters and papers, everything. Mr. Clemens gave Mr. Paine permission to go everywhere and get all the information he wanted, so Mr.

Paine went to Hartford and Elmira and to all the people that knew Mr. Clemens and was with us, wherever we lived—until the biography was done. It was quite a job, I guess, and a very interesting book.

Mr. H. H. Rogers used to come a great deal to see Mr. Clemens, I told you what a wonderful friend he was to him, all his life, and how he looked after his investments and done everything he could to make life easy and pleasant—like all of his friends. But it did seem as though Mr. Rogers could never do enough. He was always right there—right on hand, up to the day of his death.

He'd come every morning in his car to the Fifth Avenue house, just to see Mr. Clemens. Mr. Rogers was such a dear friend—oh, a good friend he was! He was a tall man, tall and thin, with a gray mustache, and very good-looking.

Well, the summer we went to live in Dublin, when Mr. Clemens was so terribly forlorn and lonely, he come down once while they was fixing the Fifth Avenue house. Mr. Clemens wanted to show the men just where to put the radiators, because he'd had to stay in bed all the winter before on account of the cold, and he said he was going to *sue* that landlord for all the days he'd had to stay in bed and couldn't work. The landlord felt terrible and told Mr. Clemens if he wouldn't sue him, he'd make it hot enough for him the next winter, so he ordered all them radiators put in. That's why Mr. Clemens come back to New York to see about it. It was so lonely, anyway, up in Dublin, he was glad of any excuse to leave for a while, I guess.

So Mr. Rogers says to him: "Why don't you come and stay in New York and not go back to Dublin?" He said he could go out in his yacht every night on the water, where it would be nice and cool, and do whatever he pleased in the daytime.

So Mr. Clemens did that for some time—stayed on the yacht nights and come home in the morning. Mr. Rogers used to drive him down about eleven o'clock to the Fifth Avenue house; then I used to get him a little lunch. He didn't usually eat lunch, you know, but I thought if I got him something he *liked* maybe he would eat. So I made arrangements with a bakery in the neighborhood to make a nice fresh huckleberry pie every forenoon, and bring it to the house. Then I'd get a quart of milk and put it on the ice, and have it all ready—the huckleberry pie and the cold milk—about one o'clock. He'd eat half the huckleberry pie, anyway, and drink all the milk.

"Oh, that was delicious, Katy," he'd say, because he just loved the huckleberry pie. The first time I put it before him, he said, "Why, did *you* make this, Katy?"

"No, Mr. Clemens, no," I said, "but I got a bakery around the corner to make it *especially* for you."

"You did!" he says. "Why, how did you ever think of that, Katy?"

"Oh, I did it," I says, "because I try to think of all the things you like—to try to make you happy."

Well, he always talked about that, said how good it was and how much he enjoyed it—and it was really a delicious lunch.

Of course the house was very comfortable that winter after we got them radiators in. It was a very nice house, and, as I told you, all the things we used to have in Hartford was brought down there. Miss Clara had her two beautiful rooms right on the corner, facing Fifth Avenue—one was her music room, the lavender room I told you about. She had her piano in it and all her things, and used to sing and practice there, and receive all her friends and callers. Clara was beginning to sing again a little, after she come out of the sanitarium. That was the third winter we was in the Fifth Avenue house. She was well again and going on with her life, and back in her father's house, which made us all happy.

She went on some concert tours a little later, and I used to go with her sometimes. Miss Clara had a beautiful voice, you know—and was an artiste really. She was very dramatic in her singing—and a fine musician as they call it. I'll tell you more about that by and by. I mustn't forget to speak about the billiard room now. Mr. Clemens had one of the rooms fixed up into a lovely billiard room and Mrs. Rogers give him an elegant billiard table for a Christmas present. He enjoyed that very much; he was just crazy about billiards and used to play every single day. Mr. Paine played with him all the time, and his secretary played with him, too. Everybody could play billiards; he would take them right in for a game. It was a great amusement for him always—that and the Orchestrelle. They had that wonderful Orchestrelle and Mr. Clemens used to love to hear it play. They took it up that summer to Dublin, with a lot of trouble and expense, but it was a real comfort to Mr. Clemens—which was the main thing. He used to play lots of nice pieces on it—some of them I knew. He used to play pieces by Schubert and that thing—Handel's Largo—he played that all the time—every night—he loved it! That was very solemn and grand, but it was beautiful. He used to play that up in Redding, when we moved there later on. He never got tired of that piece.

Of course, I can't ever tell you all the people that come to see Mr. Clemens. It seemed as though everybody in New York come! If I was to mention them all, I guess I'd have to write a biography of Mr. Clemens myself! All I can do is tell the stories, and the things and people I used to see and hear about such a lot.

I remember Mr. Collier used to come there. He run *Collier's Magazine;* he was a great friend of Mr. Clemens', and Norman Hapgood—he was another one. He was a writer, too, and he was a great friend of Miss Clara's. He used to come to see her—as well as Mr. Clemens. Of course, Colonel Harvey was there a lot and Martin Littleton (he was a very smart lawyer), he come, too, and Mrs. Littleton, and Mr. Howells and Mr. Gilder all the time. And I remember Mr. Frohman—Daniel Frohman, I mean—they was friends, he and Mr. Clemens—and Charles Frohman—his brother, too, that great theatrical manager. Mr. Clemens liked him very much and I heard him say once that you didn't never need a contract with him—just his word was all you needed—if Mr. Frohman said he'd do anything." I guess that's enough, and I'll go back to my story-telling.

But there's just one person I left out, and I'll tell about him because he wrote an awful funny book about Mr. Dooley. *Mr. Dooley in Peace and War,* it was called. It was Irish and very funny. Well, the man who wrote it was Dunne, Peter Dunne. Mr. Clemens liked him very much, and they used to play billiards together a lot.

It seems as if I should never get through telling all the wonderful things that happened to Mr. Clemens those last years. It seemed as if everybody in the world was doing him honor, but one of the grandest things that ever happened, he thought, was when that great college that's so famous in England, Oxford, sent him an invitation to come over there that summer so's they could give him what they call a degree. That means a great deal, and when you're a literary man, that's about as high as you can get. There's very few that gets it, too—only the very greatest! Well, he went over to England and had a perfectly marvelous time. They said all the newspaper reporters was down to meet the ship and all the high society in London invited him to dinners and parties and everything you could think of.

Well, he went up to Oxford College when he got that degree (Doctor of Literature, it was called), and he got a wonderful robe to wear with the Degree, and he wore that robe when Miss Clara was married later on. It was a long thing, such as the students wear—a gown—and it was gray and scarlet. Then there was a big cape that he had, too, I think, that had a big band of purple on it. He liked himself in them Oxford things and had his picture taken in them a lot.

Well, it seems the day he landed in London the celebrated Ascot Cup was stolen (that's the cup they get at the famous Ascot Races they have over there) and it seems the newspapers got out big placards all over London saying in great big letters, "MARK TWAIN ARRIVES," and "ASCOT CUP STOLEN"—something like that.

Of course, that was a big joke, and the newspapers caught on to it and kept it up. It tickled Mr. Clemens, too, I'll bet, and they kept carrying the thing on, because it seems there was something else stolen the next day, and they tried to lay that to him, too!

Well, anyway, he went up to Oxford, where that college is, and all those wonderful people went up there—professors and everybody else, and they gave him that degree right then and there. I heard Rudyard Kipling was there that time, and Mr. Clemens seen him and was very glad, I guess, 'cause he always admired him so much.

Well, it seems when Mr. Clemens stepped out on the platform to get his degree, the college boys cheered and yelled and hollered out, "Did you bring your 'Jumping Frog' with you, Mark Twain?" and "Where's your 'Golden Arm'?" they shouted (which shows they knew his story pretty well). And then somebody else yelled, "And where'd you put our Ascot Cup?" Oh! The newspapers was full of this and it was all republished in our papers over here, so we read all about it, and knew everything that was going on. I used to read every word.

Mr. Clemens kept up that Ascot Cup joke, and then at some big dinner they gave him, when he made his speech, he said "Yes," he really did steal that cup the day he arrived, and he warn't going to give it up, never! I guess that was the climax of it. But he talked a lot about it when he got home again.

There was no end to the wonderful things that happened that time in London, and there was one terrible exciting thing happened when he was there, and it got into all the newspapers and upset Miss Clara very much. I suppose the report was kind of exaggerated, 'cause the newspapers said that Mr. Clemens just trailed out one fine morning from the hotel where he was stopping (Brown's Hotel) and walked across the street in his nightshirt to take a bath at some bath club he went to! Well, when Miss Clara read that, she sent him a cable

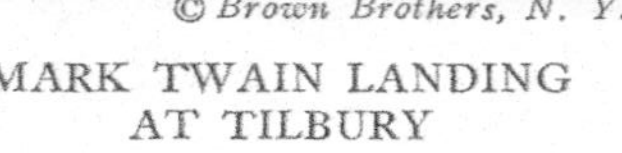
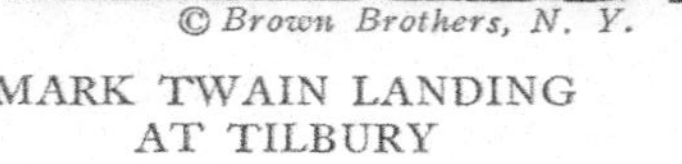

© Brown Brothers, N. Y.

MARK TWAIN LANDING AT TILBURY

MARK TWAIN AT DOLLIS HOUSE, ENGLAND

MARK TWAIN IN HIS OXFORD ROBE, AFTER CLARA'S WEDDING

pretty quick and it said, "Father, look to propriety," or something like that. She said something, anyway, to make him careful what he was doing. But I guess he didn't care very much. The story was, that when he come out of the bath place there was a great crowd hanging around, watching for him, and when he seen them, he says: "Why, what's happened? Is there a fire here or anything? What are you looking at?" And then one man in the crowd, he says, "It's you we're looking at, sir, going out in your nightshirt!"

"Well," Mr. Clemens says, "don't people go to baths in their nightshirt or bathrobes? What *else* would they go in?"

And then I guess the crowd must have laughed at that, of course, 'cause he had 'em there! It seems those reports was really exaggerated and he didn't go out in his nightshirt, but went in his bathrobe, instead—which was bad enough! But it made a good story for the papers, anyway!—which is the main thing, 'cause everything he did attracted attention, no matter where he was.

Mr. Clemens stayed in London quite a while that summer, having a perfectly elegant time with all his old friends, and then he come home. They said everybody hated to have him leave, and there was crowds of reporters and all kinds of famous people to see him off, and the English papers was just full of it. So you see, they made just as much fuss about him there as we did at home.

When he got home he was in Tuxedo awhile that summer, but it was pretty quiet there, and I guess he missed things—the gayety he'd been having. I used to think sometimes that Mr. Clemens did really miss the old days—them wonderful days with the Royalty that he used to joke at so. By that, I mean that he was getting past lots of things and growing older (though he never seemed old, as I told you before, and I could never believe really that he passed Pier No. 70 as he called it).

They were getting ready then to go into the country to live. Mr. Clemens thought he'd like that and Miss Jean would like it, too, although Miss Clara, she didn't care so much about it at first. Mr. Clemens had bought some land up in Redding, Connecticut. He bought just a little piece of land at first—I think it was Mr. Paine that first give him the idea, 'cause he had a place up there where he lived himself, and of course that would be really wonderful if Mr. Clemens come there to live, too, and make it a swell neighborhood for everybody.

Then Mr. Clemens got quite interested and excited about it, and he bought quite a bit of land—I forget how much—and they got John Howells, Mr. Howells's son—he was an architect—to make the plans for the new house. Of course they started off kind of modest and simple, but it ended by building a great big, beautiful house. It was a year almost in building, and they were all looking forward to gettin' into it.

Of course Mr. Clemens wanted to have a big Billiard

Room—that's the first thing he thought of. He wanted a big living-room, too, where he could put the Orchestrelle, but that's about all he ever said in regard to it. He'd never been to Redding himself—he'd never seen the plans of the house and didn't want to bother with them. He just told them all to go ahead an' get everything done before he seen the place—to take his bank book and draw the money out of the bank for what they needed, but not to bother him! And he said he wouldn't move in till the cats had had their breakfasts and was purrin' on the hearth. When they was doin' that, he said, he'd know everything was settled and he'd be ready to come, too. Yes, when that happened, he knew everything would be all right. He was very fond of cats and always wanted them wherever he was.

You see, Mr. Clemens had lived in so many different palaces and places, all over the world, that one more new house didn't mean very much to him, I guess, although he kind of looked forward then to the idea of getting away from New York. The winters was hard on him 'cause everybody was chasin' him so all the time, and 'cause he was always having those awful attacks of bronchitis. That winter before we moved up to Redding he had to go down to Bermuda to stay to get rid of his bronchitis.

Yes, Mr. Clemens, he just loved cats, and the children did, too. I remember once way back in Hartford, when Miss Jean was a little girl, she was all ready to go to church on Sunday and she had on a beautiful new white fur coat. It was the first time she put it on, and she ran right down to the bank of the river there and found a big black cat, dying as she thought. So she took it up in her arms with her lovely new fur coat on and brought him up to the house to her mother, who set in the carriage waiting for her.

"Oh, Jean, Jean!" says Mrs. Clemens, "what are you doing?"

"Oh," says Jean, "I'm bringing this poor cat home because he's dying."

And her mother says, "But, Jean, just look at your new coat!"

"Oh," says Jean, "that's nothing; that don't make any difference, but this poor cat must be put in a warm place. I'll take him into the kitchen." So she fixed the cat up with nice warm milk and then went to church with her mother. But she hurried right back, and then she found the cat kind of lively when she got home, so she took him to see her father, as she knew he loved cats.

"Why," he says, "what a nice little cat this is, Jean—nice and frisky!" he says. "We'll name him Satan."

Well, Satan got very gay and wild and grew up very quick, and then Satan, it seems, turned out to be a lady-cat and one fine day had a daughter, and when Mr. Clemens heard that, he laughed and said, "Well, now we'll name this new kitten Sin—the daughter of Satan, you know."

She was a little gray kitten, very pretty, and grew up—and took after her mother, I suppose.

When we went up to the farm that summer he got four more cats and he gave them all Bible names. I can't remember just what they were, only one was Deuteronomy and the other was Genesis—and there was one called Sour Mash—but I don't remember when it was he had that cat. He used to have them cats right in a chair in front of him when he was walking up and down, and he used to talk to them—and I declare I think they knew everything he said! He talked *real* talk to them, and they used to set up there looking and listening to him. Perhaps he was trying to educate them to swear! But I guess cats have swear words of their own, if you can judge anything from some of the sounds they make—nights.

Mr. Clemens borrowed a kitten one time, called Bambino, from Clara, who had him in the sanitarium, and had trained him to wash his own face in the bowl every morning—which shows that he was a very smart little cat. He used to have this kitten up in his room at the Fifth Avenue house and he taught it to put out a light, too. He had a tiny little lamp to light his cigars with at the head of the bed, and after he got all fixed and didn't want the light any more, he taught that cat to put his paw on the light and put it out. Bambino would jump on the bed, look at Mr. Clemens to see if he was through with the light, and when Mr. Clemens would bow twice to him, he'd jump over on to that table quick, and put his little paw right on the lamp! Mr. Clemens was always showing him off; he did that for a lot of people that come there to call.

One night he got kind of gay, when he heard some cats calling from the back fence, so he found a window open and he stole out. We looked high and low but couldn't find him. Mr. Clemens felt so bad that he advertised in all the papers for him. He offered a reward for anybody that would bring the cat back. My goodness! the people that came bringing cats to that house! A perfect stream! They all wanted to see Mr. Clemens, of course.

Two or three nights after, Katherine heard a cat meowing across the street in General Sickles' back yard, and there was Bambino—large as life! So she brought him right home. Mr. Clemens was delighted and then he advertised that his cat was *found!* But the people kept coming just the same with all kinds of cats for him—anything to get a glimpse of Mr. Clemens! I've got a picture that I'll give you of them four cats of Mr. Clemens' with the Bible names. I've got another nice picture of Mr. Clemens, too, taken with Lewis, the old colored man that lived up at Mrs. Crane's house at Quarry Farm for years and years. I'll tell you about that later.

Yes, the whole family loved animals, and cats especially; and Miss Clara and Jean loved them just as much as Mr. Clemens did. From the time she was a little bit of a girl, all her life, Jean was always interested in any kind of suffering, whether it was animals or humans, as I told you before. She used to be always talking about what a cruel thing it was the way the Americans treated the Indians in the early days. She felt terrible about that, and used to talk about it to her father, but not so much to me, because of course I couldn't understand it very well. She felt it was very cruel to kind of push the Indians back out of the way. She thought the Government ought to do something more about it than they had done. You see, Jean had a very tender heart for any one she thought warn't treated right.

She belonged to the humane society every single place she went, and they always did her out of a lot of money. She was just crazy about animals, Jean was, that's why she belonged to all them societies. Her father always joked her that they was just asking her for her money. Of course, he'd send them any amount she'd ask for, because she wanted to take good care of them animals. Why, she belonged to the society in Vienna and one in Switzerland, and then she got up a humane society of her own in Elmira—when she was quite a little girl—years before.

You know, there was a steep hill going up to Quarry Farm in Elmira, and she stuck up signs all along the road, "Uncheck your horses going up here." And if a man coming along didn't uncheck his horse and she'd be coming along, too, why, she'd jump out of the carriage and stop him then and there. Of course, people used to fight with her about it a lot.

One time her Uncle Charles was going up that hill and when he got to the house it seems he didn't have his horse unchecked neither! So she went right out and unchecked him herself. And when her uncle saw that, he said, "Why, who's unchecked my horse?"

"Oh," says Jean, "I did, Uncle Charles, 'cause you didn't uncheck your horse, when you was comin' up that hill."

"But," he says, "Jean, you can't really drive that horse when he's unchecked. You *got* to check him up. He steps right on his own face if he's unchecked! Don't you never uncheck that horse again, Jean," he says, "never." Well, of course, they both got mad, but she didn't pay no attention to that.

Then there was one horse, "Michael's horse," she used to call him, and she'd go out and gather up fresh grass for him. She'd have a nice big bunch all ready for him when he'd drive in. He really belonged to the garbage man, you know. That was way back in the Hartford days, when she was a little thing.

One day she was feeding this horse, and stuck her hand right in his mouth to help him eat the grass, and he almost chewed the top of her finger off—bit it right through! Of course it hurt her terrible and she come out and told me; but she says: "But it wasn't his fault, Katy, it wasn't 'Michael's horse's' fault. It was my own!

I kept my finger in his mouth while he was chewing, so of course he had to chew my finger at the same time he was chewing the grass. Don't say anything about it," she says. And she never let on and took care of that finger herself. She never told her mother about it, for fear they would stop that horse coming into the yard, and she used to wait for him every morning with a handful of grass, and sometimes a lump of sugar to feed him.

And Clara was most as bad, too. She always wanted to go downtown with me in Hartford when I went to do the shopping, and I didn't want her to go lots of times, because she was a perfect nuisance. She would go along with me, but she wouldn't come into the stores—just hung around outside and I used to say to her, "Well, Clara, what do you come for, anyway?" Then she'd say, "You go in and do your shopping, Katy, and I'll stay right here"—and then she'd go along to every horse on the curb, and pat him and rub him, and put her arms around his neck and kiss him, too, sometimes. Lots of horses she didn't know what kind they were, of course, but that didn't matter to Clara. She'd pet them just the same, and if she could buy anything to feed them with, she'd do it right there. One day a man said to me: "Here, you'd better keep that little girl away from that horse. He might bite her. He's cross."

"Oh," I says, "no horse ever bit her yet. Every horse seems to love her." They used to lay their heads right over on her shoulder when she spoke to them.

One day Mrs. Clemens says: "Katy, it's very strange, I think, that Clara always wants to go downtown shopping with you every time you go. I don't understand it."

"Oh, Mrs. Clemens!" I says. "It isn't because she wants to go shopping in the store with me, that she goes. Oh, no! She just wants to pet all them strange horses on the streets—that's what she's up to—that's why she wants to go!"

There was a family lived near us one time, and they had the wildest horse you ever heard of—he was perfectly crazy—used to kick and roll his eyes and show his teeth to everybody that come near him. The coachman used to have terrible times getting him harnessed up. Well, one day the coachman went back into the stable for something and he nearly fainted, for there was Clara, right in the stall in front of that crazy horse, feeding him! Well, this coachman, he just ran to me and says: "Why, what do you think? That little thing is in there with that crazy horse! I'm afraid to go in that stall myself, he kicks so! I'm afraid he'll kick her to death! You'd better go after her quick and get her out somehow."

So I ran over and there she was, standing—kissing that old horse and feeding him. And I called to her kind of quiet so's not to scare her, but she says, "Oh, all right, Katy. I'll be out in a minute." So she gave him another hug and kiss and walked right out and he didn't touch her, of course. When she was out, safe and sound, I says to her:

"Oh, Clara, Clara!" I says. "Didn't you know that horse is very wicked and has often kicked the coachman and tried to bite him, too? He kicks him every time he goes in there!" I says.

"Well," she says, "I might kick him, too, if I was a horse!" And of course, I had to laugh at that, because there was some truth in it, after all.

Well, now I'll go on with that little story about Lewis, the old colored man, and Mr. Clemens. There was an old cackling guinea hen up at Quarry Farm that summer, and one night that guinea hen nearly cackled her head off—such a noise! Mr. Clemens was wild about it, and he rushed right out in the night and chased that hen all over the farm, because it was disturbing Mrs. Clemens—keeping her awake. But he couldn't catch it, of course. So in the morning he called Lewis and he said, "Lewis, I want you to catch that guinea hen to-day and kill it; and for punishment, I want *you* to *eat* it, too, every bit of it yourself, so I'll know it's dead and gone."

Well, Lewis killed the guinea hen, and took it home and eat it. The family was getting ready to go to Europe right away, and it seems as soon as Mr. Clemens got to London that trip he went to a grand dinner one night at a restaurant, and the first thing he seen on the bill of fare was "*Guinea Hen*," so just for fun he thought he'd order it. Well, he eat it and said it was the most delicious thing he'd ever tasted in all his life—and when he thought of that other guinea hen that Lewis had killed up in Elmira and eaten himself, he said he felt like coming right home again, and killing Lewis!

Mr. Clemens always saw the jokes so, in everything. Any bit of fun would make him laugh and laugh. He used to laugh at his own jokes, too, sometimes when they was very funny, and once he and Jean, when she was a little girl, had quite an argument about it—which he got the best of, as usual. He'd joke about anything—even his own death—which reminds me of something he once said to Miss Clara. She went to Europe an awful lot, you know. She was always going over there, and she used to go to her father and say, "Well, father, I really think I'll have to go over this year for a little while." Of course this was all after her mother died and she was a young lady. Every summer she'd have a different excuse, and she'd go to her father and kind of break it to him, and then he'd say: "Well, Clara, what's your reason this time for wanting to go? What kind of a story have you made up for me now?" And one summer I remember he said to her, when she asked him about going: "Well, Clara," he says, "all right, all right! But what is it *this* time?" And she said:

"Oh, father, I must go this summer, because poor Leschetizky is getting so old" (he was that famous piano teacher, you know) "that if I don't go now, I'm afraid

I'll never see him alive again!" And then her father said:

"Well, go ahead, Clara, go ahead! But be careful!—for maybe while you're over there in Europe attending to Leschetizky's funeral—you may miss mine!"

But although Mr. Clemens always turned everything into a joke, he never played bad jokes on people, and never disappointed them, either. He always kept his promises, and that makes me think about something he done once for Lily Burbank. She was a friend of Clara's in the old days. We seen a lot of her in Vienna and in New York, too. She was very nice, quite a well known person in society, and she admired Mr. Clemens very much, and I remember about one time when she got up a nice little dinner party and asked him to come. That was when we was livin' in Riverdale.

It seems there was a very famous Englishman just come to New York that knew Lily Burbank—he was a scientist or something like that, and when he found out she knew Mark Twain, he was just crazy to have her fix it up so's he could meet him. Why, he said he'd rather meet Mark Twain than any person in America—anybody in the whole world, he says. So she said she'd try and get Mr. Clemens to come to dinner to meet him. She knew it would be very hard, because he was up in Riverdale and warn't going out much that winter; but she told the Englishman she'd try and fix it up for him as a special treat. And she was going to ask another man, too—

somebody from Boston that was quite famous; an author, I suppose.

Well, she telephoned up to Riverdale and invited Mr. Clemens, and he was very nice and said yes, he'd come, he'd be glad to. I suppose he did it because he knew it would please her. Well, anyway, she told him the date for the following week and he wrote it down (that is, she thought he did!) and said all right, he'd be there on time. So everything was fixed up for that night, and they was all delighted, and she was planning a wonderful lovely dinner and everything nice for Mr. Clemens and this Englishman.

Well the night *before* the dinner, she come in from shopping about seven o'clock, with her arms full of bundles, all tired out and kind of cross, and when she got to her apartment the maid opened the door and looked sort of queer, and says: "Oh, Miss Burbank, I guess there's some terrible mistake, 'cause Mr. Clemens is settin' there in the Library now and says he's come to dinner, and you know the dinner ain't till to-morrow night! I didn't know what to do," the maid said, "so I just left him settin' there!" My goodness! Poor Miss Burbank nearly fainted! She knew right away Mr. Clemens had made a mistake and come the wrong night! She hurried into the room and there he was, she said, all dressed up, spick and span, looking very fine and waiting for the dinner party to begin! Of course, I suppose she tried to explain to him, and not hurt his feelings, and say that he'd come the wrong night. "Oh, Mr. Clemens!" she said, "I'm so glad to see you, so glad, but I'm really afraid you made a little mistake. The dinner is to-morrow night—not to-night, you know."

"Oh, no!" says Mr. Clemens. "*I* didn't make any mistake! *You* made the mistake. You said the dinner was to-night, and I put it down for to-night, and I've come to-night, and here I am!"

Poor Miss Burbank! She didn't know what to say, but she tried to explain it very polite and take all the blame on herself, I suppose, but the more she talked, the more set he was that he knew he hadn't made any mistake; that the dinner was for that night! So then she said, "Did you put it down in your little book, Mr. Clemens, where you always put things down?"

"Why, yes," he says, "I did; and I guess I've got it right here in my pocket. I always carry it with me, and I'll look at it," he says, "to prove who's right."

Well, he pulled out the little book, and they both looked at it, and sure enough! *He'd* made the mistake! 'Twas written in pencil, you see, kind of faint, and it was for the next night the dinner was—not the night he'd come!

Well, he was just struck dumb! He felt terrible, and of course he was mad—mad at himself. And Miss Burbank says he said, "Well, why in hell didn't some of the family stop me before I started off! Why didn't Claude, or Clara, or somebody in the house look up that date, and see that I was going the right night? Well," he says, "there's no help for it now! I'm sorry."

And Miss Burbank, she was almost crying, and she said, "Oh, Mr. Clemens, please stay to dinner now, anyway,—just with us. We'll give you a very nice dinner. I'll get you anything you want," she says.

"Oh, no," he says, "no!" He said he was too upset for making such a mistake; he'd go on down to Mr. Rogers and eat a few nightingales' tongues, he said, or something queer like that for his sins! And so he just hurried right out, and Miss Burbank was ready to cry her heart out because she knew he wouldn't come the next night, and that her elegant dinner party was all busted and ruined! But she had to go ahead with it, anyway, because both those men was in Boston and she couldn't get word to them. So she got up her dinner just the same the next night, and the Englishman and his friend arrived, and then she had to tell them what had happened, and how Mr. Clemens had come the night *before* and had made a mistake in the date! Oh! They just felt terrible when they heard that. They was ready to cry, too. This Englishman said he just couldn't bear it. "Of course he won't come to-night. There's no hope of that. He'll never come again; and to think I have missed him!" Of course, there wasn't anything to do but make the best of it, so they tried to pretend they didn't mind so much, and have a good time by themselves; and they set down to the table pretty sad and quiet and begun their soup,

Helen S. Allen, Bermuda

MARK TWAIN AND ALBERT BIGELOW PAINE AT BERMUDA, A FEW WEEKS BEFORE HE DIED
(Courtesy Harper & Brothers)

MARK TWAIN AND HIS BIOGRAPHER PLAYING BILLIARDS IN 1907, AT 21 FIFTH AVENUE
(Courtesy Harper & Brothers)

MARK TWAIN AND LEWIS AT QUARRY FARM

and just as the first course started—what do you think! The doorbell rang very loud and long, and the maid went to the door and in came Mr. Clemens, looking perfectly wonderful in his dress-suit clothes, with a white carnation in his buttonhole—just gay and smiling and in the best kind of a humor!

Well! Miss Burbank says they all jumped up from the table and just cried and hugged him! They was so crazy with delight! And they had a perfectly wonderful dinner, and that Englishman said he never knew such a wonderful man as Mr. Clemens, never!

Now warn't that lovely of him to come the second time and make everything all right, 'cause he'd been the one that was wrong in the beginning! But that was just like Mr. Clemens. He never wanted to hurt anybody, or disappoint them, as I told you.

Well, to go back to the Redding house: When I first saw that house I thought it was beautiful. You couldn't help but like it, it was so grand. Miss Clara had been on a concert tour in Europe that summer while they was finishing it, and I was with her, of course. When we got back we went right up to Redding that first night, and Miss Clara saw it for the first time and liked it right away —it was so cheerful and nice. Everything about it was beautiful. We'd taken the furniture from the Fifth Avenue house, and everything was in apple-pie order. Mr. Clemens had taken that great Orchestrelle up there, too, to have a little music (he used to play it himself, you know), and it looked very grand in the new house—like a great pipe organ—the pipes ran way up to the ceiling. It cost lots of money, I'll tell you, to carry it way out there and install it—but 'twas worth it!

And the new billiard room was beautiful, too. That was the best part of the Redding house, according to Mr. Clemens. It was in the billiard room that he had his aquarium. It warn't a real aquarium, but just pictures of goldfish that come from Bermuda. It seems he got a lot of fish and had them pictures taken and then had them framed nice under glass, and he called it his aquarium. And then he christened them all different names for people he knew, and some little girls he knew that used to come out to amuse him—they used to write their names on the pictures. Two of them was Helen Hamilton and Marjory Clinton. He used to play billiards with some of these girls sometimes to amuse them, and he used to play with Mr. Paine's little girl Joy—Joy Paine. My! Mr. Clemens thought that was the funniest name, Joy Paine—because it's a kind of a contradiction. It always made him laugh, but he liked Joy very much.

Mr. Clemens named the place "Innocence at Home," but afterwards said he'd made enough money out of that book *Captain Stormfield in Heaven*—to pay for that house, so he thought he'd call it "Stormfield" instead; so "Stormfield" it was, though I always spoke of it as the Redding house.

Well, Mr. Clemens settled down and seemed to be

happy there. He used to play on the Orchestrelle every night before he went to bed, and he begun his billiard playing again, too. Mr. Paine was a neighbor then. He lived on his own place close by, and used to be there all the time, and he played billiards with Mr. Clemens every day.

It was really a beautiful place, and Clara liked it, too, very much. It was so cheerful and the view was so pretty. The Loggia was lovely and Mr. Clemens used to sit out there in the summertime and have the sun glare at him from all sides; and he seemed happy and contented. Of course the usual stream of visitors came chasing up there, just as they used to in New York, for no matter where Mr. Clemens went, people would follow him, so there was lots of company all the time.

It was while we were living in Redding that Mr. Clemens had another terrible blow. That was when Mr. Rogers died. Miss Clara got the news first and went to the station to meet her father so that he should hear it direct from her and not from the paper. We was expecting him up from New York, so she went to the station, and when Mr. Clemens stepped off the car, she told him the terrible news. The tears rushed down his face and he said: "Oh, Clara! Is this true? It can't be true!"

"Yes, father," she said, "Mr. Rogers died last night."

"Oh," he said, "I don't know how I'm going to get along without Mr. Rogers. I don't know how I'm going to live without his friendship any more!"

Poor Mr. Clemens was all broken up over it. He had seen so many that he loved die before, but even so, although he ought to be used to it, it just tore his heart all over again, because Mr. Rogers had been such a friend to him—such a loving, faithful friend. "The very best in the world," he used to say.

Well, we settled down there in Redding, and everybody liked the house and we had lots of company all the time. Jean was better and at home with her father, and Miss Clara, she was there a great deal. Then one summer—the second summer, I think it was—Mr. Gabrilowitsch come out to Redding, which pleased Mr. Clemens very much. He was very fond of him. He was a great pianist then—very famous.

I told you how we knew him way back in the Vienna days, when Miss Clara was a pupil of old Leschetizky, and how he was very sweet on her even then. He come out that summer, right from the hospital. He had had a terrible operation, and he come there to get strong again. He had to stay in bed at first, but after a while he was able to sit up and they all used to have lovely evenings together. They told stories and laughed and set around on the porch them beautiful summer evenings. Mr. Clemens liked it very much and wanted everything done for Gabrilowitsch, and we all took good care of him—especially me, because I told you before, I think, I was always very fond of him myself!

It was at this time that they wanted a library built in

Redding. Mr. Clemens got very much interested in it and Jean, too, she wanted the library just as much as Mr. Clemens did. She helped start it—that is, gave all the money she had. She sold that place down in the lower part of the farm that she owned and turned all the money into the library. She was always chasin' around after books for it. You know, she almost stripped the library at home to get books to put into the new one.

Then it was that Mr. Clemens said they'd get some of the neighbors—men up there—to give the land for it, and they'd give a grand concert at our house to raise money for it. They'd give it right there in the Redding house and Mr. Gabrilowitsch said he'd play, and Miss Clara was to sing and David Bispham—he was a famous baritone singer—he was to sing, too. Mr. Clemens said they'd make a lot of money out of it, if they charged the right prices. It was going to be $1.50 a ticket to set in the living-room, where the performance was, with Mr. Gabrilowitsch playing on the grand piano, and $1.00 for the dining-room where they couldn't *see* very good, but could *hear* all right, and seventy-five cents to sit in the hall where they couldn't see anything, but could hear well enough, and fifty cents for everybody that come inside the gates! Well, the people just flocked there! They drove their automobiles in—there was hundreds of them, and people come from all over—from New York and even from Hartford! You see they advertised it good and plenty that Gabrilowitsch was going to play. It was a great success and they got a lot of money out of it, and they called on Mr. Clemens and he made a funny little speech. He said what a nice concert it was and how fortunate they were to have Gabrilowitsch and Mr. Bispham—such famous artists to perform for them; and then he said, "Of course, my daughter Clara is going to sing, too. My daughter," he says, "is not so famous as these gentlemen, but *she's ever so much better looking!*" Of course, they all roared at that! And then they had tea afterwards, and kind of a party to wind up the thing. So that scheme worked out pretty well, and the library was started, and it's there now.

You know, when he was getting that library started out at Redding, he charged everybody a dollar apiece for sleeping in the Redding house, when they come out to stay overnight. He loved to have them come, of course, but then, he said, they'd got to help pay for the library. They'd have to pay a dollar before they left in the morning. There was some rich people that come that used to pay as much as five dollars. And when Mr. Clemens would go to collect that dollar, they would just hand him out a five-dollar bill. Of course, he was glad to take it for the library—'cause that was part of the way he was going to get the money to build it with. And then he'd make them all register, put their names in a book, like they did in a hotel, and they'd all tell how much money they gave, too, in that register. 'Twas a very good way, I thought, to collect money, and of course, as everybody was so crazy to be near Mr. Clemens and to come out to the Redding house, he raked in a good deal that way.

Mr. Gabrilowitsch was well by that time, but when he first come out to Redding he was pretty near dying, and, oh, I was afraid then! I used to wait on him hand and foot. I did everything I could for him. He was afraid of getting baldheaded, too, and I used to rub his head just as I used to rub Mr. Clemens', to make his hair grow —though nobody could have such hair as Mr. Clemens, no matter how much rubbing it had.

Mr. Gabrilowitsch's rooms was way off one side of the house and Miss Clara's was way off on the other, and they didn't see each other until lunch time every day. So they used to write notes every morning and I carried them notes back and forth—just as I used to in Vienna, and as I used to when he first come to New York before he was so famous, when we was living at the Tenth Street house and I used to sneak out with notes to him from Miss Clara—sneak out to the Brevoort House to give them to him in answer to notes he had sent her by a messenger boy. I certainly helped that courtship along 'cause I was always for him! When I took the notes to him when he was at Redding, he wouldn't read the note while I was there. So then I'd say, "Why, aren't you going to write anything to Miss Clara for me to carry back?"

"No," he says, "no note, only just carry my love; but then, Katy," he said, "that's so much you couldn't carry it all!" And there was no joke in that, I guess—that I couldn't carry all the love he had for her!

And so they got engaged. They was sort of engaged once or twice before, but this time it was for sure, and that night after the concert I was telling you about, Miss Clara she took a walk right afterwards, and she come in with a funny look on her face. But she didn't tell me anything. Then Gabrilowitsch was going to leave the next morning, and so I think it was that night he proposed to her for the last time.

I was getting a little apartment ready for her in New York that time where she would stay overnight whenever she went to the opera, and I was to meet her there a few days after the concert. Well, she met me in New York and said: "Now, Katy, don't bother getting the apartment ready. I'm not going to use it this winter; for I'm going to be married next week!"

Well, I almost fell on my knees —I was so delighted, and I says: "Oh, oh! And where is Mr. Gabrilowitsch?" She says, "He's coming along pretty soon." Then I told her how glad I was—that I was most as happy as they was.

And then began the awful rush to get things ready! There wasn't a minute to spare. She went to Altman's and ordered dresses and hats and all kinds of beautiful clothes, and Miss Jean and I, we ordered all the rest, all the linen and silver and everything for her house. We had only a week, and oh, my! how we hustled! And I ordered the wedding colation, too, from Maresi's (that was a swell place). I ordered everything for the wedding, and I didn't know nor care about the price of anything. I just ordered wild-like, and had the bills sent! So the wedding day was set and everything fixed up and ready. Mr. Twitchell married them and Miss Clara told him before the wedding he would have to leave the word "obey" out of the service. That made him laugh, of course—but it's a pretty good idea, I think, myself.

Well, Ethel Newcomb, she played the wedding march. Mr. Langdon was best man, as you call it, and Miss Jean was the bridesmaid. Mr. Clemens, he gave the bride away and he wore his Oxford suit at the wedding ceremony. Jean had a beautiful new white silk dress, all trimmed with lace. I got the two bouquets for her and Clara the night before in New York. Mr. Gabrilowitsch told me to get the best I could find—not to mind the expense! He wanted everything done right—the bouquets was orange blossoms and a few other things. Miss Clara's friends all come out to Redding and was crowding into her room to help her dress and put her veil on. Mr. Clemens was very quiet for a wonder—didn't seem excited nor rush around—but the guests was all running around like mad! They was all over the house and upstairs, so they had to tie ribbons across the stairs, to keep the guests in place and make them behave.

I didn't help Miss Clara dress because I was so upset and worried about things downstairs, for fear everything wouldn't go off all right. I worked all the morning and I was looking after everything and everybody was calling me this way and that. I didn't know who was there, hardly. They got me down into the kitchen, just as the wedding was about to begin, and Claude—the butler—was hopping around like a crazy man! He got awful mad at me because I asked him for something to drink. I was so dead beat, you see, I thought maybe if I had a glass of wine it might brace me up a bit for the ceremony. But he was so upset himself, he went right off the hammer—but anyway, he gave it to me after an awful lot of fuss, and it bucked me up. Then the wedding began and it was time for the bride to come—marching down the stairs. I remember just how the wedding party looked. Mr. Twitchell, the minister, was there, of course, and Mr. Gabrilowitsch and Mr. Langdon was at the foot of the stairs waiting for the bride to come down; and she was hanging on to her father's arm coming down the stairs. She did look so sweet and so little! She looked like a little cherub.

They marched right down the stairs into the living-room to Ethel Newcomb's playing of Mendelssohn's Wedding March. They made a kind of a little stop in the bay window where Mr. Twitchell was standing, and then he married them right off, then and there. Then Mr. Twitchell he made a nice little sermon to start them off, for of course he knew Miss Clara since she was a baby, and that ended that!

Mr. Clemens made a few remarks, too. He was talking and laughing all the time after the ceremony, to all the guests, telling about his nice, new son-in-law. After the feast (it was a very swell colation), the whole thing was over. We had kind of a buffet feast—everybody helping themselves (which was the style then). Then Mr. Clemens went upstairs and took off his Oxford things, and put on his white suit, and all the people went out to the front of the house and everybody was photographed. Then Miss Clara went upstairs and changed her dress and she and Mr. Gabrilowitsch hopped into the automobile and drove away. Then the guests went off, too. They was all driven down to the station and took the train back to New York. All their most intimate friends was there, and everything was a great success.

Clara's wedding was on October 6th, and it was a beautiful sunny day. In spite of my being so flustered, I shall never forget it. It was the first wedding in the family, and it struck me very deep, because the girls always seemed just like my own. I'd been there so many, many years, you know, and all kinds of thoughts and memories kept coming to me that night after it was all over and I got quieted down a little mite; and I thought how Mrs. Clemens would have enjoyed it and how happy she'd been, too, if only she could have been there. But it was a great day for all of us—gay and solemn, too—and I think Mr. Clemens felt it very much—so did all the friends that come there.

I'll never forget how Mr. Gilder stood up on the step and waved his hat, very gay, in a kind of a good-by to all them wedding guests, as he drove off down the hill to the station. I think of it now 'cause it was the last time I ever seen Mr. Gilder. It was only a few months after that he died, and that was another great loss to Mr. Clemens.

Well! After the wedding the letters of congratulation kept pouring in, because everybody was pleased of course. Mr. Clemens missed Miss Clara terribly, but he was happy there in the Redding house—"Stormfield," as he called it. He used to say he loved the place and that Mrs. Clemens would have loved it, too. You see, she was never out of his thoughts, really, after all those years. He used to love the country round there and used to take walks—he and Mr. Paine and Jean. She was there then and was interested in farming, too, and decided to become her father's secretary. She said she could do it as well as anybody, although it was a pretty stiff job; and that pleased Mr. Clemens very much, because he loved to have her with him. She wasn't ever cured of her trouble that I told you about, but she'd been much better them last few years and able to do lots of things she hadn't done before.

Oh, I mustn't forget to tell you (but that was before Miss Clara's wedding) how the burglars come up to the house one night and robbed it. There was great excitement and Claude, the butler, he shot off his pistol enough to wake the dead, but of course he didn't hit anything.

Mr. Clemens said he heard that pistol shooting off, but he said he thought maybe it was just somebody opening a bottle of champagne! So he went to sleep and didn't pay no attention to it. Well, Mr. Clemens was quite excited over it, when he found it out, and so he wrote on a piece of paper something funny which he addressed to any more burglars that tried again, and stuck it up on the front door! And he said how they only used plated ware in his house—that there warn't nothing valuable inside, except the family! and if the burglars wanted the plate to help themselves; they was welcome and could find it in a basket in the dining-room—where the cats was; they could help themselves to the plated ware, but anyway please not to disturb the cats! It was something like that—which of course would upset any burglar if he seen that nailed on to a front door! I've got what Mr. Clemens wrote copied off on a piece of paper somewhere, and I'll give it to you—the exact words.

Mr. Clemens was so fond of cats, and had just as many up at Stormfield as he had in the old days. He had two or three pretty kittens at that time, and they used to jump up on the billiard table when he was playing and shove the balls around and Mr. Clemens, he wouldn't say a word. He just stopped the game and waited patient as could be until they was all through fooling. I remember the name of two of them kittens—one was Sinbad and the other he called Billiards—and he just loved those little things. Never could have too many cats to suit him—which is a good sign in a man.

We had lots of company, as I told you before, and everybody loved the place. Mr. Howells come there and made a visit and it made him very happy, I guess, to have Mr. Clemens like the house so much, because his son John was the architect. He and Mr. Clemens had a wonderful time that last visit. They used to walk up and down in the sun together, laughing and talking just as they did way back in Hartford. Mr. Collier and his wife, too, they come up once, and that great man from London that owned so many newspapers—Northcliffe, his name was. He'd been made a Lord then—Lord Northcliffe. He come up there to visit Mr. Clemens, too. And Dr. Quintard was there quite often—he was Mr. Clemens' doctor and a great friend. He come when Mr. Clemens had that terrible pain in his chest—wasn't anything he wouldn't do for him.

Mr. Clemens used to see a lot of his neighbors, and that first summer at Redding he throwed the house wide open and invited them all over for a kind of a house-warming. And Mr. and Mrs. Martin Littleton they come up from New York at that time, and Mr. Clemens he made a speech that day and so did Mr. Littleton, who was a very bright, smart lawyer. Mrs. Loomis come up a good deal that summer, too—Mrs. Edward Loomis (she was Julia Langdon before she was married, and Mrs. Clemens' niece). Of course she was at the house a great deal, being one of the family, and I can remember her for years and years. She was a very fine woman, I thought, and she's married now to Edward Loomis, who's quite a big railroad man in New York, and settled and lives there with her family. I used to see a great deal of her in them days before Mrs. Clemens died, and afterwards too, as she was one of the family.

Quite a number of literary people lived near Mr. Clemens in Redding—Miss Jeanette Gilder had a little place up there, and so did that famous writer, Ida Tarbell. She wrote a lot about the Standard Oil—old Rockefeller—she did it all up brown, they said. She was very smart and nice, and used to drive over to see Mr. Clemens, too; and then Dan Beard—you've heard of him—he had a place somewhere near. So you see there was quite a little "colony"—as they call it. All authors again!

Mr. Clemens used to say that they had "gaudy" times. He always said that when Mr. Howells come.

Speaking of famous people, I mustn't forget to tell you that Jeanette Gilder (Mr. Gilder's sister) was a funny-looking woman—looked and dressed something like a man. She had a very deep voice, too. I once mistook her for a man when I let her into the house. It was kind of dark and I couldn't see very good—only hear her. It was many years ago, and the doorbell rang one evening and I answered it, and there was somebody standing there, that I thought was a man, and that asked for Mr. Clemens, in a very deep voice. So I says: "Yes, sir, he's in. Walk right in." And then this person said, "Will you tell Mr. Clemens that *Miss* Gilder would like to see him, please?" Of course I thought I'd misunderstood—on account of that deep voice. So I went and told Mr. Clemens, and he went down expecting to find Mr. Gilder, but found Miss Gilder instead! When he come back, he says to me: "Why, Katy, why did you say Mr. Gilder was downstairs? That wasn't a man—that was Miss Gilder."

"Well," I says, "from what I could see, she was a man. She had on a hat just like a man, and a long dark coat and she spoke in such a deep voice that I thought it was Mr. Gilder." She kind of dressed like a man—made herself look like a man, so I thought she was one. After that I seen her a good many times. She was quite famous and used to come over to see Mr. Clemens very often, and I got to know her very well.

So that's the way life went on in Redding—everything centered around Mr. Clemens and all we thought of was to make him happy and comfortable. Of course, Miss Clara was there a lot before her wedding, and we was afraid Mr. Clemens was going to miss her terribly—and he did. But it would have been much worse for him if Miss Jean hadn't been there then. It was a good thing she was home again.

But, right after the wedding, Mr. Clemens got kind

Warren's, Boston

WILLIAM DEAN HOWELLS
(Courtesy Harper & Brothers)

G. C. Cox

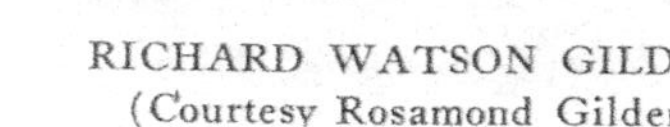

RICHARD WATSON GILDER
(Courtesy Rosamond Gilder)

Brown Brothers, N. Y.

"STORMFIELD," MARK TWAIN'S HOME AT REDDING. JOHN MEAD HOWELLS, SON OF WILLIAM DEAN HOWELLS, WAS THE ARCHITECT

MARK TWAIN'S LIBRARY AT "STORMFIELD"

of sick. The cold air brought on a pain in his chest. He had to stay in the house and complained of that pain all the time—although he looked just the same and his eyes was clear and he had a nice color in his cheeks, and his lovely white hair shone just like silver. I know, because I massaged it every morning for him most all his life. He didn't seem to get any better then, so he thought he'd go to Bermuda, and he went down there in November. I think Mr. Paine went with him, and the very night before he sailed he had the terrible news that Mr. Gilder had died! That was a blow, for he loved Mr. Gilder, and they'd been friends for many years. He said that Gilder was lucky to be able to go. Mr. Clemens was seventy-four years old then. Oh, my! It was hard to believe it when you looked at him and heard him laugh and joke—just the same as he used to when I first went to work for them in Hartford as a young girl.

When Mr. Clemens went to Bermuda the house seemed so dead and empty and it was hard for Miss Jean, too, because you always missed Mr. Clemens so. He was one of them people that just filled up the world for you. Mr. Clemens didn't stay very long in Bermuda that time. He got better, and wanted to come home for Christmas. You see Miss Clara and Mr. Gabrilowitsch had had their honeymoon and Mr. Gabrilowitsch, he had appendicitis and an operation, and he was not strong and so they had gone over to Europe, to spend the winter in Switzerland so Mr. Gabrilowitsch could recuperate there —and they was there then.

So Mr. Clemens come home and arrived at Redding just a few days before Christmas. Miss Jean, she'd been working very hard—too hard, really—with her farming and her errands and being a secretary, too. I always thought it was too much for her, but she always would do everything there was to do—never spared herself. You see, poor Miss Jean wanted to make up for all the lost time she'd had to be away from home, and sick.

There was one funny thing that happened right after he come home—just the day before Christmas, when the newspapers got some report again that he was sick and dying, so he told Jean to telephone to New York and deny it. Well, she telephoned for him to the newspaper, and the telephone message was: "You needn't say I'm dying, 'cause I wouldn't think of such a thing—not at my time of life! Merry Christmas and a Happy New Year from Mark Twain"—something like that it was.

Oh! Mr. Clemens, he was so glad to be back, and the night before Christmas, Jean was trimming the great Christmas tree there in the loggia, and had all her presents ready and packed. They was going to invite some people up from New York, and she had gifts for everybody and a beautiful Christmas tree, just like her mother used to have. When she and Mr. Clemens finished fixing the tree, Christmas Eve, they bid each other good night at the door. She had a little cold, so she said, "I won't kiss you, father, because I've got such a cold." So he kissed her on the forehead and she kissed his hand, and they said good night to each other that way.

In the morning she was going to take her presents to the station, so she told Jennie to have her breakfast very early and the horses ready at the door, and her cold bath fixed for seven o'clock. Miss Jean always slept on the porch and took this cold plunge every morning. She'd run right in from the porch and jump straight into the tub. I think she jumped into the tub that morning and the shock must have been too great for her heart—for after she'd been there quite a while and didn't come out, Jennie called me and said: "Miss Jean is still in the tub. You'd better go in there, Katy." So I ran in and there she was, lying in the tub. My heart just stopped beating when I saw her there. I picked her up, and then her head fell right over on my shoulder, against my cheek; and I knew the worst! I called to Jennie and said: "Oh, come! Come! Miss Jean is dead!" And we lifted her out together and laid her on the great towels on the bathroom floor and tried to bring her back to life—but there was no life there! We sent for the doctor right away, but 'twarn't no use—it was all over!

Mr. Clemens had heard the noise and thought we was getting ready to go to the station, and then—oh! I knew I must tell him somehow, and so I ran straight into his room for I couldn't think any more, and I cried right out, without even giving him any warning (I was so crazed with grief). I says: "Oh, Mr. Clemens, Mr. Clemens! Miss Jean is dead!" I hardly knew what I said! I couldn't think at all. I just cried it out.

He jumped right out of bed and put his two hands to his head and whispered: "Oh, God! Oh, God!"

And he ran with me to the bathroom where she lay, and when he seen her he stood very still, and just looked and looked at her, and said, "How beautiful she looks, Katy! How beautiful!" And he stood there a long time, looking at her without speaking. Then he said: "She's happy now, she's with her mother and sister; and if I thought I could bring her back by just saying one word, I wouldn't say it."

Miss Jean had been ill a great deal and Mr. Clemens always had it on his heart about leaving her. He dreaded that; he thought it was so much better for her to go before him.

The doctor came and then Mr. Langdon, and Mrs. Loomis and Mrs. Littleton came right up from New York and we made arrangements to take Jean's body to Elmira. And I dressed her in her white silk dress—the one she wore at Clara's wedding. It fell to me to do it, as I had done it for her mother and little Susy. And I put the pretty buckle on her dress that day, that her father had brought her from Bermuda for Christmas, that she had never seen. The next day we was to take her to Elmira. But Mr. Clemens was so sick—he couldn't go to Elmira with her, and, besides, he said he could never see another person belonging to him laid in the grave.

And so he wrote all that night about her, and all that day that she died—and it was called "The Death of Jean"—that piece he wrote; and it was the last time he ever wrote anything. Oh, it was beautiful—that piece about Jean. Nobody could ever read it without crying.

All that day that he wrote, he used to go down into the great music room, every little while, and sit and look at Jean as she lay there. He'd look and look at her, and then he'd go back upstairs very quiet, and write again.

Miss Jean's big dog stayed right by her all the time. He seemed to want to lie right by the head of the casket, all the time she was there, before we took her away. And every now and then he would rise up on his feet, very soft, and he'd raise himself up high so as he could look at her—so he could see her face. If anybody come into the room he'd just lay down again, so sad and quiet. But as soon as they was gone, though, and he was alone, he'd raise himself up—and make a little crying sound—he would, and he'd look and look at her to see if everything was all right. It seemed as though he was waiting for her to speak to him. She had loved him so, and he knew it, you see, and couldn't understand why she didn't speak to him.

We started the next night for Elmira at six o'clock. A terrible heavy snowstorm had come on and the snow was falling very thick and white when the hearse came up and the two or three carriages. Mr. Clemens asked Mr. Paine to play something on the Orchestrelle—to play Jean's favorite music while they was carrying her out. Then he said they must play something for Susy, too, and then play Handel's Largo, that he loved so much, for Mrs. Clemens. And they carried Jean out while the music was playing and they lit them big lanterns at the door so Mr. Clemens could see us as we went. And he stood by the window watching us go down the hill—watching us in the twilight and the snowstorm—watching the last of Jean and poor old Katy taking her to her final resting-place.

I looked back out of the carriage window and I could see his white head there, shining in the light and watching us, and it broke my heart all over again.

Somehow we got to Elmira the next day and Jean was buried that afternoon and we laid her by her mother and Susy, and then I come back all alone, as soon as I could. And I went right in to see Mr. Clemens the first thing, and he stood up and said, "Oh, Katy! How glad I am to see you back!" And he reached out his hand and shook hands with me with his two hands—and he was full of tears and grief and he said, "So, you've laid my Jean away." And I said, "Yes, Mr. Clemens, right beside her mother."

He seemed so broken-hearted I couldn't say much to him—for I was broken-hearted, too. There was nothing more we could say to each other. It was a bad time! An awful time! Christmas was over then—over forever—for us!

When I think of it all—Mr. and Mrs. Clemens and the children—well, Mr. and Mrs. Clemens, of course I knew they would die sometime, but somehow I didn't never think—never dreamed the children ought to die so fast—that is, Susy and Jean. I thought I would be able to stay with them right up to the end of my time, and that they'd always be there till I was gone.

The house was so desolate after this that Mr. Clemens wanted Mr. Paine to move up there with his family to be company for him. So Mr. and Mrs. Paine come, and the children, and was there when I got home from Elmira. It was a good thing for Mr. Clemens, but oh! It was awful to see any other family there instead of my own.

Mr. Clemens only stayed at Redding two weeks after this. He felt so sick he couldn't bear it there, and he wrote to Miss Clara and he told her that he was glad Jean was safe—safe at last! Of course they'd cabled Clara and Mr. Gabrilowitsch about her, and Mr. Clemens didn't want them to come back to America. It was no use then. He said he'd go to Bermuda and try to get well.

So he went right away and Claude the butler went with him. Mr. Paine stayed with us. Mrs. Loomis, she come up to spend that last evening with him at Stormfield, and then they went down to New York and he sailed the next day for Bermuda. Mr. Howells went to see him at the hotel, just before he sailed, and I think that must have been a comfort to Mr. Clemens—that was the last time he seen him—but of course neither of them knew that then.

Mr. Howells loved Mr. Clemens, I suppose, about as much as anything in this world, for Mr. Howells said one time, why, he'd feel it an honor if any one said he was born even—in the same country and breathed the same air—as Mark Twain!

Well, Mr. Clemens got better just at first. He loved Bermuda and wrote that he was comfortable and happy, and didn't say anything about being sick, so we hoped he was all right. But towards spring, he got sick again and we were very anxious; and he wrote he wanted to come right home. When he said that, we knew that he must be pretty bad. So they cabled Miss Clara to come back. And Mr. Paine started right off for Bermuda. Mr. Paine found him there at the hotel and Claude taking care of him, and he had very kind friends there, too—Mr. and Mrs. Allen—who had been doing everything and was very devoted to him. Mr. Paine said afterwards that Mr. Clemens looked pretty good when he seen him first, but he seemed weak and thin, and couldn't lie down at all, because of that terrible pain in his chest—and he couldn't breathe. It was like a spasm, almost. Then they brought him home. That must have been a terrible voyage back for Mr. Paine, with poor Mr. Clemens so sick, for he got worse on the boat and they thought he'd never live to get home—but he did, thank God! He wanted to live to see Clara again.

Of course his friends went down to meet the steamer—Dr. Quintard and Dr. Halsey was there, and they brought him right up to Redding in a special train.

Dr. Quintard thought it best to bring him right home and make him comfortable there as quick as they could, and so they did. They had two nurses with them, and they said he seemed a little more comfortable—could breathe better, on his way out. We was all waiting at the house, for the carriage to roll up, and it come right up to the door and they used a chair to lift Mr. Clemens out with. He set on that chair and they lifted him in it right out on the porch, where we all stood, waiting.

And they was going to carry him into the house then, quick, but Mr. Clemens says: "No, boys, let the chair down now on the porch. I'm going to stand right up here now," he says, "and say 'How do you do' to Katy and Mrs. Paine, because," he says, "I want to shake hands with them *standing up!*"

And, oh! I was so glad! I says: "Oh, Mr. Clemens, you're welcome home. I know you're going to get better now, and we're all going to do everything to bring you back to health and strength again." And he said: "That's nice, Katy. That's nice. For I'm so glad to be at home!"

Then they took him upstairs and put him to bed, and both doctors stayed all that night, for he was very weak; and Dr. Halsey never left the house again. And Dr. Quintard he come back every night. Then Miss Clara was going to arrive. She was on the ocean, you know, hurrying home—and we was expecting her any day. She got there about two days after Mr. Clemens did, and Mr. Gabrilowitsch, he telephoned up from New York that they was there and coming right up; and they come the next morning.

Mr. Clemens was feeling more comfortable that morning, and stronger, and Miss Clara rushed right in to her father as soon as she got there, and they had a long embrace, and quite a little laugh, too. Why, I heard him out in the hall laughing; and then they talked a little.

Then he says to her, "Oh, Clara, I'm so glad you're back again!" and he says, "Clara, you're going to sing for me a little song," he says. That was the day she got there. And she says, "Any time you want me to, father, I'll sing for you"—though it was terrible hard for her to say that, I know, and he says, "Well, maybe to-morrow, Clara." And the next day it was that she sang to him. And he wanted her to sing "Flow Softly, Sweet Afton," and she done it for him.

Oh! He was so happy when she sung. It was very beautiful and pathetic. Her voice trembled so, it was full of tears, but she sang it all through for him, and oh, he was so glad to have her! After she went out he said, "Wasn't that beautiful, Katy, and isn't it nice to have Clara back again?" And then he waited a moment and kind of whispered to himself, "Oh, God! She's all alone when I'm gone." And then he seemed to remember that Clara wasn't alone, that she was married now, for he said sort of to himself: "No, she has Gabrilowitsch now—and I'm glad—glad! Thank God!"

Mr. Clemens never seemed to realize that he was going to die. He wasn't like most people who was sick. He didn't say anything about going then. He hated the thought of sickness or medicine, or anything like that. Even when he was very bad and the doctors come and fixed him up a little, as soon as it was over, he'd seem to forget it.

It was angine pectoris he had. That is the worst kind of heart trouble. I used to stay with him those few nights when the nurses would go down to supper. He didn't like the nurses to set with him all the time. He'd say to them, "Now, when you go to your supper, tell Katy it's her turn to sit here." Then I'd come up and talk to him a little bit and he'd speak a little too, sometimes; but he was not able to talk very much then.

Miss Clara used to come in every night, the very last thing, and sit with him until he went to sleep. It seemed a long time to us who was watching and hoping, but it was only a week really that he lived. He died just one week after he got home.

There was one night, I remember, he was feeling a little stronger, and he had a book in his hand when I went in. I have that book yet. I shall always keep it, because he read two pages in it to me, and he said, "Do you like it, Katy?" I said, "Yes, Mr. Clemens." Then he says, "Well, then, I'll read you a little more."

"Oh, no," I says, "no, you mustn't. You'll tire yourself out."

"All right," he says, "just as you say, Katy!" Yes, I got that book yet. I always kept it. It was a funny little story, a nice story, but it didn't matter what it was, really. It was the idea that he wanted to read it to me.

He was so weak then that he really had to mind. There wasn't very much change the day he died. Of course the doctors could see there was, but we couldn't, because he'd talked that day. He never lost consciousness at all—not at all. He talked with Mr. Gabrilowitsch a little while, and he asked him to give him a drink one time, " 'cause," he says, "you're the only one can understand me." And so Mr. Gabrilowitsch he gave him the water and held him while he drank it. We was all with him then, Mr. Langdon, Clara and Mr. Gabrilowitsch, Dr. Quintard, Dr. Halsey, and myself.

He'd been very sick that day and it was about five o'clock when the doctors said he couldn't live but a few minutes more. I went in and looked at him. He seemed to look up and open his eyes and know me. Clara was standing up and had ahold of his hand, and Mr. Langdon was there. And I went and stood at the foot of the bed, and he was very quiet. Then he just breathed hard—a little bit—twice—and then he turned his head on the pillow—his beautiful head—and then he passed out.

Oh, my! It was awful to think that last breath had gone. I shall never forget that minute when he died. I'll never forget how I went in and looked at him that night when he was dead, how I went and looked at him and says to myself, "Mr. Clemens, aren't you never going to speak any more?"

It was a terrible, cruel thing to have him die, really, because he was too young—that is, he *felt* young, you know, and that made him young; and he could have said a good deal more. Yes, he could have written some more. He could have kept on talking and writing more. I know he could, and he ought to have gone on, because what he said was *worth* saying.

I don't know of anything that was such a shock as that—his dying! It was the awfullest feeling anybody ever had. Like some great earthquake—something terrible! To think he would never speak again! I have had my own people die, my father and my mother and sisters and brothers, but oh, there was nothing ever like the day Mr. Clemens died! It almost cut my heart in two when I looked at him for the last time. I felt like my life ended then! That I had lost the best friend I'd had in the world. It was hard! It was hard! To have such a person as Mr. Clemens die—to be still forever, you know. Never to hear that voice again! Never to hear him talk any more—nor laugh!

After he died, they brought him to New York and he lay in state there, in the Brick Church, they called it, on Fifth Avenue. The funeral was there. Dr. Van Dyke was the minister. And Mr. Twitchell, his lifelong friend, who'd married him way back in the old days ("Uncle Joe"), he come from Hartford, and he said the prayers. And his heart was broken, too, Mr. Twitchell's was, for Mr. Clemens, and his own wife who was dying in Hartford, and that he went right back to after the services.

It was a great funeral and hundreds and hundreds of people (all kinds of people) come to take their last look at Mr. Clemens and say good-by to him.

He wore his white clothes that he loved so much and he looked so beautiful as he lay there. His skin was just like ivory, and he was so peaceful-looking, so grand, too—just like a god would look, and so quiet—just like he was asleep. And his beautiful hair that I had massaged every day for years, it looked like silver—it shone so; but I could hardly see it that last time for crying.

Hundreds of people passed by that casket, because everybody loved him so. Rich and poor, they all come—some crossed themselves, too, when they passed by and some stopped just a minute and took a long, long look at him, but they all cried. And the church was full of flowers that his friends had sent him, and on the casket was a great big laurel wreath that Dan Beard had picked up in Stormfield and sent down. Mr. Howells, he was at the funeral, too, and it must have been a bad time for him, as it was for all of us—for all the world! Yes, a bad time for all the world. The whole world knew it when Mark Twain died, and they was mournin' in every land that knew his name; for he was beloved from one end of the earth to the other, I might say. The name "Mark Twain" was known and honored in every land. Oh, 'twas a sad day for the world when he died, April 21, 1910. That was the day. I'll never forget that date; and it was a great day for the world, too, when he was born into it, more than seventy-four years before that, November 30, 1835. I'll never forget them two dates—never!

After the funeral he was taken to Elmira to the Langdon house and laid there in the big parlor where Mrs. Clemens and Susy and Jean had all laid, and where he was married so many years ago. Oh, the people that flocked there to see him! It seemed to me that everybody in Elmira came. And there was another funeral all over again there, and it seemed harder than the first one, for then we all knew it was the end of Mr. Clemens, and it seemed then like the whole world had stopped. I couldn't help thinking that day about lots of things he'd said—about religion and his belief, and how he hated meanness. And I kept wondering where he was, and what he knew now about the "Undiscovered Country" he used to always be talking about—the place most of us call heaven, I guess.

After the funeral Claude and I came back from Elmira and went up to the Redding house. Clara and Mr. Gabrilowitsch came, too, and we all lived there peacefully until August when Clara's baby, Nina, was born.

Mr. Gabrilowitsch used to practice every day in the music room, and one morning he was playing something about Marguerite from *Faust* and I was making Clara's bed at the time and straightening the room, and she said to me, "Oh, Katy, how can you keep on working when that's being played?" This was a few days before Nina was born, and Clara, she just stood there by the door drinking in all that lovely music.

The night before Nina was born Clara was very sick and Mr. Gabrilowitsch, he was playing all the time for her, and she was lying on the sofa listening to him. I was in the room when Nina was born. The doctor handed her to me—that little baby. The doctor wrapped her in a blanket and laid her on my lap—and I looked and looked at her, and I thought how pleased Mr. Clemens would have been to see her. And, oh! If Mrs. Clemens could have seen her! For she loved children so. She used to say to Miss Clara: "Oh, Clara, when are you going to get married? We want a baby in this house." Miss Clara said to me afterwards, when Nina was a few weeks old—"I had hoped it would be a boy, Katy, because then it might have been like father."

Those was hard weeks right after Mr. Clemens' death, before the baby come. It was awful there, without Mr. Clemens. Of course, Clara and Mr. Gabrilowitsch made up a great deal, and I was so glad to have her home. We began to straighten up the house and put Mr. Clemens' things away, after the funeral, and it seemed as though I couldn't do it. I picked up everything from his bureau and tables and put everything into a trunk. I did it when Susy died, and I did it when Mrs. Clemens died; I did it when Jean died, too; and then I did it for the last time, when Mr. Clemens died!

It was a terrible thing to take his pipes and empty boxes of cigars and pencils and everything that he'd used, off that table by the head of his bed. Why, I used to fix that table every day of my life, sharpen them lead pencils, fill his boxes with matches—and the pins he used to get so mad about; and put out a fresh box of cigars, fill the bottle with whisky and put them all there every night for him.

And then—to have to take them all off and put that table away—forever! Oh, it was awful! Every morning while I was putting the things in order, I always locked the door so nobody could come in, because I would cry over everything I picked up—every single thing—because I knew he never would use it again. It was so terrible to think he wouldn't be ever any more in that room. The odor of tobacco was so strong there I used to feel when I first went in, in the morning, that he *must* be there, smoking—just as he used to be. His presence was so vivid in that room, I could almost see him settin' there, and hear him, too.

It was a desolate house, I'll tell you! It took me more than a week to straighten that room, because I couldn't do but a little at a time. I really couldn't do my work—for the crying. Miss Clara couldn't bear it any more than I could, and I tried to save her all I was able.

Well, finally we got everything put away, and then we settled down to live again. I used to massage Mr. Gabrilowitsch's head every day—rub his head good (I got that job back, you see), just as I used to do it for Mr. Clemens.

It was lovely in Redding that spring. It was coming on summer, you know, everything was beginning to form and grow, and budding to come out nice, and oh! to see everything coming up new again and no Mr. Clemens to enjoy it! He used to love the summer so, looking out at the trees and the birds singing, and seeing all the things grow into life. It didn't seem right to have summer come without him, and I was glad to go away from there.

In August after Nina was born, Clara and Mr. Gabrilowitsch planned going back to Europe, made arrangements to go to Munich to live. They packed everything up in the house and had the great vans come to take the things straight down to the steamer. All them beautiful things was packed and put in the vans, and I saw them go off, and knew we was nearing the end. Miss Clara took everything for her new home in Europe, except the things she gave me. It made me sick to see all that furniture going out—and know I wasn't going with it. The first time in all my life I was to be really separated from the family.

Clara gave me lots of things from the house—anything I wanted. But I'd had so much trouble then, that the furniture didn't mean much—after the family was gone. But after a while, later on, that furniture was a great comfort to me. I always felt I was with the family still, when I was looking at them things, and it made me happy just to have them. The last day at Redding I went all over the house for the last time, and oh, it was lonely! I went into Mr. Clemens' room to say good-by to it. I went in and locked the door—and stood there all alone, and I looked around and I smelled his tobacco just the same as when he used to be there. Then I said good-by to it all—forever.

I come to New York then, because some of my family was in New York and I had a house at Ninety-seventh Street and I took lodgers. It was nice and comfortable in that little house, and I was grateful for it because 'twas Miss Clara and Mr. Clemens that had fixed things up so I could always be comfortable and not worry about money the rest of my life. That was wonderful of them, warn't it? There warn't no end to their goodness to me—'twill see me right through to the end of my days.

Well, I tried to keep myself busy in that little house in New York, so's not to think about the family at all. I couldn't bear to set down quiet and think. I couldn't never realize that they was gone. I missed them every day, but I had the feeling that I was with them in some way, don't you know, and maybe it was that furniture that I had that belonged to the family. I used to set and look at it and try to imagine that they was settin' in them chairs—the family. I tried to bring them back to life that way.

I was with them for more than thirty years, day to day—from the time I left Miss Clara. 'Twas the 19th of October that I said good-by to her at the hotel and she went to Europe; and it was the 19th of October that I went to Mrs. Clemens—so it was thirty years, from day to day. A long time, warn't it?

Miss Clara and Mr. Gabrilowitsch and the baby stayed at a hotel in New York until they was ready to sail. That helped to make the break easier, for I saw them every day. I loved Miss Clara so much. Oh, dear! I would have loved to have taken care of her and the baby. But I couldn't. I wasn't able. So we made up our minds we'd part. I couldn't go to see her off at the steamer. I said good-by right there in the hotel. I couldn't have borne to see her sail away without me. I was anxious to have her go, although it was so sad, because it was best for her to get away from all the hard things and have a new home of her own, away from all the sadness.

So I busied myself as busy as could be, to keep myself from thinking. I missed them, though, every day I was keeping house in New York, but even in the beginning I had a feeling that I was with them in some way. It was the furniture, I guess, that helped to bring them back a little—the old familiar things—them chairs and tables. I used to look and look at them, and tried to feel I was with the family again, and try to imagine the old days once more.

I think I miss Mrs. Clemens now as much as I ever did because she was so good to me—because I went to her for everything and she always helped me. I miss her just as much now as I did in the beginning. But Mr. Clemens! When I think about him I don't know what to say! How nice he was to me—how kind he was to every one! I've said it a hundred times and I'll go on saying it the rest of my life. So many things come back to me. He was so jolly and he told things so funny. And how he used to make fun of me, too! And then after he'd made fun of me for something I'd told all wrong, and I'd say, "Well, I don't know how to say it right"—then he'd say, "Why, *of course* you don't, Katy!" And then he'd tell me *how* to say it and explain everything to me—all the little things I didn't understand. Oh, I miss him! Everything I do seems to bring it all back again. He was a big loss, I'll tell you, to anybody who knew him.

I don't think people ever realized how good Mr. Clemens was—no outsider knew how lovely he was in his home. For a man that was so brilliant and knew so much, he was so easy to approach, and to tell anything to. He would listen, no matter what you wanted to say, just like he would listen to a little child's story, and help you. He was never too tired or busy to hear what you had to say. You'd think, wouldn't you, to a man like him, that any little insignificant thing would bore him to death, and that he would get impatient? But he didn't. He had a big heart. He understood things. He had such a way with him.

After Miss Clara was gone, I kept pretty busy as I told you, and when I thought at all, it was always about the past. I realized what a wonderful life I had had all those years—what a great stroke it was for me when Mrs. Clemens first took me in. As a young girl I didn't think much about it, of course. I just drifted on and had everything I wanted—and not a thing to worry about. Life went on then like living in a bed of roses, and every place we went to, and everything the Clemens family did, always seemed just perfect to me. Other servants didn't seem very happy in the families that I knew—I guess they didn't work to be happy, either. They worked just so many hours a day and wouldn't put themselves out one bit. They had their time out and their time in—that was all that mattered to them. I never had any time out regular. I never wanted it. Because where the Clemens was seemed just like my home, and I spent all my time thinking of what was best for them. I didn't think of the money I was earning, and I never wanted to do anything to annoy them in any way, you know. As for doing things that I wanted to do, if it interfered in any way with them, I wouldn't ever do it—they came first. And I did it because I loved them and they was so good to me—just like I was one of their own.

No, I don't think people always understood Mr. Clemens, as I said before. So many things would get in his books, you know, like his very own self. He was so interesting. Why, just the way he'd walk and tell you something—just the movements he would make, when he would walk around, would hold you. Just to look at him, you would admire him every inch. He could be very exciting, too, and as I said, you couldn't get it in his words exactly, but through his personality. He was so funny—everything he told was funny and there was always a joke at the end of what he said. He was sad, too, sometimes, and homelike and cozy; and always so loving to his children. There was nobody I could compare him to, really. Just his voice was so charming—to hear it in another room even. It was perfectly beautiful—even when he was talking a little loud and a little bit cross—it was nice to hear him then. Why, he used to get terrible mad—sometimes when he'd get a new suit of clothes. The tailor was a damned fool, he'd say, that made that suit! he was an idiot! this was wrong and that was wrong! the pockets were too small—and oh, how he'd fuss! But even that was nice, very nice. Yes, I loved to hear him even then. When he talked that way it didn't mean that he was cross—it warn't really in an *angry* way. It really sounded more like a joke to me when he used them words—nobody thought anything about it when he raged round and said them things.

When I first saw him I knew there was something wonderful about him—even before I knew he was a famous man. And every time he talked I used to run to hear him, wherever I'd be! I'd run to get anything he wanted, just to hear everything he said. I used to stand behind the door, just to hear him laugh and joke. Oh, I loved to hear him talk, because nobody could really be in the same house with him without caring for him. And his talking would bring you kind of closer to him—I mean, make you want to be where he was. And when he used to read every night in the parlor to the family, I used to sneak behind the door and listen. Oh, my! I loved that! He read *Tom Sawyer* and *Huck Finn* for little Jean one winter when she was sick. I used to be in the room. I stayed anyway to hear him. I'd make what I had to do last a long time so's I wouldn't have to leave the room. Oh, how he used to laugh when he read some of them sentences in *Tom Sawyer*! He said:

"Jean, I can remember that just as well to-day as when it happened."

"But," she said, "father, why do you laugh so much at your *own* work? I wouldn't laugh so much about my jokes," she said, "if I were you."

"But I can't help it, Jean," said Mr. Clemens. "It makes me laugh hearty, because it is as real to-day as the day I done them things!"

And that was so. Things was always very real to Mr. Clemens—it didn't matter how far back they was. You see, Mr. Clemens was really Tom Sawyer, when he was a little boy. Them stories was true happenings about himself and his mother—she was Aunt Polly in *Tom Sawyer*.

She used to tell how she would lick him, and how he'd jump up on the shelf and hide from her. They used to laugh a lot together about it. I remember Mr. Clemens' mother very well. She used to visit us—she came twice to Hartford, and she used to tell Susy about going to dancing school and how the dancing master always danced with her, because she was the prettiest girl and the best dancer. She looked like Mr. Clemens—he resembled her very much. She was tall and slim and straight and had her face shaped just like Mr. Clemens'. Nice blue eyes—very clear and sharp. Her name was Jane Lampton. She was celebrated for her beauty, they said, able to dance all night and all day, as I told you. I suppose a good many of the things that made Mark Twain famous come from her—his sense of humor, too. He was very delicate and sickly as a child, and very mischievous, too, she said—always up to all kinds of pranks and jokes.

His mother used to tell lots of stories about him, I remember. She said he gave her more trouble than any child she ever had. She told him this when she was very old and came to visit us. He said, "Well, mother, I suppose you were afraid I wouldn't ever live to grow up." And she answered, "Oh, no, I was afraid you *would!!*"—which was only a joke, but shows she was about as good a joker as he was.

When he was a little boy, if anything happened with the children, he was the one that always was punished, and his mother would say, "If you didn't deserve a whipping for *that*, you certainly do for something *else!*" Oh! She was always talking and telling about the things he did when he was a little boy.

She didn't visit us very long at a time, because she was kind of old then. But he was very nice and sweet with his mother and joked and laughed, and they used to tell all the old stories about the time when he was a boy. I know she was very proud of him. She looked as though she was, I tell you. You should have just seen the look in her eyes when he come into the room. It must have been something to be proud of to have brought a child like that into the world. And that's what I wonder about Clara's child, Nina. And I wonder what she will be—a writer, a pianist, a singer or what?

Mr. Clemens used to talk a lot about the days when he was a boy—he just loved everything about that time and all the people he knew then. Of course, his boyhood days was full of excitement and adventures. I used to hear them telling about it. He done all kinds of things when he was a young man, because he was a poor boy and had to earn his living. You know, he was a pilot once, on a river boat on the Mississippi River. He was crazy about that, and loved the Mississippi almost as much as he loved a person, and he was always talking about it—what a wonderful river it was. That's where he first got the idea of the name "Mark Twain," and I'll tell you how that come about. That's a river term, "mark twain," and they call it out as they go along, and it means two fathoms of water. He thought that was an unusual name, and signed his first writings with it when he was working on the newspapers. He was right. It was an unusual name, and he made it one of the greatest in the world! He was a miner, too—that is, he went and dug for gold—"staked a claim"—prospecting, they called it, in Nevada and California, and he was at just all kinds of jobs when he was a young man, before he started to become a writer. And he just loved everything about that time and the people he knew then. He never forgot when he become famous. He loved everybody connected with them times—especially the miners, his old chums, that he knew when he was mining in the gold mines in Colorado.

They loved to see him after he become famous and he enjoyed seeing them, too. They'd come to visit him in the old Hartford days. Those miners was the roughest-looking old boys you'd ever seen, but that didn't make no difference to Mr. Clemens. They'd go walking around and smoking around, all over thc house.

"Why," the miners says, "your wife don't allow you to smoke in these lovely rooms with all these wonderful hangings" (on the bed). You see, we had them lovely satin hangings, and it struck these miners, I guess, as something wonderful—and it was.

"Oh," Mr. Clemens says, "my wife thinks there's no place in this house too good for me to smoke in, and so I smoke everywhere—in the bedroom or in the parlor—any place I like. There's only one thing," Mr. Clemens says, "I never smoke more than *one* cigar at a time. People say I smoke a great deal, too much. But you never saw me smoke but *one* cigar at a time, now, did you, boys?"

Them miners, they was pretty rough, but they perfectly adored Mr. Clemens. Only about two come at a time, but he used to entertain them royally, I'll tell you. Of course, he wouldn't give them great dinner parties or anything like that, because the miners didn't have no dress suits nor nothing, but every night Mr. Clemens

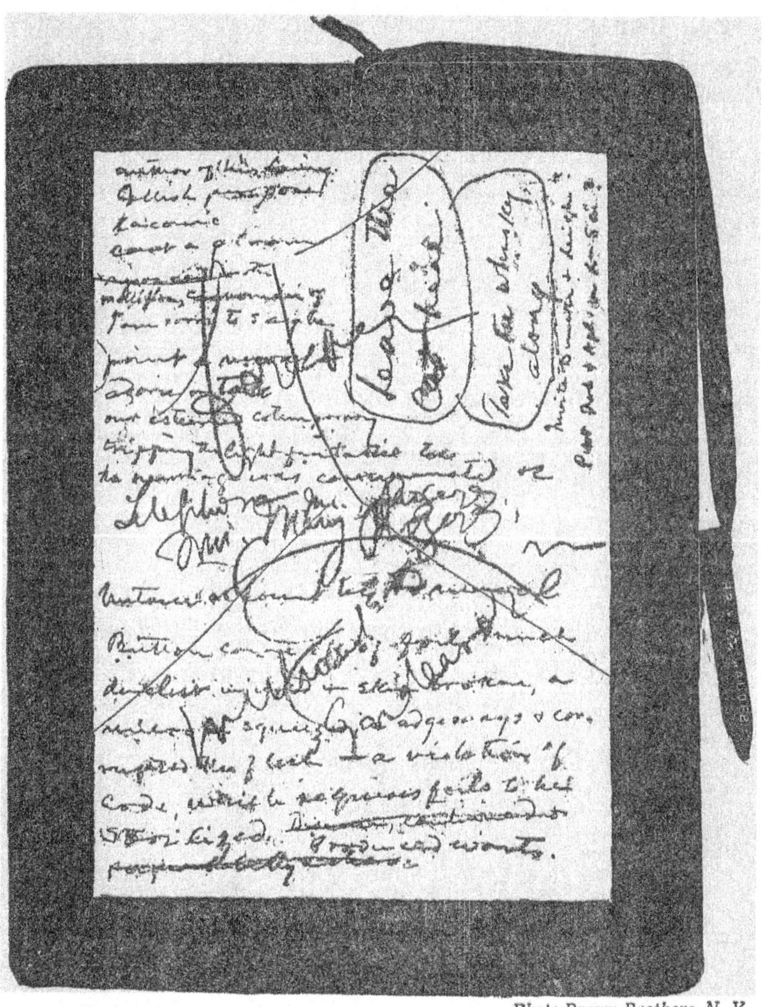

Photo Brown Brothers, N. Y.

MARK TWAIN'S SLATE NO. 34.

gave them a hot Scotch toddy before they went to bed, as a final nightcap, I guess. He played billiards with them and took them for drives and walks and give them plenty of elegant food (and drinks, too) whenever they wanted them, and a good bed to sleep in, and kept them there as long as they liked to stay. Mrs. Clemens was very hospitable to them, and really lovely. She tried to do so much for them to make them feel comfortable and at home. They really had grand times together. And in the evening, after dinner, they used to set by the fire and swap stories and laugh and laugh, and smoke their great cigars. They wore great big high top boots and big brown coats—rough-looking—and them great big hats like the cowboys wear; but they was so nice and tried to be so jolly and polite that you forgot all about their clothes and that they was the rough miners that they were. I remember them well and I liked them.

You see, Mr. Clemens never forgot his old friends; the past was always wonderful to him—made him feel like a boy again.

And I guess that's so with all of us—I know it is with me. Nothing matters any more, now that the family is gone, and it comes back every day—the wonderful life I had with them. It's always in my thoughts them years we had together, way back in the beginning, stretching up to now. It seems like a long, long road to me, but all of it was happiness, and when I shut my eyes, or even when they're open, I can see them all around me again

Each person is born to one possession which outvalues any he can earn or inherit — his last breath.

Mark Twain

Let us endeavor to so live that when we come to die even the undertaker will be sorry.

Mark Twain

INSCRIPTIONS FROM THE HUMORIST TO MARY LAWTON IN PERSONAL COPIES OF HIS WORKS.

and sometimes the old furniture, as I told you, helps to bring it back, and it all comes true again—just like a fairy story would. This morning, when I was kind of half awake (it must have been, because I *know* it wasn't a dream) I kind of started up and I says: "Why, I wonder what Miss Jean had for breakfast; she never told me what to get for her breakfast. Now I wonder where that child is!"

I couldn't get it through me, somehow, where Jean was. I set there for the longest time, trying to think, and then—suddenly I realized that she was gone—gone forever. Oh, if I could just speak to them once more, if I could just see them once more! If I could speak to Mrs. Clemens and hear Mr. Clemens' voice again! Oh, if I could only hear that old alarm clock ring, as it used to, way back in the old Hartford days—when it made me so mad to hear it clanging out at ten o'clock (because that meant my beau must go)! If I could just hear Mr. Clemens shouting out again: "Ten o'clock, Katy. Ten o'clock! Time to lock up!"

Well, I guess it's about time for me to lock up now—lock up for good.

They're all gone—not even a beau left! But I guess it's all Fate, as I said before—all blocked out—our lives. I think God makes it that way.

And although it's terrible lonely when I get to thinking about the past, I have the comfort of having them with me in my thoughts, anyway. And sometimes it

Huck Finn
Tom Sawyer
MARK TWAIN
AT HOME
1895

almost seems as if they was right here in the room—just as I thought Jean was, the other morning. That they are here just as they used to be, and I can go on serving them to the end. It won't be for so very long, I guess, and I hope to meet them all again when I go. Yes, I have the hopes of meeting them—if I am worthy—of meeting them in heaven—as they say.

But then, any place would be heaven where they was!

THE END

CPSIA information can be obtained
at www.ICGtesting.com
Printed in the USA
BVOW08s1647190717
489750BV00006B/331/P